JESUS

Among Secular

GODS

The Countercultural
Claims of Christ

JESUS
Among Secular
GODS

The Countercultural
Claims of Christ

RAVI ZACHARIAS
and VINCE VITALE

New York • Boston • Nashville

FaithWords
Hachette Book Group
1290 Avenue of the Americas
New York, NY 10104
faithwords.com
twitter.com/faithwords

First Edition: January 2017

FaithWords is a division of Hachette Book Group, Inc. The FaithWords name and logo are
trademarks of Hachette Book Group, Inc.

The publisher is not responsible for websites (or their content) that are not owned by the publisher.

The Hachette Speakers Bureau provides a wide range of authors for speaking events. To find out
more, go to www.hachettespeakersbureau.com or call (866) 376-6591.

Edited by Lance Wubbels Literary Services, Bloomington, Minnesota.

Library of Congress Control Number: 2016954495

ISBNs: 978-1-4555-6915-1 (hardcover), 978-1-4555-6914-4 (ebook)

Printed in the United States of America

10 9 8 7 6 5 4 3 2 1

Ravi Zacharias

To Chris and Raiko Blattner: devoted friends and great examples in my life to help me pursue the vision God has given to my heart. Ever grateful to you both.

To Hayden Kho and Vicki Bello: devoted friends whose lives have experienced God's miracle and whose friendship has been an inspiration beyond words. My heartfelt thanks to you both.

To Philip Ng and Edmund Cha: lives that inspire and hearts that have touched my heart in ways that words alone cannot convey. Thank you, Philip and Edmund. God bless you and your families.

Vince Vitale

To Jo: my love; lover of Truth.

CONTENTS

Chapter 1

Altars Against God

Ravi Zacharias

It was years ago when I was speaking at an openly and avowedly atheistic institution that I was fascinated by a questioner who asked what on earth I meant by the term *God*. The city was Moscow; the setting was the Lenin Military Academy. The atmosphere was tense. Never had I been asked before to define the term in a public gathering. And because I was in a country so historically entrenched in atheism, I suspected the question was both hostile and intentional. I asked the questioner if he was an atheist, to which he replied that he was. I asked him what he was denying. That conversation didn't go very far. So I tried to explain to him what we meant when we spoke of God.

It is fascinating to talk to a strident atheist and try to get beneath the anger or hostility. *God* is a trigger word for some that concentrates all his or her stored animosity into a projectile of words. But as the layers of their thinking and experience are unpacked, the meaning of atheism to each one becomes narrower and narrower, each term dying the death of a thousand qualifications. Oftentimes, the description is more visceral and is discussed with pent-up anger rather than in a sensible, respectful discussion. More than once I have been amazed at the anger expressed by members of the atheist groups at one or other of the Ivy League schools in the United States to which I have been invited to speak, anger that I was even invited and that I had the temerity to address them.

In theory, the academy has always been a place where dissent serves a valuable purpose in helping thinking students to weigh out ideas and make intelligent choices. And, dare I say, had I been a Muslim speaker, there would have been no such dissent as I faced. Evidently, being able to instill fear in people has a lot to do with how much freedom of speech you are granted. But alas! For some, at least, civil discourse is impossible. To her credit, at the end of a lecture, one senior officer in one club stood up and thanked me, a veiled apology for the resistance vented before the event. I did appreciate that courtesy.

This unfettered anger on the part of some is quite puzzling to me. I was raised in India where I was not a Hindu and, in fact, never once gave it any serious consideration. For that matter, I'm not sure if I even really believed in God. I was a nominal Christian but never gave that much thought, either. Most of my friends were either Hindu or Muslim or Sikh, with a few others of different faiths. I never recall feeling any anger or hostility toward those who believed differently than me, no matter how ludicrous their beliefs may have seemed to me. Nor do I remember ever being on the receiving end of such anger and hostility because I did not have the same belief.

But the likes of Richard Dawkins are renowned for their bullying and mocking approach toward opposing views, an attitude from an academic that makes one wonder what is really driving such an intense temperament. A questioner at a gathering in Washington, DC, once asked Richard Dawkins how one should respond to a person who believed in God. "Mock them," he actually replied. "Ridicule them." When someone at an event asked me what I thought of that response, I reflected that, were Dawkins to practice that same method in Saudi Arabia, chances are he would not need his return ticket. One thing is for sure—he would at least find out that not all beliefs in God are similar and not all imperatives, equal.

But his "ridicule them" posture remains unchanged. In an interview in *The Independent* with Maya Oppenheim (May 23, 2016), he said, "I'm all for offending people's religion. It should be offended at every opportunity."[1] Really? Is this how one arrives at whether or not a belief is valid? He went on to add, "In the case of immigrants from Syria and Iraq, I would like to see special preference given to apostates, people who have given up Islam."[2] If Donald Trump had said the same, there would have been a session in the British Houses of Parliament to decide whether or not he should be allowed into the country anymore. But Dawkins says it and it's acceptable, because atheists who love him and his style of atheism have their own absolutes and their own legitimized prejudices.

Intolerance, prejudice, disrespect, hatred, and offense are all within the fruit of Dawkins' philosophy. In creedal form, his philosophy is hate, discriminate, judge, mock, castigate, eliminate, stop... do whatever you need to do to put an end to belief in God. Ironically, he condemns God for being prejudiced, hate-filled, egotistical, judgmental, and demeaning to those who don't agree with Him. He derides the attributes of God by making a caricature of Him, but justifies the same attributes in himself without caricature. I would rather trust the judgments of a good and gracious person than one who spends his time and energy in mocking people and their sacred beliefs. And he is not alone. The hallmark of the so-called "new atheists" is the anger and ridicule that is hurled toward anyone's belief in the sacred.

Need I add, not all atheists have the same disposition. In fact, many find the hostility of the new atheists an embarrassment. I have met many a cordial conversationalist who is atheistic in his or her belief, and we've had the best of conversations. Many have remarked that they have been able to take only so much of Dawkins and his followers and then stopped even reading them. Whatever worldview we espouse, dialogue and debate should take place with civility and courteous listening. But our times make that ideal so elusive. Holding a supposedly noble belief and reducing it to ignoble means of propagation makes the one who holds that belief suspect.

To be sure, many in the so-called "religious" category have provoked strident responses. The pulpit can sadly be a place of bullying people into guilt and remorse and other emotions that make them want to escape from the voice hammering away at them, to say nothing of the anti-intellectualism among Christian ranks that brands even a hint of philosophy or science heretical.

History has taught us to beware of extremists in any camp that sacrifice cordial conversation at the altar of demagogic enforcement. Views and opinions are aplenty in our world of tweeting and Instagram, but civil discourse is rare. And rarer still is the ability to defend one's beliefs with reason and experience. I sincerely hope that as my colleague Vince and I examine the differences among secular belief systems (that are, in fact, also religions), we will be able to effectively demonstrate where these differences really lie, and that the Judeo-Christian worldview has the most coherent answers to the inescapable questions of life that we all have, regardless of our beliefs.

Questioning the Question

The story is told of an Indian sitting in a plane next to Albert Einstein. To pass the time, Einstein proposed that they play a game. "I will ask you a question, and if you can't answer it, you pay me fifty dollars. Then you ask me a question, and if I can't answer it, I will pay you five hundred dollars." The Indian knew he was no match for Einstein but figured he had enough philosophical and cultural knowledge to be able to stump Einstein sometimes, and with a ratio of ten to one, he could manage to stay in the game.

Einstein went first and asked the Indian how far the earth was from the moon. The Indian was not sure of the exact number and put his hand into his pocket to give Einstein fifty dollars. Now came the Indian's turn, and he asked, "What goes up the mountain with three legs and comes down with four legs?" Einstein paused, pondered, finally dipped his hand into his pocket and gave the man five hundred dollars. Now it was Einstein's turn again. He said, "Before I ask you my next question, what *does* go up the mountain with three legs and comes down with four legs?" The Indian paused, dipped into his pocket, and gave Einstein fifty dollars.

Like that Indian, we often ask questions that are manufactured to trip up the other person, while having no answers to the question ourselves. In his book *The New Atheism and the Erosion of Freedom*, Robert Morey points out the seven leaps atheists have to explain: How…

Everything ultimately came from Nothing
Order came from Chaos
Harmony came from Discord
Life came from Nonlife
Reason came from Irrationality
Personality came from Non-personality
Morality came from Amorality[3]

But more than that needs to be asserted. The questions in life are not just in the sciences. They are not just of mathematical or empirical measurement. Two people sitting next to each other in a plane may both be going to the same destination. They may know how many hours the journey takes and how many miles they may cover. One may be going to give a talk on science and the other may be going to bury his grandson. But think about this. The scientist may have his subject well in hand, but still have unanswered questions on the meaning of life, while the person next to him may have unanswered questions on the value of the constants in the early formation of the universe, yet have the knowledge of what life really means. He may have in his heart the deep conviction that this present sorrow is only a punctuation mark because eternity awaits. One discipline may answer "how" in a material explanation, but the most important question answers the "why." Why is it that we are here in the first place, and who will see us through the anxieties and pains of life itself? These questions are different yet equally relevant, but for different reasons. Life requires some understanding, and the struggles we face need explanatory power. It is when we get the two subjects and their reasons for existence mixed up that we end up with verbal attacks and needless hostility.

Many an atheist asks questions for which he or she admittedly has no answers or believes the answers to be "on hold," but we are expected to give credence to the whole worldview for merely raising the question. I understand. As a young man I was like that, thinking that putting another person down automatically justified what I had said in response to his position. This book is about examining the "gods" secular thinkers "worship" and how repeatedly they leave their own questions unanswered.

The points of tension within secular worldviews are not merely peripheral. They are systemic. Indeed, they are foundational. I have dealt with the philosophical debate on these matters in other writings. Here, I wish to examine their answers to questions about life and its meaning in distinction to the answers Jesus gives to the same questions. That's where our philosophical rubber meets the road of life. But hopefully, more than that, we will state why the answers of Jesus have stood the test of time, truth, and coherence.

Remember the insight of G. K. Chesterton in his book *Orthodoxy* that, for the atheist, sorrow is central and joy peripheral, while for the follower of Jesus, joy is central and sorrow peripheral. The reason that statement is true is that for the atheist, the foundational questions remain unanswered while they have answers for the peripheral questions; hence, sorrow is central and joy peripheral. For the Christian, it is reversed: The foundational questions have been answered and only the peripheral ones remain in doubt.[4] Hopefully, as the content of this book unfolds, Vince and I can sustain that claim.

Life Seeks a Balance

My favorite essayist, F. W. Boreham, has written an essay entitled, "A Baby's Funeral." Anyone who has read Boreham knows the beauty of his language and the depth of his writing. He has authored over fifty volumes of essays. In this particular essay, which I have references in two of my previous books but in this new context perfectly illustrates how all of life must be grounded in truth, Boreham begins by describing the scene of a distraught woman he saw one day walking back and forth outside his home, pausing as though wanting to enter his garden and then backing off.

Finally, Boreham stepped out of his home and wished her a good morning. She asked if he was the pastor of the church nearby and he admitted that he was. She entered the house at his invitation and struggled to pour out her story. She had had a baby, born terribly deformed, who had died shortly after birth. She desired for the baby to have a proper burial and wondered if he would do that for her.

Boreham promptly responded that he would. He took out a pad to get the information. Did the child have a name? Who was the father? So went the questions. She answered them and the date for the funeral was set. The woman left and Boreham and his wife continued with their plans for a picnic that morning. Throughout the day the woman was on his mind and he told his wife that there was something that didn't quite sound right about her narrative. He did not know what it was but hoped he would have more clarity before the day of the burial.

When they returned home, the woman was standing outside their home and asked if she could come in. She sat down, rubbing her hands nervously, and said, "I have not been honest with you. The baby was born illegitimately, and I have given you a made-up name for the father." The story unfolded and Boreham comforted her as best as he could.

The day of the burial came. It was pouring rain, and to add to the desolate reality, the cemetery was a new one and this was to be the first body interred. Boreham remarks on the total feeling of aloneness for this poor woman. An illegitimate, deformed baby. Pouring rain as the three stood under their umbrellas, the grave digger standing by ready to lower the casket into the soggy ground. A tiny body about to be buried in a place where no other had ever been laid to rest. No one else, just the minister and his wife and the bereaved mother present for this tragedy, and they too were strangers.

Boreham suddenly switches the scene and begins to write about being on a train journey years later with a superintendent in his denomination. It was a whistle-stop trip where, at every station the superintendent would step out, meet with a group of his ministers, listen to them, pray for them, and then would leave these parting words with them, "Just be there for your people. Be with them in their needs, in their hurts, in their pains. They will never forget your presence and your kindness."

Boreham continues that as he listened to this advice being given to the younger pastors, his mind flew back over the years to the day a young woman walked distractedly back and forth in front of his home, a woman whose child he had buried in a lonely cemetery. He realized that through the years, rain or shine, every Sunday since then that same woman had been in his church and lived a life in a quiet relationship with her Savior.

This very type of story was reinforced just two days ago. I had just finished speaking to a full church in Jakarta, Indonesia, and there was a silence as the music played softly for the closing moments. I was near the platform, having stepped away from the lectern, and my eyes caught sight of a young mother with two little children. Her arms were gently bent at the elbows, palms open, reaching outward while the two little ones, one on each side of her, held on to her skirt. As soon as the benediction was over, the two of them ran up the stairs to give me a hug, though I had never met them before. And as they left, my interpreter said to me, "Almost exactly to the day, a year ago their father was murdered. The little boy looks just like his dad."

What a statement that suddenly changed the context and my emotions from witnessing a young family at worship, absent the father, to realizing a young single mother reaching out to her heavenly father and raising her two children without bitterness or anger. I spoke to her afterward and my heart still recalls her words. "Yes, I'm alone now, but my God is with me."

You see, there is an intellectual side to life but also a side to life where deep needs are experienced. We falsely think that one side deals with truth and the other with fantasy. Both need the truth, and the elimination of one by the other is not the world in which God intends for us to live. A mockery of the sacred reveals an animosity that staggers not just the mind but shows the character flaw in one such as that. The words of Blake are appropriate here:

> Mock on, mock on, Voltaire, Rousseau;
> Mock on, mock on, 'tis all in vain!
> You throw the sand against the wind,
> And the wind blows it back again.[5]

It is my hope that the reader will stay the course with an open mind to judge fairly how unique and splendid is the message of Jesus

Christ, reaching to the deepest hungers and questions of the heart and mind. To be truthful, I wouldn't waste a solitary moment in this task if I didn't truly believe that as the world is skidding out of control—politically, socially, economically, and racially—Jesus' answers are unique and true and provide the only coherent worldview, combining truth with relevance to bring hope and meaning.

Every day, the news carries stories of tragedy and atrocity. News is thrust into our consciousness whether we want the information or not. Behind many an act and behind all responses is a worldview that filters reality. The follower of Jesus sees what is happening through the lens of how Jesus describes the human condition and the answer He gives. The contrast with the secular gods of this age is huge. A fair-minded person must at least give a hearing as to why that is so and, if indeed the answers of Jesus open up vistas for one's own individual life, see the world through a different set of eyes. With that goal in mind, I enter into this journey of thought.

Your Worldview Matters

The Great Books of the Western World, published in the 1950s, gave the longest space to the theme of "God," addressed by the most notable Western thinkers of the day. When Mortimer Adler, the editor, was asked why that theme occupied such length when many other notable themes were given less space, he answered without hesitation, "Because more consequences for life and action follow from the affirmation or denial of God than from any other basic question."[6]

The questioner was silent and nodded.

Yes, indeed, more consequences, on every matter of value and relationship, follow from one's genuine belief or disbelief in God than from any other issue. This alone ought to remind us just how critical is the foundation to every life when it comes to God. The follower of Jesus Christ must take serious note of this. That belief has meaning and must make a difference.

I will never forget talking to a former Muslim who had committed his life to Jesus Christ and who gave me a fascinating word picture. He drew two circles and put a small dot in each of them. Pointing to the first, he said, "As a Muslim, I believed the circle to be my faith and the little dot to be my life." Then he pointed to the next circle and said, "Now, as a follower of Jesus, I have seen the difference in the cultural tension. To many Westerners, the circle is his life and the dot is his faith."

In other words, a Muslim believed that life was expendable, his faith paramount. The Westerner, he charged, regards his life more important than what he believes. "That is why," he added, "the West will ultimately be overrun. Faith, in the West, is sort of an extracurricular interest and a mere aspect of life for the sake of inner peace. But faith seldom enters the conscience as a conviction."

That was truly a sobering revelation of just how faith is viewed by most in the West, let alone the plurality of faiths that exist. In fact, the very word *faith* is now used in less than flattering terms. The real world is considered intellectually rigorous, and the world of ultimate reality—faith—fanciful, not to be entertained in factual terms. How fascinating that is. So the values by which we live are parked on the shifting mix of quicksand the skeptic calls "faith," while the world of pragmatic and real understandings is supposedly built on the bedrock of the sciences called "reason."

Is my friend right?

If he is right, I will go so far as to say that the West is on the verge of collapse at the hands of its own secular intellectuals. It is only a matter of time. The Christian faith brings with it convictions by which to stand and build a moral framework. The secular thinker, with his implicitly amoral assumptions, imagines that knowledge without a moral base has enough sustaining power. It simply doesn't.

Watch Europe cower under the heel of Islamists who have not forgotten that they were stopped from overtaking Europe and beaten back by Charles Martel thirteen centuries ago. Now, with patience and the clever control of demographics and a gullible media, they stand by, ready to one day take over the structures and edifices built by a different ethic and a different belief system. It is only a matter of time, and they are in no hurry. Thirteen centuries ago, Europe was able to stop the theocratic Islamic tidal wave because it had a faith to defend. The value-less culture of today will not be able to withstand the attack.

Years ago, while Hitler was making plans to overrun the world and some were attempting to placate him in order to save themselves from having to make a moral justification for war, Winston Churchill made a telling speech in the House of Commons on October 5, 1938. ("The Munich Agreement" is also known by the title "A Total and 'Unmitigated Defeat,'" referring to the mollifying treaty brought back by Neville Chamberlain.) Quoting from Scripture, Churchill declared, "You have been weighed in the balances and found wanting" (Daniel 5:27 ESV). Then he ended his speech saying, "And do not suppose that this is the end. This is only the beginning of the reckoning. This is only the first sip, the first foretaste of a bitter cup which will be proffered to us year by year unless by a supreme recovery of moral health and martial vigor, we arise again and take our stand for freedom as in the olden time."[7]

After Hitler visited Paris in 1940, André Boulloche, a courageous member of the French Resistance, penned a letter to his father, saying: "The country can only be saved by a complete moral resurrection, something that will require the work of all men of good will.... I think I can contribute a great deal. And if more troubles lie ahead, isn't my duty present?"[8]

Indeed, the preservation of a nation's ethos is at stake at all times. This is especially true of a nation such as America whose values of trying to balance liberty with law were clear from the beginning. That balance is easier stated than done. John Adams said it well: "Our Constitution was made only for a moral and religious people. It is wholly inadequate to the government of any other."[9]

So I ask: Should one's belief in God and destiny be more important than life itself?

The answer truly depends on what that belief is and whether it is true. The irony is that for the atheist, the answer can only and ultimately be found in one's political theory or, by default, in one's cultural cradle, and cannot be mandated by a supervening worldview that pursues truth as an objective fact over and above all else. Every other discipline is dismissed as being outside truth, reflecting merely cultural and career desires. That's all life is about. The naturalists control truth and then give license to other disciplines to live without absolutes. That is the deadly fallout.

In a commercial I saw recently, a couple of bandits are holding the tellers at a bank at gunpoint and demanding money. All the customers are ordered to the floor. One man whispers to a security guard, "Do something, you're armed!" The security guard replies, "I am on duty not to do anything but only to determine if a robbery is underway." Then he pauses and reassures the customer, "Yes, indeed, this is a robbery."

The naturalist is somewhat like that. Unable to respond to where the truth leads, he is useless to a person hungering for rescue and safety for life itself. He just states what is and does nothing about what should be.

Why do I make the connection between a nation, a people, and a culture? In the current climate, the political arena is fraught with language and views that are scary and disorienting. In one instance, a trail of lies makes no difference to the electorate, proving that the most valuable thing in human discourse, truth, is an expendable value if power is obtained. In another instance, even extreme and sometimes pejorative statements on people and views don't seem to matter, and the dignity of office is replaced, once again, by the quest for power.

Candidates coming to the fore propound ideas that are creating anger and protests that make the future very fearsome. For one, "dishonest" sums it up. For the other, "disrespectful" or worse, "prejudice" is the charge. Whether these are legitimate assertions or not is secondary to the assumption that morality matters.

Ironically, the protestors protesting the candidates themselves resort to injurious means. But what is obvious is that statecraft has become soulcraft, and a nation that formally wishes to deny God finds its imperatives in a deadly mix of conflicting worldviews and hate-laden words on a path to power. What has happened? The answer is clear. The discussion in the public square is now reduced to right or left, forgetting there is an up and a down.

These matters alone remind us that we had better understand this philosophy called atheism and why it leads where it does. Strange, isn't it, that atheists in the West want the term *marriage* redefined while their counterparts in Russia and China will have nothing of that redefinition? Both have their own reasons, and there is no common point of reference. That's precisely the edifice built on the bedrock of naturalism. Each person is a law unto himself.

Remember in the Old Testament when people wanted a king and God said that He wanted to be their ruler? The people fought back and said they wanted to be like every other nation and, in fact, have somebody else to fight their wars while they could go about their lives. They got what they wanted and found out that the greatest battles were ultimately for the rule of one's heart. Once that becomes autonomous, culture and politics become lawless. And when those battles are lost, the war that looms is of huge proportions. This is, at best, the unintended consequence of atheism.

As Old as the Hills

We think atheism is some kind of newfangled thinking, that science and its bequest gave way to autonomy and our solitude in the universe. That is simply not so. The formalization of it and giving it intellectual respect may have taken time, but the question goes back to the beginning of time. Right from the start the question was not the origin of species but the autonomy of the species. We are more prone to quote from the Wilberforce/Huxley debate or the Galileo/Church conflict than to look back and see where such real tensions began.

We think Darwin buried God, but in fact, in Genesis 3, the very first in the created order wished to bury Him too. All the way to Calvary, the first attempt at death was the death of God. The killing of God was followed by the killing by Cain of his brother, Abel. The Bible addresses this conflict from the pre-Mosaic era. After all, the battle in Genesis was really based on two questions. The battle between theism and atheism is the oldest philosophical debate. It didn't take the French philosophes or the British empiricists to get it all going.

What are the two questions that existed for humanity from the beginning of creation? The first salvo hurled against God in the Garden was "Did God really say?" In the gospel story, the temptation of Jesus resurrects the same question, either by questioning a text or by wrenching it free from its context. The test brought to Jesus in the desert, the same test brought in the Garden, was "Has God said?" and "Is it true?" Those questions implicitly asked whether there was an up and a down. Is there a prescriptive backdrop to life? Can I not be my own definer of good and evil? Am I subject to some higher non-tangible authority?

In his article on "Religion," Thomas Paine picks up this tension as if it is something new and makes some incredible statements questioning whether one should actually believe that God reveals and speaks. Here's what he says:

> As to the bible (sic.), whether true or fabulous, it is a history, and history is not revelation. If Solomon had seven hundred wives and three hundred concubines, and if Samson slept in Delilah's lap, and she cut his hair off, the relation of those things is mere history, that needed no revelation from heaven to tell it; neither does it need any revelation to tell us that Samson was a fool for his pains, and Solomon too.
>
> As to the expressions so often used in the bible, that *the word of the Lord* came to such an one (sic.)…it was the fashion of speaking in those times…. But if we admit the supposition that God would condescend to reveal himself in words, we ought not to believe it would be in such idle and profligate stories as are in the bible…. Deists deny that the book called the bible is the word of God, or that it is revealed religion.[10]

That is a fascinating mix of prejudice and perversion. One feels he must ask if Paine was present in the Garden right from the beginning. He takes the stories of Solomon and Samson and puts them in a "history" category. Would he do the same with the crucifixion and the resurrection or does a different kind of narrative now take place?

The key here is that he simply does not believe God would reveal Himself in propositional truth. Paine didn't invent that predicament. It existed from the beginning. Revelation was not in a vacuum of belief. Revelation was sustained by evidence and propelled by a reality check, time and again. The very means by which we ascertain truth is not merely an inner voice but the rationale of why we are here in the first place.

The question should really be why we even think of a supreme being. Why do we ask if there is a sovereign power over the universe?

Is it because we are deluded into thinking there should be, or is it because reason demands a cause and a purpose? Is it possible that deep within our hungers is this quest to know why we are here in the first place, and the naturalist's cavalier dismissal of that question falls upon questing souls that search for a reason as much as the body yearns for water?

There were no professors of science in the original created order to question revelation. From deep within the human soul arose the challenge for autonomy over against a boundary within which to live. So let's get over two blunders—the one that thinks this is modern man in revolt, and the other that thinks intellectuals disbelieve in God and only the naïve or stupid continue to believe in God. I have met intellectuals on both sides of the issue, and it is not merely an intellectual struggle. It is a struggle of bridge building, of trying to tie theoretical structures to heartfelt and heart-hungering realities.

As Real as Now

The second question that originated in Genesis came in the form of a challenge: "You will not surely die! You will be as God, defining good and evil." For Darwin, as for our polite modern thinkers, hell is anathema. Why would any self-respecting human being think up hell? Interestingly, these who challenge the existence of God are the very ones who are willing to punish others for their beliefs. "Destroy the livelihood of those who believe in the sanctity of marriage!" "Don't give them a place in academia if they really believe God exists!" Such is the retribution of self-worship, imposed by those who call God vengeful, a "joy-killing monster," and "a freedom-restricting tyrant," if you don't give Him His due place. Fascinating how we wield power when we own it and then mock others with power for giving in to the same expression.

The enemy of our souls basically counters the claims of God, not merely by questioning them, but then by asserting that by disobeying God's commands one will actually be promoted to taking God's place. Once again at the heart of all temptation is the desire for autonomy and power. The human scene was steeped in the battle for autonomy and power right from the beginning. Did God speak? Is it true what He says about good and evil? Are we going to believe the truth, or are we comfortable with the lie because of the power it promises to give us?

It seems as though the ultimate destination point, then and now, is the power to control culture and destiny. Very recently, a Russian business tycoon gave Stephen Hawking one hundred million dollars toward his endeavor to find extraterrestrial intelligence. Hawking has opined that it is critical for us to find them before they find us, saying that if we don't find them before they find us, they could wipe us out of existence. After the slaughters in San Bernardino, Belgium, Paris, the Boston Marathon, Turkey, Baghdad, Orlando, Dallas, and the list goes on endlessly, we want to get to other planets without fixing our own and destroy them also?

I found his comment fascinating. My first reaction was cynical. Yes, I thought, since we don't see much intelligence on this planet any more, let's go looking for it elsewhere. Then another thought kicked in. It is fascinating that the "world's brightest mind" thinks an intelligence possibly exists out there that could destroy us, but no intelligence exists as Creator.

Then yet another thought. Professor Hawking himself, had he been left at the mercy of a pragmatic "life is not human in the womb," or not worth saving by virtue of a degenerative disease, would have been destroyed and we would never have seen the likes of his genius. It would have been our loss. You see how intrinsic value decisions are in the choices we make? The scientific single vision does not give us values; it gives us only what is and cannot give us what ought. Is it any wonder that in this scenario where science is our single vision, existence is the circle and what we believe—our values—are merely a dot, as described by my friend?

Another personal note, from having lived in Cambridge in the early nineties: Hawking's first wife, Jane, was and is a devout Christian, an intellectual in her own right. Hawking himself has paid her the finest compliments. Living side-by-side with one of the brightest minds in the world did not take away her deep belief in Jesus Christ and in the created order. That alone should tell us that what is at issue is not as simplistic as an intellectually determined faith. Much more goes into this.

So then, right from the beginning, in the face of choices, two questions determined the future: 1) Did God say? 2) Do you really think you're going to die or can you become like God, determining good and evil?

The Theoretical Backdrop

What does it mean to be an atheist? What does the "ism" of the atheist hold? Is it monolithic? Are all atheistic systems the same in political theory? How did that philosophy become a formal system, and how does one respond to its claims?

Let's go back to the philosophical and categorical roots of this so-called belief, to its philosophical and cultural viewpoint. The very Greek word from which we get *atheism* is really a simple conjoining of the negative with the divine. The *alpha* is the negative and *theos* is the word for God. At its starting point, from the very structure of the word itself, the philosophy of atheism means no personal, self-existent, autonomous, intelligent first cause of reality.

Ironically, in particular cultural milieus the word gets watered down so that in the days of the early Church, Christians were called atheists because they denied the existence of the gods of Greece and Rome. By the seventh century, Muslims branded Christians polytheists because of their cardinal doctrine of the Trinity. One can readily see how important it is to understand, from the orthodox point of view, what the beliefs really are rather than attributing cultural nuances to a system.

In two of my previous works, I have quoted the standard texts and definitions that provide the starting point for this discussion. I would like to refer back to that before I move forward and bring the positions up to date. Frankly, in a subject such as this, there really is ultimately nothing new under the sun. People such as Dawkins, Hitchens, Harris, Krauss, and others who promote the aggressive side of this belief muster not a single new argument to defend their position. That is why even other prominent atheists or agnostics consider them an embarrassment and say so. In fact, Dawkins' remark on Harris's explanation in *The Moral Maze*—that he provided the last strand against theism—is embarrassing to other atheists, to say the least. I doubt he truly believed that.

The well-respected *Encyclopedia of Philosophy* edited by Paul Edwards defines atheism as follows: "An atheist is a person who maintains that there is no God, that is, that the sentence 'God exists' expresses a false proposition...a person who rejects belief in God."[11] In his book on atheism, Étienne Borne says, "Atheism: the deliberate, definite, dogmatic denial of the existence of God."[12] So while the bottom line of the view is a denial of God's existence, in fairness it is really within the spectrum of agnosticism that ranges from a soft-boiled agnosticism where one claims not to know whether God exists to a hard-boiled agnosticism that postulates that one simply cannot know. The next stage is a rigorous denial of the existence of this Being we call God. That is the hard-nosed idea that God is not in the realm of meaningful statements, and that if He/She/It does indeed exist, it is up to the theist to prove it.

Now this latter assumption is terribly prejudiced by culture and, one might dare say, flies in the face of how philosopher Alvin

Plantinga, a longtime member of the faculty at Notre Dame, would describe belief in God—a "Properly Basic Belief" so common and so self-evident to the masses of humanity that, to them, no defense is needed. Of course, other philosophers take issue with that and say that in any debate this description would not stand the test of argument. Plantinga contends that the masses of people are not in the arena of debate; they intuitively believe that there is a power greater than themselves, and they seek ways in which to connect with that supreme being. Raised in India, I have seen this firsthand. Though it was not my personal belief, it was indisputably intrinsic to the mainstream of life, both for the unsophisticated and the highly educated.

It is important to recognize that the Greeks, who really are the forerunners in systematic philosophical thought in classical philosophy (and as an extension of that came democratic government), attempted to define ultimate reality in abstract terms. Their musings and ponderings on ultimate reality cause some to even argue that Plato was probably moving toward a high monotheism. Whether one accepts that or not, what is important is that in their view, ultimate reality was inseparable from virtue and ethical norms.

For many in Greek thought, the power of reason was supreme, and the freeing of philosophy and science from the mystical was a deliberate and purposeful discipline. But, I repeat, for the Greek thinkers, though they did not posit a God, one thing was certain— virtue and harmony were the emergent implications for life.

There is a striking similarity between our so-called doctrine of tolerance and the early Greeks. For example, the oration at the funeral of Pericles gives fascinating insight into the hub and spokes of their reflections on life and destiny. We owe to Thucydides the reconstruction of that eulogy. Here it is:

> [J]ust as our political life is free and open, so is our day-to-day life in our relations with each other. We do not get into a

state with our next door neighbor if he enjoys himself in his own way.... We are free and tolerant in our private lives; but in public affairs we keep to the law....

When our work is over, we are in a position to enjoy all kinds of recreation for our spirits...in our own homes we find a beauty and good taste which delight us every day and which drives away our cares....

Our love of what is beautiful does not lead to extravagance; our love of the things of the mind does not make us soft.... As for poverty, no one need be ashamed to admit it: The real shame is in not taking practical measures to escape from it.

We make friends by doing good to others, not by receiving good from them. This makes our friendships all the more reliable.... [E]ach single one of our citizens, in all the manifold aspects of life, is able to show himself the rightful lord and owner of his own person, and to do this, moreover, with exceptional grace and exceptional versatility.[13]

Tolerance the New Virtue

Actually, that philosophizing would fit into Buddhism, Hinduism, Jainism, and the new tolerance of Western Secularism. That is the new god of this age. One look at this and you can see how a political framework addresses the soul of a people when God is not known or sought. We can readily see how critical it is that values be upheld for the public good. In reality, this is possibly the basis of a noble humanistic credo, but we shall deal with that later.

For now, we see how the early Greek philosophers and early nontheistic spirituality or mystery religions believed in a structure of virtue for one's individual life and destiny. There were, however, very important differences in terms of *why* they thought this way and what they believed the purpose of life to be. That, to me, is key. As I have travelled for some four decades and have literally met with thousands of individuals, either one-on-one or in small groups after the public forums, there are really a handful of questions that emerge.

The first question is of life's purpose and meaning: What does life and living really mean? Then there comes the question of pleasure and enjoyment: How do I fulfill my desires? The pursuit of pleasure is at the core of our existence. We work, we earn a living, we return to our homes, but then we make decisions for our enjoyment: Are there any boundaries for pleasure? Then there is the third question: What does one make of all the suffering and pain we see in this world?

There you have it. Meaning, pleasure, pain. And all of these hang on the hinge of the fourth major question, a very defining one: How and why am I here in the first place? This was the very bedrock of questioning that Solomon pursued. He was not raised a Greek. He was raised in David's family, a Jewish family with a definite belief in a personal God. There had to be a father-son disjunction here for Solomon to live as a hedonist but be regarded as a moralist, renowned for his wisdom.

That defining question is answered confidently by the atheist that we are here by accident. Turn back the clock and try the same thing again and it will never happen once more. Our presence is a cosmic accident for which there is no script for life or preassigned purpose. But let us be absolutely clear: The atheist has placed all other definitions of life's imperatives on this one hinge, that we exist on this earth and struggle with human personality, morality, and reality without a personal, moral, or real first cause. That's the leap of faith—to believe that ultimately life is matter and that it therefore doesn't really matter. If you submit to the first conclusion, you are inextricably bound to the rest that follow.

Take for example Stephen Jay Gould:

> We are here because one odd group of fishes had a peculiar fin anatomy that could transform into legs for terrestrial creatures; because comets struck the earth and wiped out dinosaurs, thereby giving mammals a chance not otherwise available (so thank your lucky stars in a literal sense); because the earth never literally froze entirely during an ice age; because a small and tenuous species, arising in Africa, a quarter of a million years ago, has managed, so far to survive by hook and by crook. We may yearn for a higher answer—but none exists. This answer though superficially troubling, if not terrifying, is ultimately liberating and exhilarating. We cannot read the meaning of life passively in the facts of nature. We must construct these answers ourselves—from our own wisdom and ethical sense. There is no other way.[14]

Gould states unequivocally that meaning is not decipherable by us. No higher answer exists, he says, and we have to find the answers on our own terms. This incredibly answerless answer is what sends Western values on the slippery slope of nihilism. But there is more. If meaning is not within the purpose of our existence, the second struggle is whether to seek a boundary for pleasure or eliminate all boundaries.

The difference between a nontheistic religion and an atheistic worldview is literally worlds apart. The difference comes from the explanation for theistic thinking. Both the realities of pleasure and of pain demand answers and explanation, whether life has meaning and whether there is a solution to the problem of pain. To arrive at a formal and creedal denial of a supreme being opens the door to all kinds of debates and arguments on the entailments of such a hopeless foundation.

From that starting point the remaining three answers are literally up for grabs, so let's see how the religious nontheist and the secular atheist deal with the entailments of their starting points. When you start off with "no god," you end up with the strangest of mental manipulations to keep you from the logical arc of reasoning. And the first mistake for the atheist is to position science into doing what it was never supposed to do.

Scientists themselves question their fellow authorities in this field. The agnostic physicist David Berlinski has written a trenchant critique of Dawkins in his book *The Devil's Delusion*, a challenge to Dawkins' *The God Delusion*. On the inside flap of the book, introducing his subject, he writes,

> Has anyone provided a proof of God's inexistence?
> Not even close.
>
> Has quantum cosmology explained the emergence of the universe and why it is here?
> Not even close.
>
> Have the sciences explained why our universe seems to be fine-tuned to allow for the existence of life?
> Not even close.
>
> Are physicists and biologists willing to believe anything so long as it is not religious thought?
> Close enough.
>
> Has rationalism in moral thought provided us with an understanding of what is good, what is right, and what is moral?
> Not close enough.

Has secularism in the terrible twentieth century been a force for good?
Not even close to being close.

Is there a narrow and oppressive orthodoxy of thought and opinion within the sciences?
Close enough.

Does anything in the sciences or in their philosophy justify the claim that religious belief is irrational?
Not even ballpark.

Is scientific atheism a frivolous exercise in intellectual contempt?
Dead on.[15]

One has to commend Berlinski and others like him for calling the bluff of those hiding behind science and making sweeping assertions against belief in God. In fact, there is so much contradiction even within the exact sciences that anyone who speaks for all obviously does not respect the different disciplines within science. I know scholarly thinkers in the field of chemistry who have issued challenges to others, asking them to show evidence from chemistry that the move from primordial slime to Homo sapiens is even theoretically possible. Professor James Tour of Rice University is one such scholar. In fact, cosmologist John Barrow said to Dawkins, "You have a problem with these ideas, Richard, because you're not really a scientist. You're a biologist."[16]

Interesting, isn't it, how the methodology and implications vary between the disciplines? It was this very challenge that caused Chandra Wickramasinghe and Fred Hoyle to postulate that an earthbound theory explaining origins is mathematically impossible. But that is the foundation on which all the debunking of religious belief takes place. My colleague in this book will be dealing more extensively with the hazards of a scientific single vision. For my purposes here, let us agree that the extension of the discipline takes it outside its range.

That, then, brings the implications of the existential struggle into the no-man's-land of meaninglessness.

A Rootless Culture

In Western cultural speak, we have basically gone from being a rootless society to a ruthless society. In America, we say that we are a nation of laws. That sounds fascinating. Are we implying that other nations are nations without laws? No culture on earth has more laws than the Islamic world. Their laws extend to what you eat and when you eat, how you marry and whom you marry, how you bank and with whom you bank, when you fast and how much you give, which way you face when you pray and how many times…laws ad nauseam. They pride themselves on it.

So we are a nation of laws. Let's move further. To use a metaphor, law forms the roots from which our culture is built. The trunk then becomes the political system; the branches and the leaves or the fruit of the tree become the expression of the culture. That's the figurative description of how we build a culture. When you think about it, it is actually circular. We act as if law just came into being and is self-evident. The question should really be, what holds the law in place?

The laws that legitimized slavery were railed against by a moral intuition that this exploitation and dominance of a people was morally wrong. Ironically, in their songs both the slave and the slave owner called upon God to rescue them or validate them. They weren't calling upon nature to do so. Even in the context of the dominance of the Indian people by the British, Bertrand Russell, of all people, said that it was doubtful the plea from reason would have succeeded against the British except that it appealed to the conscience of a Christianized people.

This is where worldviews come into play. What holds the laws of a nation? It is the moral soil that must hold the roots. As G. K. Chesterton put it, lawful and legal do not mean the same thing and the moral soil is indispensable to aesthetic flourishing:

> We are always near the breaking point, when we care only for what is legal, and nothing for what is lawful. Unless we have a moral principle about such delicate matters as marriage and murder, the whole world will become a welter of exceptions with no rules. There will be so many hard cases that everything will go soft.[17]

> Nothing sublimely artistic has ever arisen out of mere art, any more than anything essentially reasonable has ever arisen out of pure reason. There must always be a rich moral soil for any great aesthetic growth.[18]

Recently I saw a movie titled *Irrational Man*. The well-known actor Joaquin Phoenix plays the role of an esteemed and attention-drawing professor of philosophy. Before he arrives at the school at which he will be teaching, he already has a reputation as a bit of a loner and an eccentric. As the story line builds, we become aware that his goal is to influence his students toward the ethical system he subscribes to, built on the existentialists.

One day he overhears the story of a woman who was wrongly victimized by a judge's ruling and becomes irate over that injustice. He ponders how to set this right and decides to kill the judge. That accomplished, one of his students discovers that he is the killer and, aghast, gradually pins him down with the truth. He has one option left, to kill her as well, even though he was romantically involved with her. In the end, in a struggle near an open elevator shaft, she gets the better of him and instead of her, as he had intended, he is crushed under the weight of the elevator.

It is interesting that though reason was his discipline, he was crushed by the weight of the immoral reasoning he had justified in his own heart as the right thing to do…until he was found out and had to explain it.

Law, philosophy, love, education, justice…all are built not on reason alone but on *moral* reasoning. This is the discipline under which atheism fails, and the ideas of atheism will be crushed under the very system constructed to make the one who points the guilty finger ineffectual.

The hunger of the human heart is for meaning, reason, purpose, and value, and atheism simply does not have either the answers or the explanatory power to make it possible to build a life on the foundation it offers. That is why some of the best of them discover at life's termination point that their philosophy was reasoned into irrationality and their temporary victory, pyrrhic—it cost the victor more than it cost the vanquished.

To wit, Antony Flew and A. N. Wilson, two prominent thinkers who climbed the tree of atheism to great renown, only to concede that its trunk is hollow and its branches, deadly. The unanswered questions made Flew question the philosophy. An Easter Sunday walk to church with his family where he observed the followers of Jesus and heard the truth claims of their resurrected Lord made the difference for Wilson, the difference between life and death, substance and hollowness, purpose and meaninglessness, love and hate, living a lie or living by the truth.

The chapters to come show the difference between Jesus and secular "isms" in the why of life itself. Our first comparison will be a deeper exploration of atheism—the general "ism" underlying all other secular worldviews. Then we proceed chapter by chapter to confront the secular gods that guide our neighbors and our nation. So far we have glimpsed only the tip of the iceberg. Let's see where the differences really take us.

Chapter 2

Atheism

〰️

"There is no God."

Ravi Zacharias

Since Dawkins is the new guru of atheism, I will take his major criticism against belief in God—God, the moral monster—and consider his assertions and conclusions. Others have dealt with the supposed use of science to defend his case, and Vince will address this in his chapter on scientism. My intention is to respond to the philosophical implications and ramifications of Dawkins' belief in contrast to the real message of Jesus Christ. Indeed, Dawkins reserves his strongest attacks for the Bible and the "unfathomable atrocities" that God commanded. He lists them ad nauseam to make his point. To give him the full benefit of the doubt, I will let you read his words for yourself as he writes in his book *The God Delusion*:

> The God of the Old Testament is arguably the most unpleasant character in all fiction: jealous and proud of it; a petty, unjust, unforgiving control-freak; a vindictive, bloodthirsty ethnic cleanser; a misogynistic, homophobic, racist, infanticidal, genocidal, filicidal, pestilential, megalomaniacal, sadomasochistic, capriciously malevolent bully.[1]

31

A few years ago, some of these words weren't even in the dictionary. One is tempted to ask, "How do you really feel, Richard?" Dawkins himself is not known for being a particularly humble, irenic, and gracious person. But that is not the issue here. I grant that at first blush this is very powerful, and it is troubling that God should be open to this kind of characterization. I would like to add that anyone who believes that a thinking Christian is not troubled by it hasn't talked to the serious-minded thinker. Of course it is troubling, deeply troubling!

Whether we like it or not, we are all to a certain degree a product of our own experiences. I could hazard a guess that there is some such deep antipathy toward God in many atheists though it may never surface, even in their vitriolic outbursts. But it is not hard to see. I look back over the years and see how I was shaped through the lens of what I witnessed and heard. All one has to do is be present in a real war zone, where devastation and death are all around, to move from questions about individual suffering to those over mass suffering. Hate, anger, and cruelty are seen up close and questions crowd the emotions.

In my twenties, I covered the length of Vietnam during the height of that war. Late one evening I sat on the front porch of a missionary's home about twenty miles from the demilitarized zone and listened to the firepower being unleashed just a few miles away, reflected in the amber-colored sky. I was a safe distance away from where it was really happening, but I was close enough, and the sound of incoming and outgoing artillery was constant. I asked myself to what end was all this? How can such realities be part of an eternal plan?

Just a few feet in front of where I sat was the mass grave of six missionaries who had been murdered in cold blood three years earlier, just because they were there. They were noncombatants, there to touch the souls of the people, whether friend or foe. They were there to help others, and they paid with their lives, their children left orphaned. Late into the night my hosts and I talked of the horrors of war. I attended church services where airmen in uniform prayed and were prayed for immediately before being deployed on a mission, uncertain of their return.

On another occasion I was driving in a car with some missionaries from Dalat to Saigon when our car broke down on a rather desolate part of the road. After several minutes and some uneducated tinkering, the car started and we continued on our way, only to come upon a terrifying scene a few miles up the road. A car that had overtaken us while our car was disabled had been ambushed and all the occupants lay mangled and bleeding to death on the side of the road. In the distance, we could see the attackers melting away into the jungle.

At twenty-five, I had seen enough of warfare and bloodshed. I had heard enough political speeches. I had read enough of the journalists and their pontifications from a distance. I had heard all the dissent I needed to hear from professorial lecterns; communism versus capitalism, freedom versus demagoguery. Walking away from the body of a loved one being lowered into the ground is a heart-wrenching experience. Seeing it multiplied in the deaths, deformities, and destruction around me, I found myself crying out to God, "Why all this in the name of humanity and survival?"

I was doing my thinking as a young man. Years went by, and I read the philosophers and philosophies of war and the attending theories. I questioned, I struggled. It would have been enough to question the entire theistic framework. It didn't take an atheist to raise the question of violence, injustice, and evil.

Many of the prophets in the Bible raised this issue directly to God and sought answers from Him. "How long, LORD, must I call for help, but you do not listen? Or cry out to you, 'Violence!' but you do not save?" is the question Habakkuk raised (Habakkuk 1:2). Jeremiah did the same and asked God to stand in the witness box. In Jeremiah 12:1, he says: "You are always righteous, LORD, when I bring a case before you. Yet I would speak with you about your justice: Why does the way of the wicked prosper? Why do all the faithless live at ease?" Later in the book he even accuses God of deceiving him and in frustration he says, "Cursed be the day I was born!" (20:14). And in Psalm 10:1, David asks God, "Why, LORD, do you stand far off? Why do you hide yourself in times of trouble?"

No one questioned the Almighty more about the pain and shame of human evil and personal loss than the biblical writers. But here's the rub. They always raised it while still recognizing the nature of good and evil, victim and victimizer, human limitation and divine power. They not only understood the categories, they questioned where a sovereign God was in the midst of all this. And they found answers. Habakkuk particularly found his way to some solid footing. We will get to that. What is dramatically real is that they do not raise it to question God's existence, nor do they raise it to prove that good and evil are not real. They raise it to find the answers to God's existence within the framework of the good and evil they undeniably see around them.

In contrast, looking at the same evidence as the biblical writers, the conclusion Dawkins draws is to deny the existence of God, and he is forced, therefore, to dismiss evil and good as absolute categories. And therein lies the deep-seated difference. What do I mean?

Where Do You Get Off?

These terrible descriptive words for God that Dawkins uses put him in a real philosophical and existential quandary. He begins by saying that the God to whom these actions are attributed is really a "creature of fiction." If God is indeed a creature of fiction, he is in effect mounting this great effort against a nonexistent entity to whom such actions are attributed by some very gullible people. So wherein lies the evil? If God doesn't exist, the evil that Dawkins is railing against is really coming from human beings playing God, isn't it?

This is key to underscore. If atheism is correct, his nauseating list from genocide to infanticide does not describe God's character but the people who claim to believe in God. Ironically, this comes from an intellectual who writes at a time when the killing of babies by abortion is at an all-time high, legitimized by intellectuals as one's moral right. Thus, the killing of millions in the name of individual rights is okay, so long as humanity declares it is so. So the source of both scenarios is human, not divine by his paradigm. If God is dead, then in the words of Malcolm Muggeridge, we are left with "the pursuit of power versus the pursuit of happiness, black-and-white television versus color, the clenched fist versus the raised phallus."[2] In other words, it is either megalomania or erotomania, Hitler or Hugh Hefner.

If God does not exist except in the minds and writings of His followers, who are human beings (of whom Dawkins is one), it is they who are genocidal, misogynistic, infanticidal, homophobic, etc. How in the name of reason does Dawkins think that his own judgment, as a human being, is a fair and correct assessment of other people? If evil does not exist, his is merely a "preferred flavor"…as is theirs.

Intuitively, people react against the behaviors Dawkins is warring against. But in order to vilify them, or the people he blames for them, he has to agree that these things are evil, a category he struggles to locate. By saying that there is no God but that these attributes of God are evil, he has put himself in a bind and is playing God himself. He may as well put a picture of himself in his living room and bow down to it every morning.

Elsewhere, this same Dawkins goes on to say that at the base of it all there is no good and evil; we are all dancing to our DNA.[3] What on earth has he created? He vilifies a monstrous God and throws Him away but presents a monstrous philosophy of life as the most reasonable. At best, his reasoning is either circular or self-defeating. Philosophically, his thinking really assumes and deduces the following:

Assumption 1: If an all-powerful and all-loving God exists, He would not do such evil things as we see happening. Therefore, the God described by the religions of the world is fictitious and cannot possibly exist.
Conclusion: There is no God.

Assumption 2: Since there is no God, these terrible things are really thoughts and actions of the human heart.
Conclusion: Because there is no God to declare good from evil, these things are really not evil per se. They are just the means of survival and expressive categories of human beings.

Assumption 3: Since there is no God and therefore no evil, everyone is merely dancing to his or her DNA. We each do what we do because we are soft wired and hardwired to do what we do. It is not our choice, and we bear no responsibility for it. This is a nicer way of saying, "nature red in tooth and claw," now scientifically postulated.
Conclusion: Since there is no such thing as good and evil, the accusation that God is evil becomes invalid since the very challenge is merely a DNA dance. Even so, the religious dance is more evil than the nonreligious one.

Assumption 4: Since religion is therefore a phenomenological matter rather than a matter of verifiable truth, all religion should be treated as fictitious.
Conclusion: Mock and ridicule people who still believe in God because it is nonsense. God's anger is perverse, but

man's anger against God is the zenith of knowledge. That religious people may be deeply hurt from such verbal bullying and ridicule ought not to be a concern for the one who lives by the reality of a world without God, because God is the ultimate bully.

There you have it in a nutshell.

Now, contrast the Christian worldview. Strangely, this slippery slope in thinking and the degeneracy that follows when humanity turns its back upon God is addressed in the Bible. In Romans 1:18–25, the Apostle Paul says,

> The wrath of God is being revealed from heaven against all the godlessness and wickedness of people, who suppress the truth by their wickedness, since what may be known about God is plain to them, because God has made it plain to them. For since the creation of the world God's invisible qualities—his eternal power and divine nature—have been clearly seen, being understood from what has been made, so that people are without excuse.
>
> For although they knew God, they neither glorified him as God nor gave thanks to him, but their thinking became futile and their foolish hearts were darkened. Although they claimed to be wise, they became fools and exchanged the glory of the immortal God for images made to look like a mortal human being and birds and animals and reptiles.
>
> Therefore God gave them over in the sinful desires of their hearts to sexual impurity for the degrading of their bodies with one another. They exchanged the truth about God for a lie, and worshiped and served created things rather than the Creator—who is forever praised...

What we have here is the exact opposite of the atheistic worldview. Atheism declares that belief in God is "foolishness." And in that denial there follows an ultimate denial of the essential definitions of good and evil. Everything becomes desacralized. In the Christian framework, the denial of God *is itself foolishness* and leads to a degeneration that is perverse and celebratory of things commonly considered perverse. The judgment that falls upon willful evil is ever greater evil.

In short, by denying God's existence, the atheist doesn't solve the problem of evil, he just uses the horrors of evil to deny its moral context, and if hate follows, so be it. In Christian terms, that very denial of evil has everything to do with evil. And that is just for starters. There is more. The human scene is even more fundamentally flawed. You see, for moral reasoning to exist, one must at all times assume the freedom to choose.

Within a nontheistic, mechanistic, accidental cause for the universe where "blind and pitiless chance" molds and shapes our choices, determinism is the inescapable conclusion. With the absence of God, true freedom goes as well; thus, as Dawkins says, we dance to our DNA. Even Stephen Hawking grudgingly granted this conclusion, quantum theory notwithstanding, in a lecture at Lady Mitchell Hall, Cambridge, in 1990, a lecture at which I was present. Determinism is the logic of our chance existence. And the journey into contradiction begins. Psychologists such as B. F. Skinner latched on to this inevitable reality and have been writing on this subject for years.

Determinism and Destination

Determinism dictates that we are hardwired to think in the terms that we do. That makes truth claims invalid since we are really not free to think in any other way...out of flux, nothing but flux. Determinism removes the possibility of free options and can only result in preset conclusions. We are actually computers with prescriptive feelings for specific realities.

With that hardwiring, even love becomes illusory and merely a mechanistic preference that is no choice at all, just an action.

You see the result: The foolishness of denying God as the first cause also, in the end, puts both truth and love in jeopardy. Truth and love as ultimate realities are lost in the quicksand of a deterministic foundation.

This is reversed in Romans 1. It is very important to understand that belief in God means that we start off free and volitionally choose that which is corrupt and corrupting. That corrupted mind/heart slides further into darker choices till we are conditioned to think in opposite categories to those with which we started. Good becomes evil and evil becomes good. Those choices we made three sentences back determine and reconfigure our mind-set and destination. Determinism is, in fact, the end state, *not* the beginning.

That is why evil is the final choice and now, with a thoroughly impaired judgment, we have made God also to be evil and ourselves to be wise. Those who have freely chosen to reject God end up in the very place they started in their own thinking; thinking themselves to be determined, though they were free, they end up determined and shackled. The lie they believed to start with becomes the entrenched truth that started as a wish to become like God, determining good and evil, and becomes a death wish. That, after all, was the same warning given in Genesis 3.

This is the path to an incredible destination of deception and degradation that seems noble. The gods of this world have deified themselves unto death. Genesis 1 begins with "In the beginning God," and Genesis 50 ends with Joseph in a coffin. The God of creation warns us of the folly of rejecting God. Secularism is by definition "this worldly," concerned with the things of this world. The life and death of human reasoning takes place in time and space. As one writer puts it, "The worst effect of sin is within, and is manifest not in poverty, and pain, and bodily defacement, but in the discrowned faculties, the unworthy love, the low ideal, the brutalized and enslaved spirit."[4]

I can hear it already. There's the word that is so despised: *SIN.* We hate the word because it brings with it all the collective prejudice of an anti-God state of mind to shout back, "It is the same old thing." C. S. Lewis reminds us that the fear of the same old thing is the strongest passion the Evil One has put into our hearts to resist any sense of self-indictment. So let me give sin its softest definition: A violation of purpose; an addiction to the profane.

The Prison of Darkness

Some time ago, I was visiting death row in one of the largest maximum security prisons in America. When I came to a particular cell, the young lawyer who had arranged for us to be there immediately turned away and left the group. She said that the man I was about to talk to was a serial killer and in her days at university, she recalled him spreading fear throughout her campus as he had brutally tortured and killed his victims, all young women. She did not want to make eye contact with this man who had committed such monstrosities.

One of my colleagues and I stopped by his cell to talk to him. The conversation, had we not been separated by bars, would have been terrifying. He repeatedly and belligerently demanded us to tell him whether we were for or against the death penalty. I told him that I would answer his question if he would answer one of mine. I asked, "What do you miss the most?"

He paused and said, "My wife and children."

So here he was, convicted of killing numerous women who were somebody else's children, irate at the fact that a system would choose to separate him from his wife and children and outraged that someone would sentence him to death for what he had done. The very thing he had done to others he despised when applied to himself. Young, intelligent, strong, yet condemned by his own choices, he couldn't even make sense any more. He had chosen his own path of darkness and now reviled those who would protect others from his dark and eerie world. He made a hell around him but wished a heaven for his destiny. Which of the two worlds was proven by his life, the world of self-deification that presented itself in grandiose terms as promoted by Dawkins or the world of Romans 1 and the unleashing of evil it describes?

I recall a conversation with a man who told me of the time Billy Graham was visiting Disney World. As he left, Mr. Graham said to Mr. Disney, "This is quite a world of fantasy you have created here." Mr. Disney is said to have replied, "Actually, you have that reversed. This is the real world. As you leave this place, you enter the world of fantasy."

That is an incredibly powerful analogy. Walk through Disney World and experience the contagious laughter of children! Look into their eyes and see how they shine with excitement and wonder! My little grandson insisted on riding the same ride seven times till we had to plead with him to give it a break.

Contrast this with another illustration. I know a family totally distraught over their teenage daughter's addiction to cutting. She would take shards of glass and cut herself till she would bleed, which only created in her a strange desire for more self-destruction, destruction predetermined by a destructive choice.

The paradigm of the world and the paradigm of God are opposites with strange points of terminological convergence. In the first, assuming we are determined, we freely choose to believe a lie, further eroding our conscience till we mock the truth and lose our capacity to love. We determine our own destiny of determinism.

In the Christian way of thinking, we disavow determinism and freely choose the truth to inform our conscience toward a destiny of a confirmed freedom to love. Freely, we choose the true joys of freedoms that are based on God's truth. The child in laughter symbolizes true freedom. The young teen with a broken piece of glass represents true determinism. The serial killer, the ultimate corruption of judgment.

The atheist, of course, does not like to present it in such fashion. The most sophisticated pronouncement of what he or she believes is that there is no way an all-powerful and all-loving God of the universe can justify such a creation as He has made. Since this unjustifiable order exists, it has to be that there can be no all-powerful, all-loving first cause.

The resulting philosophy is that time becomes eternity; the body becomes the soul; man becomes God; the sacred becomes profane. This moral quicksand is what we now live with in the West. I would like to unpack these four struggles in what follows.

The Difference in Jesus

In contrast, when one looks at the teaching of Jesus, one sees a new paradigm of life and destiny: *Eternity; morality; accountability; charity.* These four parameters define life in completely different ways than atheism. Let me take them one at a time.

Eternity

I have always maintained that time is the canvas on which we portray our individual lives. Eternity is the keyhole through which we see the whole gallery. Philosophical descriptions of time can get sophisticated and almost incomprehensible. The renowned philosopher Charles Hartshorne, when celebrating his one-hundredth birthday, remarked that time was the most mysterious thing about life. But in day-to-day parlance, we see time as a calibration of change. If the now is all we have, and there is no ultimate reason for our being except what we determine for and from our own reasoning, we have a vacuum for a starting point and a pollution of ideas from which to emerge. Time moves in a linear fashion as a calibration of change. We talk of the present, the past, and the future.

The Scriptures remind us that time is a creation of God's and that He dwells in the eternal realm, above and beyond time, because He is unchanging. As Vince will expound in detail in the next chapter, God is self-existent and uncaused. Only that which comes into existence from nonexistence needs a cause. I know all the arguments naturalists try to present against this. But they only do so to mount a case against theism. They never follow that same logic in every other reasoned position of an existent reality. To deny an ultimate efficient cause is to walk into a logical arena of anarchy and unreason.

God did not come into being. He is uncaused, because God is not material. He transcends materiality. Solomon reminds us of this when he says that God has put eternity into the hearts of men, yet we do not know the beginning from the end. As much as we do know, there are two moments in life over which we have no control, birth and death.

One might argue that we can control our death to a degree, but to do so we have to make two assumptions: that the time of one's death is unknown to a sovereign God and that we are absolutely certain that when the body dies, that is the end. Neither of those two realities are part of the biblical worldview. We are told that every day that is given to us was written in a book long before it came to be. It doesn't mean that it was preordained; it at least means it was pre-known.

Everything majestic and stupendous reminds us of the unfathomable vastness of the universe and the eternal. I remember being paid a visit by two astronauts who had travelled in space. One of them was the pilot of the module returning home. Among some of my CDs he had taken on his space mission was one titled, "Who Are You, God?" They paid me one of the highest honors in visiting me and presenting me a beautifully framed collage of the entire space team, the US flag, the Indian flag in my honor, and a copy of the CD. It hangs on one of our walls and I treasure it. The nation of my birth and the land in which I now live, together. They are but two specks when viewed from space but a part of this grand universe.

The pilot spoke of looking out of his spacecraft and thinking of the verse, "What is man that You are mindful of him, and the son of man that You visit him?" (Psalm 8:4 NKJV). Think of it: The vast stretch of unfathomable space, thousands of miles from earth; a small, blue speck in the distance that we call home; yet, the greatest is this little creature we call man. How does such a being as the designer and the creator of the spacecraft with all its intricacies arrive on the scene by accident? He didn't. He is the creation of an Eternal Being and designed to live in eternity. That is why the psalmist says, "You have set your glory in the heavens. Through the praise of children and infants you have established a stronghold" (Psalm 8:2).

The heavens may speak of the glory of God, but only the lips of a child or a man or woman can speak His praise. When that praise is not coming, the destructive capacity is enormous, because the mind steals that which belongs to God and the sacred becomes profane. Eternity defines the sacred; time can make things profane. If I only live for the moment, I do not count the cost. If I live for what is eternal, no temporary sacrifice is too great for the eternal joy of being in the presence of the One who shaped me.

The scientist Arthur Peacocke describes the journey of the first astronauts to reach the moon and remarks that it was not at all surprising that when they saw Earth rise over the horizon of the moon for the first time the words irrepressibly came from their hearts, "In the beginning, God." It would be a travesty if they had said, "In the beginning, nothing." How ludicrous to think that a handful of people who have read a handful of books and been given a handful of degrees by other finite beings actually have the cerebral capacity to kill God and take His place! It would be like a child jabbing at Joe Louis and thinking he was stronger because Louis didn't hit back.

Eternity is an indispensable reality if two of the most painful struggles of life are to be adequately addressed. After the sudden and tragic loss of his son, Yale philosopher Nicholas Wolterstorff said, "When we have overcome absence with phone calls, winglessness with airplanes, summer heat with air-conditioning—when we have overcome all these and much more besides, then there will abide two things with which we must cope: the evil in our hearts and death."[5]

Evil in our hearts and death: the quest for justice in a world of evil and the harsh end of life in death. I see a world of terrible injustice where the weak have no voice, the poor have no hope, the broken know no healing. How do we walk by? Jesus talked about such things, and the Bible tells us that those who heard Him marveled at His answers.

The Dawkinses of this world are manglers of truth. They take the finger of a story and conveniently ignore the fist of the entire narrative. Imagine if you walked into the play *The Phantom of the Opera* and all you heard was the phantom screaming, "Go!" "Go!" "Go!" You might think it a dreadful piece of music. You would miss the splendor of how even the ugly was given hope and how even the wounded could not stand in the way of a love pursued and desired against all odds.

The Eternal Quest for Justice

For the Greeks, virtue was indispensable to democracy and governance. But we might well ask, whose virtue and why justice? These are not self-defining terms. Content is poured into them. And whatever happened to justice? What is the difference between the teaching of Jesus and the naturalist's framework on these issues?

Let's take them in turn and examine the assumptions and challenges of atheism in this context. The first of these assumptions is that nature is all that there is, that nature and what is natural explain everything. For the biologist this means natural selection, for the scientist it means gravity, for the empiricist it is scientific methodology, and for the metaphysician, the supremacy of reason over faith. All of them have the same starting point and the same destination; that there is *no* evidence for God and that the handmaiden of the autonomy of the will and the supremacy of law naturally follow. Political correctness is the escape clause for the inescapability of values, and so they find a home for morality in politics.

Fascinating, isn't it? The institution least trusted by most people and most proven false is the storing house for values. What does that say? Corrupted values find a corruptible system in which to store and define corruption. Rights replace right, power replaces freedom, laws become morals, and what is legal becomes what is just. We talk about human rights, seldom about the right to be human. Yet the quest for justice continues.

In 1994, former National Football League star O. J. Simpson was accused of brutally murdering his thirty-five-year-old estranged wife, Nicole Brown Simpson, and her friend Ron Goldman, a restaurant waiter. The nation was held captive by this trial. Even a barking dog knew a crime had been committed, but O. J. was acquitted. Recently a television interviewer, herself a successful lawyer, asked the lead lawyer on the case whether justice had been served by Simpson's acquittal. His answer was, "There is legal justice, and there's moral justice, and, in this case, legal justice was served."[6]

That is the seduction of reasoning without morality. That is the lie of perverted justice. I would have liked to hear his answer if it had been his daughter who had been so savagely murdered. I cannot but wonder, would it be the same? We have become professionals without morals and judges apart from being lawful. Our courtrooms have become theatrical performances where arguments risk the lives of people and countries, and reasoning has become rationalization for the most debased acts.

With God denied and evil necessarily gone, justice will soon be a thing of the past, as the very generation that cries out for justice has empowered legions of thugs to behave unjustly when their own desires are jeopardized. This is a society without moral moorings. Such are the shenanigans we play in the name of reason.

But where else can this thinking lead? The governing boundary is that the sciences deal only with phenomena. They deal in the real world of matter and with the laws of nature. Nothing supernatural, please. So even justice, the foundation of all civilized societies, is sacrificed at the altar of self-worship. "Legal justice was done." The danger of that kind of thinking is that it risks destroying reason and justifying killing the innocent. Nazi Germany is an example of what can happen to a culture when a legal system perverts justice.

Here is the irony. Those who declare themselves atheists lay claim to nature and deny that the miracle can ever take place because nature's laws are inviolable. But when they consider the laws of a land, they find every conceivable way in which to justify its violation. So while arguing for science, they deny the exception. When arguing for ethics, they invoke the exception. Reason? They wish to play God, and once the destination is determined, the path of least resistance is chosen.

So with constant manipulation, the guiding principle and the constrictions of the material world are supposedly determined by empirically verifiable laws as the basis. These are not proofs for God's nonexistence. These are the assumptions of a worldview that is built only on physical law and then toys with moral law. This is the cry of a society where people are behind bars who cannot understand the justice of bringing them to a place of accountability. But even one of these claimed to love his own wife and children. The O. J. Simpson defense trial lawyers evict the claims of moral law to keep people free, and put their own families at risk. Genesis tells us how such killing within the family began. It all began with the conflict within a man over what belongs to God and what belongs to his own whim. Cain ran the rest of his life.

How do these two beliefs, that nature is all that there is and that the empirical sciences are the final authority, even if only argued from silence, disprove God? Where does that lead in the quest for justice?

Time, which became the friend of naturalists in explaining origin, has become their enemy as they look for justice. Eternity is swallowed up in an unanswerable tension between our intuition and our reasoning. The difference is even greater in what follows.

Morality

Whatever happened to *good*? In trying to explain away God and evil, the critic actually misses the larger point. The Christian worldview is much wider in its scope and more penetrating in its claims than just a definition of evil and an explanation of its origin. The removal of God may bring some temporary satisfaction to an argument that seems unbeatable as presented. There remains, however, a counter side that is totally ignored. If evil makes belief in God indefensible, where does one find a definition for good? Is good also indefensible? This is key and critical.

Some years ago we had a beautiful dog, a Border Collie that we had brought from England. We named him G.K. after G. K. Chesterton. Chesterton would have been honored, because Border Collies are considered one of the brightest and most teachable of the canine species. He was really my wife's dog. She took care of him and his entire upkeep. During his last two or three years, he suffered quite a

48

bit with various ailments. Margie was always there for him. Although he didn't quite like his visits to the vet, when Margie took him, he never fought her on it. Gradually, his ill health got the better of him and we knew his days were numbered.

One afternoon, when I returned home I found that he could not even stand on all fours. One look at him and I could see the life slipping out of him. I called Margie and told her G.K. was at his worst and she had better come home if she was to see him before he was gone. She got into her car and headed home. Several minutes later, G.K. heard the car pulling into the driveway and the sound of that engine that was all too familiar to him. Then he heard the garage door open. He raised his head while lying down to see if she would come into the house. As soon as the knob turned, I watched as he struggled to rise on all four feet, slipping and staggering, and literally stumbling over to her as she entered and collapsing at her feet. He could stand no more.

The Scriptures tell us that even the ox knows its owner and the donkey its master's stall. May I ask, from whence comes this affection on the part of an owner to its animal and the reciprocal understanding of the household pet? In fact, of all species the dog is one of the most fascinating. From the animal world, it actually grows to be more attached to its human owner than to the world with which it shares its DNA. In the same strange way, the human being of flesh and bone leans so much more to the things of the spirit and naturally expresses both love and gratitude to God. These extraordinary reminders speak of an inherent goodness that we celebrate and embrace. We are moved by such expressions of love and kindness.

Love is real and needed.

This perspective is very unique to the Christian faith. Let me take an illustration of greater depth, given to me by a Palestinian young man. We were sitting in a coffee shop in Jerusalem and he spoke in soft tones. He mentioned to me that he had observed a conversation between a leading Muslim sheikh and the Christian worker Brother Andrew. The sheikh had recently ordered the killing of eight Israelis because the Israelis had killed four Palestinians whom they had accused of crimes against the Jewish people. Brother Andrew asked the sheikh, "Who appointed you judge and jury and gave you the authority to order such killings?"

The sheikh replied, "I am not the judge and jury. I am merely an instrument of God's justice."

There was a moment of silence and then Brother Andrew asked, "What place is there, then, for forgiveness?"

The sheikh replied, "Forgiveness is only for those who deserve it."

Now there was a real protracted silence. The young Palestinian said to me, "I thought at once, this explains everything and nothing. If forgiveness is merited, then it's not really forgiveness, is it? But I remained silent," he said, "because I saw two completely different worldviews at work, both with a common starting point about God, but with radically different views of God."

Grace is real and needed.

There it is, the heart of the matter. Our starting points are key, but even they need to be defended. The teaching of Jesus goes beyond mere morality. It goes to what even morality cannot do. We are creatures who are flawed from within. We lust, we are greedy, we are proud, we are selfish. We need these countered not merely to be good but for the sake of what is at the essence of true value. We have to value one another not just ourselves. At the core of the gospel message is "God so loved the world that He gave…"

To subsume all religions as one and, further, wrench texts out of context and make a caricature of God that is repugnant is to play to deceit and to evoke emotions that are conditioned by error. If there is anything that stands out in the teachings and the person of Jesus Christ, it is the notions of love and grace, not hate and killing. Is there not a nobility to grace and admiration for courage that stops the domino effect of evil?

It is not enough to define evil and be repelled by it. We must make a case for the good. The starting points of religious worldviews may bear surface resemblance to one another, but the character within the theistic framework has a direct bearing upon the justifiability of good or otherwise. Goodness and love are equally lost as categories when a naturalist such as Dawkins cavalierly dismisses such expressions as good and evil, grace and love as dancing to our DNA.

Just hours ago, I was talking to a man from a Muslim country. He was asked the difference between the Muslim God and the Christian God. He said he reflected for a moment and replied, "If you want to know what the Muslim God is like, read and observe the life of Muhammad. If you want to know what the Christian God is like, read and observe the life of Jesus. Between the two lives you will see the character of God displayed." He said that settled it for the person who had asked the question.

Our academics once again are so clever and intoxicated with their credentials that they often manipulate ideas to reach a pre-planned conclusion. The God of Christianity and the God of Islam are simply not the same. The Muslim knows that, and the truly committed Christian knows that. If they were not different, why is there any need for a second religion, as Islam began after Christianity? And why was there a movement within Islam to ban Christians from using the generic word *Allah* for *God* in the Bible? Not all religious beliefs are the same. There is a difference, and that difference is justifiable based on a moral difference.

But the same is true of versions of atheism with a dramatic difference. The Marxist-Leninist doctrine of government and the Maoist communist government were both atheistic with different political theories emerging. Both had the same starting point: atheism. Their political theory and their slaughter of millions in the formation and sustaining of government made for a different final destination with similar means—killing, fear, the silencing of dissent, the slaughter of millions. They have a common starting point, different to theism.

Though theists all believe in God or gods as their starting point, their different notions of God lead to different political theories. Atheists share the identical notion of no God and material man, and that has led to the ultimate demise of any absolutes and to the place that any political theory can be justified. Man is nothing more than dust in the path of ideological idealism. So the similarity in essence for atheism is the reason for the atrocities against humanity. The dissimilarity in theistic frameworks makes the difference in what it means to be human. But here the most critical question emerges. Is the atheist right in making man the measure of all things and reducing the opposing person to his own measure? The powerful obliterate the weak because an idea becomes more important than a person. This is when atheism gets hoisted on its own petard.

God's character matters and is needed.

Amorality and the Cost of Truth

An atheist such as Dawkins needs to consider two tensions he must face. The first is a descent into the erosion of the categories of good and evil that may result in others who take what he says to heart. Dawkins may make the case that neither Maoist nor Leninist political theory are his. Fair enough. So let's consider his view of scientific materialism. I begin by asking a simple question. Suppose a case can be made that upon reading Dawkins' books, several people have taken their own lives because what they read shattered their lifelong beliefs about the nature of reality. Would that stop Dawkins from writing these books?

This is not merely a hypothetical question. I know people whose parents have been on the verge of suicide because their children have departed from the family's faith. I have met mothers with broken hearts who said some professor somewhere knocked all belief in God out of their son or daughter. That loss of faith set in sequence a belief system that minimized the value of relationships, plundered marital commitments, engendered an antiestablishment state of mind, and split up families. I have heard these stories. Will seeing the negative impact of his books on others, albeit unintended, be convincing enough for Dawkins or any atheist to stop writing their books? Will he see himself as the author of destruction? I doubt it.

And strangely, maybe rightly so, he might well say, "I am not to blame. I should be free to express what I believe is true." But then I plead and create a scenario to argue that some of those who have committed suicide have left their families destitute; in fact, one of them was doing cancer research that could have greatly rescued humanity from that dreadful disease. In other words, people involved in noble causes have cut their lives short because of the philosophy of atheism that sent them into a nihilistic frame of mind. Should the purveyors of such thinking be held accountable for such deaths? Such writings as Dawkins' need to stop.

Picture another illustration. After reading a convincing argument for atheism, a pilot goes into depression and crashes a plane with men, women, and children on board. I could go on and demonstrate a domino effect from the negative fallout of the book, but would that be enough to convince the atheist not to write those kinds of books anymore?

No! They would insist that their books speak the truth and that those who had believed a lie paid the price. Isn't that what they would argue? Friedrich Nietzsche's books had an impact on Hitler. Copies were presented by Hitler to both Stalin and Mussolini. Atheistic writers make an impact and can shape terrible realities. But should that stop them from their honest expression that we are without a personal moral first cause?

Here then is the second tension for the atheist. If, indeed, the value of the truth as he sees it is worth the numerous tragedies that can ensue by virtue of those who have believed his idea of truth, why is it that he denies the Creator of the universe the same commitment to truth? The simple reality, albeit painful, is that when truth is resisted, tragedies and atrocities come to be. At least in defense of God, the Creator of life can also restore that life into even more pristine circumstances, something atheists simply cannot do.

It is key to know the truth and its implications for life. The repugnance for evil may create questions about how God can exist. The freedom to propagate truth eclipses the wrong-headed decisions made by those who choose to believe a lie. The inexorable tug of goodness and its attractiveness still has an intuitive power over the human heart. This makes atheism not only uneasy on the conscience but untenable in reality.

I knew a prominent businessman in the city where I live. He was immensely successful and had a big heart for charitable causes. His wife was a lovely woman, wishing to protect the neediest in society. He invested mistakenly in one huge venture. He put all his money in a scheme that he thought would make his material success even greater. And he lost everything. Everything. On a given night, while his wife was asleep, he made several notes and pinned each to a different piece of furniture or jewelry, bequeathing each of their possessions to different members of his family. Finally, he wrote a note of regret, took his gun, killed his wife who was still asleep, and then shot himself.

Having lost his entire wealth, he ended the life of his wife and himself. Did he not know the grief and pain he was inflicting? He genuinely thought he was making a decision for the better. This is the reality, isn't it? We can take the risk of destroying lives, thinking we are doing it for the better and that a greater cause is being served. Be it in the name of academic truth or existential pain, we simply cannot point the finger at God and say He ought not to be allowed to permit all this pain when, given the choices, we do the same thing for our own supposed noble reasons. Causing pain doesn't stop us from doing what we feel is right. In Dawkins' case, he exonerates himself for the pain and disillusionment he causes, saying it is in the interest of truth. This other gentleman justified the pain he inflicted because of a looming catastrophe.

People such as Dawkins make these accusations against God because they assume that what is true is valuable and that, when violated, it breeds death; that freedom is a gift to be treasured and not abused; that we have no right to take another's life and, more to the point, to take our own life because we victimize others in the process; that we are interconnected with our fellow human beings, and oftentimes those who had nothing to do with someone else's decision pay as much, if not more, of a price for the actions of another.

But are these not the assertions of a theistic worldview? How does one explain such realities emerging from a nontheistic, accidental collocation of atoms? These very ideas and values are actually borrowed from a theistic framework. They are illegitimate deductions within naturalism. Determinism cannot give us true freedom and true moral categories.

Let's go further. However we try to mitigate the reality, there is a difference between a tragedy and an atrocity. We like to blame God for the atrocity, but we exonerate ourselves for the atrocities we cause. So we then point to tragedy because it is easier to absolve ourselves from a causal role. In the grand scheme of things, God is sovereign over tragedies and we simply cannot explain His role away without invoking the very categories we disavow of good and evil. So beneath the weight of all this struggle lie these twin realities. Some things are good in themselves and some things are evil in themselves. Atheism cannot sustain the definitions.

Truth matters and is needed.

Morality and Beauty

I am sitting in a plane, writing this on a flight between Seoul and Atlanta. I have entered the skies of the United States. It is about six a.m., and as I look out the window I see a spectacular sunrise. The clouds below are soft and almost appear like marshmallows. I marvel at the beauty. Oscar Wilde remarked that while I may be in awe at its splendor, the sunrise cannot return the compliment to the viewer. It is the person who frames such realities of beauty. Beauty as an abstraction does not revel in itself. But I move to a higher plane and think of how a poet would respond to such splendor. And then I ask myself, have I ever read poetry that no poet had written? Have I ever heard a song that no singer had sung or instrument played? Had I ever read a book that no author had ever written? Have I ever been loved when there was no one behind that love?

To be sure, the atheist can also enjoy the sunrise. But the atheist stops at the door of beauty or goodness with no one behind that beauty and goodness. It is the ultimate dead end of an idea and decapitates the cause behind the creation and the one who is in awe. Personhood and genius are destroyed at the doorstep of ideas. It is natural to see a painting and look for the signature, to read a book and look for the author, to see a war and ask who started it, to see a grave and ask who is buried, to see a baby and ask who are the parents. The intrinsic and creative or destructive worth of a person.

The atheist in fact talks of the true, the good, and the beautiful, but never asks why we admire or pursue such categories. These are ideas by which we judge everything, as Mortimer Adler points out. The same applies for liberty, equality, and justice. These are ideas by which we seek to live. Wars are fought over them. Books are written because of them. If such categories exist, which of the worldviews is able to explain them or justify them or sustain them? Atheism simply cannot do it. To be sure, it has been tried. Sam Harris writes on it in *The Moral Landscape*, as does Stephen Hawking in *The Grand Design*. But, alas, there is no designer and there is no objective moral lawgiver. We make laws and claim credit. We design beauty and claim the credit. But is the backdrop of these categories free from such necessary connections? The counterintuitive conclusions are indefensible. We will write books that can break up lives and defend freedom, but we deny God the same prerogative. We cannot restore life. He can. We do not have infinite knowledge. He does.

Ideals matter. They all matter because of eternity and because of the character of God. Eternity, morality, and, next, accountability.

Accountability

With the jettisoning of eternity and morality, we return to the inevitable: Are we as human beings accountable to anyone or to anything? Or is it just that we need to avoid being caught? So I go back to my first challenge: When Dawkins brands God with all these nasty descriptions, what is he saying? Is he saying that such a God exists and is not worthy of our worship? Or is he saying that no such God exists and is the creation of people?

Aha! That's it, isn't it? It is the people who believe in God that he is lampooning, not God. He doesn't believe God exists; he is slandering the thinking and beliefs of people. So when people such as Dawkins mock God, they are really mocking people who believe in God. It is the wretchedness of humanity that he is talking about, not God. It is precisely what happens when man plays God.

For the Christian, then, the question still remains: How can "God command these" things if we claim that this is God's word? These atrocities listed by Dawkins, at times so ridiculously and tendentiously stated, still need some contextual explanation. Were they really ordered by Him? Was God used as a foil to do one's own bidding? Was there a reason for some of the hard to understand judgments? Are there contextual explanations? Is there a difference between some of the real consequences of turning one's back upon God and so-called arbitrary interventions by God? Were there built-in covenantal entailments for a covenant agreed upon for a nation's good? Are there differences between ceremonial profanities and moral resistance?

All these and numerous other contextual matters have to be carefully considered, in contrast to the brash and angry responses of Dawkins. He clearly desires an end position and manipulates texts to get to that emotional outburst. A Bible scholar, he is not. God becomes a very easy target when we wish to create a caricature of Him. The angry outbursts tell us more about the resistance within the heart of man than it does on the reach of God for our hearts. We must get to these issues in response, and we hope to get to these as the material unfolds and present some greater context in my final chapter.

Charity

Some time ago, I was at a university open forum and a student asked me for my view on gay marriage. I knew right off the bat that it was a question designed to put me, as a Christian, with my back to the wall. So I responded with a question of my own: "What kind of culture are we living in? Theonomous, heteronomous, or autonomous?"

A theonomous culture believes that God's law is so engraved into the human conscience that by design we think His thoughts and are naturally driven toward His higher calling. Though this perhaps used to be the dominant thinking of Western culture, it no longer is.

The second kind of culture is heteronomous. *Heteros* means another, and a heteronomous culture is one in which the thinking of the masses is dictated by a demagogue or a power base that forces its own morality upon them. In religious terms, Islam is a heteronomous culture. In secular terms, Marxism is a heteronomous culture. In the West, we repudiate that kind of dictation of morality.

This means we are neither theonomous nor heteronomous. We are, strictly speaking, an autonomous culture. We are self-governing in our moral choices. The questioner granted that conclusion.

At that point I said, "Now let me ask you this. If we are an autonomous culture, will you give me the privilege of making my own moral choices, or the moment I do so, will you switch to a heteronomous mode and dictate my choice?" He remained silent. Charity is not an easy deduction in an anti-God state of mind. But it is the logical outworking of a Christian worldview.

This is the Christian ethic at work. I am given the freedom to choose, and I am loved even when I make the wrong choices. But I am graphically reminded in the mission and work of Jesus Christ that, though I can choose my behavior, I cannot transpose the consequences that are inextricably bound to a particular choice. The greatest reality is that even in my wrong choice, I am still loved by God who woos me back to Himself by making the most sacrificial gift of all—a Savior for my rebellious heart.

Charity is a soft word. A sacrificial love is the substance of that expression, a love that reveals the pain of wrong choices by paying the price in One who did not make that choice. That is why the supreme expression of the gospel is the word *grace*. Some languages have a hard time even translating it. It is the richest word for the most impoverished heart, and it is the inheritance of one who merely asks of the Judge of all the earth to extend that to the one who has wronged Him.

Remember the conversation with the sheikh who said that forgiveness is only for those who deserve it? Or the mocking of Dawkins, for whom grace is probably a foreign concept? Grace and forgiveness are at the core of the message of Jesus Christ. That truth stands tall in the light of secular gods, or for that matter other religions of the world.

For the atheist, man becomes god; the body becomes the soul; time becomes eternity; the profane becomes sacred.

In the teaching of Jesus, eternity, morality, accountability, and charity define the nature of our existence and the pattern of our behavior. Is it any wonder that the Christian faith is the richest faith in music and worship? It is based on a relationship, expressed in worship, demonstrated in charity, a great leveler of humanity, and it reaches into eternity. It can take captive the mind of a child and set free the greatest philosopher—both can express wonder in the most simple yet sublime terms.

The best known verse in the Bible is John 3:16. In fewer than thirty words we have everything stated: "For God so loved the world that he gave his one and only Son, that whoever believes in him shall not perish but have eternal life." Unpack this profound verse with me:

> The starting point is filial;
> The giving is unconditional;
> The gift is relational;
> The range is eternal;
> At the core it is judicial.

Contrary to the criticism of a naturalist such as Dawkins, there is a law by which this world operates. The law of God is existentially necessary and was empirically verifiable in the life, message, death, and resurrection of Jesus Christ. That is why in countries that were once totally atheistic, the masses still clamor for His message and, even at the risk of death, will cling to that belief and hope. Jesus has been repeatedly crucified and buried, but He rises up to outlive His pallbearers in history and in the hearts of billions of His followers.

Next, we turn to one of the most influential rumors of God's death: Science has buried God. The scientism that posits the all-sufficiency of science is perhaps the most widespread form of and supposed justification for atheism. But can it be sustained?

CHAPTER 3

SCIENTISM

~≈~

"Science has disproved God."

Vince Vitale

The first time I met people who encouraged me to consider God, I was in college. I began by reading the gospels, and I found myself attracted to the Christian message. I found myself especially attracted to the person of Jesus and the beautiful life that He lived. But, to be honest, I assumed that belief in God was for people who didn't think hard enough. I assumed that smart people somewhere had already disproved belief in God. More specifically, I assumed that there was some purely scientific way of understanding the world, and that miracles had no part in it.

I can remember picking up a book in a university bookshop around that time and reading the back cover, which summarized the book as an attempt to hold on to a form of Christianity while explaining away all the supposed miracles of Jesus in scientific terms. And I remember hoping it could be done, because I was longing for the person of Jesus, but I thought the traditional account of Christianity was just too extraordinary to believe.

I had this assumption that the *burden of proof* for belief in God must be higher, because God is such an extra-ordinary option. Richard Dawkins puts it this way:

> If you want to believe in...unicorns, or tooth fairies, Thor or Yahweh—the onus is on you to say why you believe in it. The onus is not on the rest of us to say why we do not.[1]

I bought into that way of thinking—that God is the crazy option, whereas a fully naturalistic and fully scientifically explainable universe is the sober, sensible, rational option. Without ever really reasoning it through, I accepted the cultural myth that we used to need God to miraculously explain thunder and lightning, rainbows and shooting stars. But now that we have scientific explanations for these things, we should stop believing in God.

That's actually not a very good argument. A good engineer doesn't need to keep stepping in to override systems and fix malfunctions. If God is a good engineer, isn't the ability to explain His design in terms of consistently functioning processes exactly what we should expect?

Moreover, we no longer think we need the moon to explain lunacy. (Lunacy comes from the word *lunar*, because people used to think the position of the moon explained madness.) Does that mean we should no longer believe in the moon? Should we become not only a-theists but a-moonists?[2] Of course not. Even if the moon doesn't explain madness, there are many other things, such as the tides of the oceans, that it does explain. Likewise, the reasons for believing in God extend far beyond just scientific reasons and include historical, philosophical, moral, aesthetic, experiential, and relational reasons.

Without thinking it through, I jumped from science to scientism—from the fact that science can explain a lot to the assumption that it can explain everything. However, just because the advancement of science has taught us new things about how the universe works, that doesn't tell us whether there is a *who* behind the *how*.

I can give you a full scientific explanation of *how* Microsoft Office works (well, I can't, but a computer expert could; he could sit you down with the design instructions for Microsoft Office and give you a full scientific explanation of *how* it works). But that would not show that Bill Gates doesn't exist; it wouldn't show that there is no *who* behind the *how*. To the contrary, it would show that Bill Gates is really smart!

The *how* question (a question of mechanism) does not answer the *who* question (a question of agency), and it also doesn't answer the *why* question (a question of purpose): Why was Microsoft Office created? We can only get an answer to that question if Bill Gates chooses to share it with us, if the creator of the system chooses to reveal it.

Some of the standard arguments against God based on science are actually not very good. But I think there are a lot of people out there like I was. People who might be open to Christian faith, but who have just assumed that science has made that impossible. They've bought into a cultural myth about the battle between science and religion without actually thinking it through.

In my own life, I'm so thankful to have met some friends, seventeen years ago, who were able to communicate to me in an accessible way their reasons for God, including their reasons for thinking that science and God are in no way incompatible. I found myself persuaded. In fact, today I would agree with Peter van Inwagen, one of the world's foremost philosophers, when he says that "No discovery of science (so far, at any rate) has the least tendency to show that there is no God."[3]

I would actually go further. Not only do I think science is in no way incompatible with belief in God, but I actually think that science points strongly to the existence of God, and I want to share with you four reasons why I believe this:

1. The universe has a beginning.
2. The universe is knowable.
3. The universe is regular.
4. The universe is finely tuned for life.

I believe all four of these facts about our universe are best explained by the existence of God.

1. The Universe Has a Beginning

Let me begin by challenging my old assumption that Christianity is too extraordinary to believe.

Right now, I am standing on a rock that is rotating at one thousand miles an hour and flying around the sun at sixty-seven thousand miles an hour, as part of a galaxy that is hurling itself at over a million miles an hour through a universe with laws so orderly that human life exists. Things are not always as ordinary as they seem!

Dawkins implies that God is too extraordinary to believe in. But a given hypothesis is only probable or improbable relative to what alternative hypotheses are out there. So what are our alternatives?

When we consider big picture explanations of the universe (How did this all get here?), there are only three options:

Option #1: God created the universe. Now, admittedly, that's a pretty extraordinary claim. But let's look at our other alternatives.

Option #2: The entire universe just popped into existence from nothing, without any explanation whatsoever. This is a very odd option. The physical stuff in our everyday lives does not pop in and out of existence with no explanation. If it doesn't now, why think that it did at the beginning?

Option #3: The universe, or perhaps some series of universes, has always existed, extending infinitely back in time. But this just pushes the oddness one step back. Now perhaps each part of the universe can be explained by some part of the universe that came before it, but we still have absolutely no explanation for why there is a universe at all. This too is very odd.

These three options exhaust the relevant alternatives, and all three of them are extraordinary; all three of them are well outside the realm of the ordinary. Now, you may say, "Okay, I can see that all the options are a bit crazy, so I'm going to remain agnostic and not commit myself to any of them." Nevertheless, you're still committed to the belief that one of these three crazy options is true, and that's just as crazy!

The conclusion: We live in a miraculous world! Regardless of whether you're a theist, an atheist, or an agnostic, no one can get around that fact. No one has the choice to believe only in the ordinary. We have not been left with that option. I call this the *normality of the supernatural*, and I find that many people just haven't considered it. They've just gone about their days with their heads down, not realizing that the fact that they are walking around as part of an observable universe nearly one hundred billion light years in size is absolutely astonishing.

Reflection on the only available options challenges the assumption that the burden of proof is more strongly on the theist than the atheist. But now I want to go even further than this and suggest that the burden of proof is squarely on the atheist. Let's take a closer look at each of the three options I've just mentioned. I'll work backward:

Option #3: Can the universe have always existed? Can it extend infinitely back into the past with no beginning?

A hundred years ago, most scientists would have answered yes; it was assumed that the universe had always existed. But one of the most significant developments in cosmology in the last one hundred years is that this thinking has been overturned. Today, the majority of scientists believe that the universe had an absolute beginning at the Big Bang. We now have instruments that can detect that the universe is actually expanding in size, and not only that but it is expanding more rapidly the more it expands. Moreover, unless scientists are radically wrong about the amount of mass in the universe, the universe is never going to contract again by natural means. So the picture that results from this, if we trace the expansion of the universe backward in time, is a universe that began with an utterly dense singularity, where all the mass of the universe was consolidated into a single point and then exploded into the universe at the Big Bang.

A second scientific reason for thinking that the universe had a beginning comes from the Second Law of Thermodynamics, which says that "entropy will increase to a point of thermodynamic equilibrium." That's fancy language, but basically it means that the universe has a certain amount of usable energy, and eventually all that usable energy will be used up. When it is, the universe will be said to have suffered a *heat death*.

Think of the coffee you had this morning. Its heat signifies usable energy, but if you leave it long enough, all that energy will be used up and it will sit at room temperature. Well, if the universe had existed infinitely into the past, it should already be at room temperature. Why? Because however long it would take for it to cool down, that amount of time would already have passed. But the universe is not at room temperature; there is still usable energy; we're still drinking hot cups of coffee! And that suggests that the universe must have had a beginning.

The Cambridge physicist Stephen Hawking is by no means sympathetic to Christian claims, but nonetheless he confirms this conclusion:

> All the evidence seems to indicate, that the universe has not existed forever, but that it had a beginning, about 15 billion years ago. This is probably the most remarkable discovery of modern cosmology. Yet it is now taken for granted... [T]he universe has not existed forever. Rather, the universe, and time itself, had a beginning in the Big Bang.[4]

So the science seems to imply that the universe had a beginning. But even setting science aside, we can also reach this conclusion philosophically.

There is philosophical reason to think that an actually infinite number of things or moments is not possible. Take a beginningless universe; the claim is that an infinite amount of time has already occurred before the present moment. But how could the universe have already traversed an infinite number of moments? Infinity never runs out! However many moments have been traversed, there would always be an infinite number more required to get to the present moment. So, if the universe was beginningless, we never could have gotten to this moment, and therefore the fact that we have gotten to this moment implies that the universe must have had a beginning.

Here's one more way to see the philosophical problem with infinity. We had a big waiting list for an RZIM conference this year, but I've told our organizers not to worry because I've solved the problem for next year. Next year we are going to move the conference to a very special hotel. It's an *infinite* hotel with an infinite number of rooms.

And here's how that will help. Imagine that next year the conference again gets completely booked—we have an infinite number of guests staying in the infinite number of rooms at our very special hotel. Every room is in use. The conference is completely booked. No room at the inn!

And then we get a call from someone who says, "I know I missed the deadline, and I know you're fully booked, but I *really* want to come to the conference. Can you *please* help me?" Normally this would put us in a tough spot. But now, thanks to our very special infinite hotel, we can say, "Of course, no problem! We will book you a place straightaway."

How can we do that if the hotel is completely booked? Like this: We will move the person in room #1 to room #2, the person in room #2 to room #3, the person in room #3 to room #4, and so on and so on out to infinity. We will ask everyone at the hotel to move down one room. Bizarrely, doing this leaves room #1 vacant for the new guest, even though all the rooms were fully occupied at the start and none of the guests have left!

And we can keep doing this as often as we like. Even if an infinite number of additional guests call us looking for a space, we can just keep saying, "Of course, no problem. Book your flight!" Every time a new delegate shows up, we'll just move the person in room #1 to room #2, and the person in room #2 to room #3, and so on. There will never again be a waiting list for this conference. And people say philosophy isn't practical!

But do you see the problem? The hotel is fully booked. Every room is occupied. Yet, when more delegates show up, we can say, "Come right in; we have plenty of available rooms!" That's an absurd result. It's a contradiction for every room to be occupied—there are no free rooms!—and yet, at the same time, for there to be available rooms for as many new guests as you like. This is the sort of incoherent result we get if we accept that there can be an actually infinite number of things or moments, and what that shows is that such an infinity is actually not possible.

Not only scientifically but also philosophically, there are strong reasons to hold that it is impossible for the universe to have extended infinitely into the past. As the first pages of the Bible affirm, the universe had a beginning. Therefore, if someone still wants to deny God, what they are left with is *Option #2: The universe, or some series of universes, just popped into existence from nothing, without any explanation whatsoever.*

This is a very odd claim. Here's one depiction of it that I saw recently:

> ATHEISM: The belief that there was once absolutely nothing. And nothing happened to the nothing until the nothing magically exploded (for no reason), creating everything and everywhere. Then a bunch of the exploded everything magically rearranged itself (for no reason whatsoever) into self-replicating bits that then turned into dinosaurs.

That's having a bit of fun, but it's also making a reasonable point. Things don't just pop into existence out of nothing for no reason. None of us have ever seen a table or a tiger or the person sitting next to us just pop into existence. William Lane Craig, the philosopher who has done the most influential work in this area in the last thirty years, puts it this way:

> To suggest that things could just pop into being uncaused out of nothing is to quit doing serious metaphysics and to

resort to magic. Nobody *sincerely* believes that things, say, a horse or an Eskimo village, can just pop into being without a cause.[5]

Even the eighteenth-century arch-atheist David Hume agrees:

I have never asserted so absurd a proposition as *that any thing might arise without a Cause*.[6]

Things don't just pop into existence for no reason. If the universe began to exist, there should be an explanation for its existence, and from this reasoning results the following simple argument (the Kalām Cosmological Argument):[7]

1. The universe began to exist.
2. Everything that begins to exist has a cause.
3. Therefore, the universe has a cause.

What would this cause have to be like? Well, for it to be the *cause* of the universe and not just some part of the universe, it would have to be outside of space and time, for it would have created space and time. And for it to be able to make the entire universe, it would have to be highly powerful and highly creative. The conclusion is that the cause of the universe is something highly powerful and highly creative that is outside of space and time, and it's hard to think of a better candidate for that description than God.

Objection: Who Made God?

Perhaps the most common objection to this argument is this: God is not a good explanation for the universe because we don't have a good explanation for God. Richard Dawkins makes this objection, saying, "As ever, the theist's answer is deeply unsatisfying, because it leaves the existence of God unexplained."[8]

I sympathize with this objection. When I was a kid, my brother and I used to leave letters in the chimney to be whisked away by Santa, telling him what we wanted for Christmas. And when I was six, what I left in the chimney was the following question written on a paper plate in my best cursive handwriting: "Dear Santa and God, was God ever born?" I like how I covered all my bases. Between Santa and God, one of them was sure to know the answer.

It's a common thought: *If God made the universe, who made God?* There are a few things I would want to say in response to this objection. For starters, I don't believe in a "made" God. Unlike the universe, the Christian God is not bound by time, for He created time and space. And remember premise 2 of the Cosmological Argument: "Everything that *begins* to exist has a cause." It is specifically things that have a beginning in time that require a cause. Why? Because such things did not exist at one time and then they did exist at a later time. That change cries out for explanation. God, on the other hand, was never nonexistent; He never *began* to exist, and therefore reason does not suggest that He had a maker.

However, the primary thing to say in response to this objection is that in order to recognize that an explanation is a good explanation, you don't have to have an explanation of that explanation. Say we were exploring on an extrasolar planet and found a deserted city. We wouldn't have to be able to explain where the aliens who constructed the city came from or how they originated in order for them to be the most reasonable explanation of what we had found. In fact, we wouldn't need to know anything about the aliens at all, and yet our belief that they were responsible for the deserted city would be perfectly reasonable.

In the same way, no one thinks Isaac Newton had to have some explanation for the existence of gravity in order to be justified in positing its existence to explain his observations. In fact, if all good explanations required explanations themselves, as Dawkins suggests, this would lead to an infinite regress of explanations. You would always need an explanation of your explanation, and an explanation of your explanation of your explanation, and an explanation of your explanation of your explanation of your explanation, and so on and so on and so on. The result would be that you could never get to an explanation that didn't itself require an explanation. Nothing could ever be satisfactorily explained! So Dawkins' objection can't be right. In fact, it's ironically an objection that is completely incompatible with the scientific enterprise.

I was in a taxi a while back and was asking the driver about his beliefs. Motioning beyond the taxi, he said, "Of course I believe in God. If God doesn't exist, where did all this come from?"

What good philosophy and good science suggest is that this taxi driver is absolutely right, as was my father-in-law, thirty years ago, when he looked out over the Grand Canyon as a skeptic and sensed God saying, "I made this." He then spent the next three days riding a bus back to the East Coast, wrestling with what it meant for his life if God not only made the Grand Canyon but also made him. Today, my father-in-law is a pastor and has devoted his life to sharing with others that "God made it," and that God made *them*.

Good science and good philosophy point to God. And that raises the question of whether it is primarily intellectual obstacles that keep people from God or rather obstacles of the heart. Divine creation of the universe is not less rational than the other alternatives, but it does demand more of us. If it's true, it's not just an abstract theory asking for our intellectual assent; it's a Person asking for our whole selves. It's an invitation to relationship, and relationships require sacrifice, commitment, and trust.

2. The Universe Is Knowable

A second feature of the universe that points to God is the knowability, or the comprehensibility, of the universe.

It was Einstein who said that the most incomprehensible thing in the universe is that it is comprehensible.[9] I think that's right. In fact, I think it follows that, without God, there is no good reason to trust *any* of our beliefs. This is something that Charles Darwin worried about.[10] C. S. Lewis also had the concern,[11] and the philosopher Alvin Plantinga has developed the thought more fully in recent years under the name "The Evolutionary Argument Against Naturalism."[12]

Here's the basic idea. If you're an atheist, it's common to believe that the sole guiding principle of human development is evolution. But then a piercing question arises: Why should we trust our cognitive faculties if they came to exist and function solely as a product of atheistic evolution?

Put crudely, evolution holds that species adapt genetically according to the principle "survival of the fittest." Apart from any supernatural guidance, atheistic evolution would cause us to develop our reasoning faculties in ways conducive to survival, not truth. And survival and truth are not the same thing. In fact, true beliefs often are not advantageous for survival. It's true that a child is likely to break her leg if she jumps out of a second-story window to avoid being killed by an encroaching fire, but it is far more advantageous for her survival for her to believe that she is likely to land safely on her feet, because then she will be more likely to jump and hence more likely to survive the fire.

Or another example that comes to mind: Geary and Mary Jane Chancey could have saved themselves from a derailed Amtrak train that was sinking in water, but instead they remained in their compartment just long enough to thrust their disabled eleven-year-old daughter, Andrea, out of a window and to safety. Their daughter was saved, but Geary and Mary Jane went down with the train and died.[13]

It is true that their child was worth dying for, but that belief was not advantageous for Geary's and Mary Jane's survival. It was specifically that true belief that led them to their death. True beliefs are not always advantageous for survival; oftentimes they are particularly disadvantageous.

Here's my point: If you think unguided, atheistic evolution is the sole determiner of human development, then you only have reason to believe that your beliefs are beneficial for survival, not that they are actually true. As Plantinga puts it, "Natural selection doesn't care what you *believe*; it is interested only in how you *behave*."[14] Our cognitive faculties are just deceiving us, because they don't care if our beliefs are true; all they care about is that we survive.

To believe in atheistic evolution while thinking your beliefs are true is like stepping on a scale and thinking it will tell you the time. Scales tell weight, not time. Likewise, atheistic evolution aims at survival, not truth.

Note also that the belief of atheism is no exception! Ironically, the payoff of this argument is that if you believe in atheism, you have good reason not to believe in atheism, for that belief too is—on atheism's own assumptions—the result of a process that is not aimed at truth.

Perhaps most disturbing is that this argument also applies to moral beliefs. If atheistic evolution is the sole guiding principle of human development, we might have reason to think our moral beliefs are useful for our survival, but we have no reason to think they are actually true. In the words of philosopher Michael Ruse, "Morality is just an aid to survival and reproduction...any deeper meaning is illusory."[15]

This is just what Richard Dawkins affirms. When challenged by an interviewer that "Ultimately, your belief that rape is wrong is as arbitrary as the fact that we've evolved five fingers rather than six," Dawkins responded, "You could say that; yeah."[16]

If we take atheistic evolution to its logical conclusion, we get highly disturbing claims such as this. Morality is just an arbitrary evolutionary byproduct. It *happened* to have developed one way, but under different conditions it just as well could have developed in a radically different way.

Charles Darwin saw the same problem:

> If…men were reared under precisely the same conditions as hive-bees, there can hardly be a doubt that our unmarried females would, like the worker-bees, think it a sacred duty to kill their brothers, and mothers would strive to kill their fertile daughters; and no one would think of interfering.[17]

This is not the morality we believe in and care about. The morality we believe in is not just an expression of evolution; it's not just about valuing and doing whatever has the most survival value. It's about valuing the *individual*, even when he or she is not contributing to the survival of the species. The elderly, the disabled, those on the margins of society, Andrea Chauncey—they are just as valuable and worthy of dignity as anyone else. A purely naturalistic understanding of the universe cannot explain this. That we are all equally created in the image of God and equally loved by God explains the intrinsic dignity and value of every human person.

It takes only a superficial awareness of the history of the twentieth century to see the great danger in thinking that people are more valuable if they are capable of outsurviving others. We are valuable because of what we are—creations of God—not because of what we do or how useful we are or how much we procreate or how much money we make. We are valuable because of what we are—beings created in the image of a God who refused to seek His survival at the expense of anyone else, but who gave up His life that others might survive.

3. The Universe Is Regular

A third feature of the universe is its regularity. This is another thing that we take for granted without realizing how absolutely remarkable it is. We just assume that when we wake up tomorrow the universe is going to carry on in the regular, stable way that it always has, without pausing to consider what an astonishing assumption that is.

Think about all the predictions that you make about the next five minutes that need to come true in order for you to live a coherent and meaningful life. You assume that the objects in your vicinity are going to remain more or less where they are, that gravity is going to continue to do its thing, that atoms and molecules will continue interacting as they always have, that the color of the things around you will remain constant, that the sun will continue rising and setting, that language will continue to operate as it does, that sound waves will continue to carry as they usually do.

Why? Why do we assume that the universe is going to continue to operate with regularity? We might respond, "Well, that's how it's always operated in the past." But that's not an answer; that's precisely the question! *Why?* Why has it always done so, and why should we think it will continue to do so tomorrow?

If you were blindfolded, and I asked you to reach into a bag full of hundreds of white Ping-Pong balls and to pull out the one red ball in the bag, you wouldn't like your chances. Why? Because there are such a large number of possibilities that are not red and only one that is red.

Well, the same is true when we consider the regularity of the universe. There are all sorts of crazy things that we can conceive of physics doing tomorrow—an infinite number. There is an infinite number of different strengths that gravity could take. But there is only one way that gravity can stay the same—second after second and day after day and year after year. Every second we are reaching into the bag blindfolded, and every time, over and over and over, we are pulling out the single red ball!

On logical grounds alone, that regularity time and time again is incredibly unlikely. What can make sense of it? We just take for granted that the universe will of course operate with regularity. The truth is that this is a great mystery.

However, if God exists, we have a perfectly reasonable explanation for why the future is likely to resemble the past. Why? Because the universe is regulated by Someone who cares for us, and who therefore wants us to live orderly and coherent lives that we can make sense of and find meaning in.[18]

Theist and atheist alike go about life in a manner that only makes sense if we are committed to believing that God is in control of the universe. We simply take regularity for granted, but only God explains it.

4. The Universe Is Finely Tuned for Life

There is one more feature of the universe that I want to call our attention to: It is finely tuned for life.

Imagine that by this point in the chapter you are unbearably bored (hard to imagine, I know). You're struggling to stay awake and you're praying the universe will swallow you up into a black hole. When that doesn't happen, you turn on the TV and the first channel you try is showing the world championship of poker. You begin watching, and in the next twelve rounds the same player gets twelve straight royal flushes.

What should you think? That's right, the person is cheating. Why? Because, even if she's a very honest woman, it's so incredibly unlikely for someone to get twelve straight royal flushes just by chance that someone must be messing with the cards.

Over the last thirty-five years, the "Fine-Tuning Argument" has suggested that we should come to a similar conclusion with respect to God. The universe we live in could have taken many different forms, and scientists have approached a consensus—not just Christian scientists but scientists in general—that there are dozens of fundamental features of the universe that needed to be precisely as they are for life to be possible. Not just life on the planet Earth or life as we know it, but any form of life anywhere in the universe.

These features of the universe include the strength of gravity, the amount of dark energy (the energy that causes the universe to expand at an accelerating rate), the strong force (the force that binds nuclei together in atoms), the ratio of electrons to protons in the universe, the strength of electromagnetism, and numerous other features.[19] In academic literature, these have been called "anthropic coincidences"—"anthropic" because they favor the appearance of life, "coincidences" because their life-permitting values are highly unlikely. In fact, "highly unlikely" is a tremendous understatement.

Take just one example: The explosive force of the Big Bang had to be within 1 part in 10^{60} of what it actually was in order for life to be possible. In other words, the percentage difference that you could have while still accommodating the possibility of life is a 0, followed by a period, followed by fifty-seven zeros, followed by a 1. That's 0.0000000000000000000000000000000000000000000000000000000000000001%.

If the Big Bang had been even the slightest bit weaker, gravity would have made the universe collapse back in on itself almost immediately, far too quickly for any form of life to develop. If the Big Bang had been just the slightest bit stronger, particles would have dispersed literally into thin air. They would have dispersed so quickly and wound up so far from one another that all we could have gotten would have been cold, simple molecules—nothing like the sort of complex chemistry required for any form of life.

That's just one example, and there are dozens more. The precision necessary for meeting some of these conditions, even on their own, can be compared to being blindfolded and spun around, and then being given one shot with a super high-powered gun to hit a one-inch target on the other side of the observable universe, almost fifty billion light years away, and hitting the target. That is the sort of odds we're talking about.

And we need not just one but *all* these conditions to be finely tuned precisely as they are for it to be even possible for the universe to produce any form of complex life. How unlikely is that? Sir Roger Penrose—emeritus professor at Oxford, one of the world's leading mathematical physicists, and joint winner of the Wolf Prize in Physics with Stephen Hawking—suggests the precision necessary is less than 1 part in 10 to the power of 10 to the power of 123 ($1/10^{10^{123}}$).[20] I would write out this percentage as I did above, but, even if I were able to turn *all* the matter in the universe into paper, I still would have far too little paper to print the required number of zeros.

On chance alone, the odds of life are much worse than being asked to randomly choose one designated particle from all the particles in the universe, and picking that specific particle on your very first try. Sir Fred Hoyle, the British astronomer and one of the twentieth century's most significant scientific thinkers, compared the random emergence of even the simplest cell to the likelihood of a tornado sweeping through a junkyard and just by chance assembling a perfect Boeing 747 airplane.[21]

William Lane Craig summarizes that "Improbability is added to improbability until our minds are reeling in incomprehensible numbers."[22] Even *The Stanford Encyclopedia of Philosophy*, the top secular encyclopedia of philosophy in the world, includes the same claim: "The apparent probability of *all* the necessary conditions sufficient to allow just the formation of planets (let alone life) coming together just by chance is utterly outrageously tiny."[23]

How are we to explain these amazing "coincidences"—these royal flushes turning up hand after hand after hand? We should come to the rational conclusion: Someone got their hands on the cards and arranged the system.

Even if you thought there was only a 1% chance that someone would cheat before they started playing poker, if you saw them get dozens upon dozens of royal flushes in a row, you'd have no choice but to conclude that someone was cheating. Scientists tell us this is exactly what's going on in the universe—one royal flush after another. Even if prior to hearing about the fine-tuning evidence you judged the probability of God's existence to be very low, once you learn of the royal flushes turning up time and time again throughout our universe, there is only one rational conclusion: Someone designed the universe.

The Fine-Tuning Argument has been very influential, so much so that even outspoken atheists have had to take it seriously. When antitheist Christopher Hitchens was asked what is the strongest argument against atheism, he responded, "I think every one of us picks the 'fine-tuning' one as the most intriguing.... It's not a trivial [argument]. We all say that."[24]

Sir Fred Hoyle had this to say after reflecting on how precise some of the universe's features had to be to allow for life:

> Would you not say to yourself...Some super-calculating intellect must have designed the properties of the carbon atom,

otherwise the chance of my finding such an atom through the blind forces of nature would be utterly minuscule. Of course you would.… A common sense interpretation of the facts suggests that a superintellect has monkeyed with physics, as well as with chemistry and biology, and that there are no blind forces worth speaking about in nature. The numbers one calculates from the facts seem to me so overwhelming as to put this conclusion almost beyond question.[25]

Hoyle was an atheist until that time, but said that the apparent fine-tuning of the universe left him "greatly shaken."

Objection: What If There Are Many Universes?

The most popular objection to the Fine-Tuning Argument is to suggest that maybe there is not just one but many universes (a *multiverse*), and, if so, then perhaps it is not so surprising that by sheer chance one of those universes would wind up life-friendly. Given enough chances, every improbable kind of thing might happen eventually.[26]

This objection is actually a backhanded compliment to the Fine-Tuning Argument, because it admits that the fine-tuning evidence demands an explanation and goes looking for one. But there are problems with claiming that multiple universes can be that explanation.

First, there is no hard evidence that even one other universe exists, let alone the exorbitant number that would be necessary to get the odds right. Richard Swinburne, the most influential British philosopher of religion of the last sixty years, says that "…it is the height of irrationality to postulate an infinite number of universes never causally connected with each other, merely to avoid the hypothesis of theism."[27] Likewise, the world-renowned theoretical physicist John Polkinghorne says the multiverse theory is "not science," calling it merely a "metaphysical guess."[28]

But, most importantly, even if there *were* strong evidence for multiple universes, the multiverse objection to fine-tuning would still fail. Here's why: Consider again a poker game where you see someone get twelve royal flushes in a row. You conclude that someone is cheating, and rightly so.

Now, suppose one of the players turns to you and says, "No, you've got it all wrong. No one is cheating! What you don't know is that we play cards all the time; in fact, we've played cards all day every day for years." If someone said this, and you had reason to believe them, should you change your conclusion that someone is cheating?

No, you shouldn't. Why not? Because for all you know this person has been cheating for years and getting royal flushes several times a day throughout their whole playing history! Your data is still only that *these* twelve hands—the twelve hands you have just observed—all came out as royal flushes, and that is just as unlikely no matter how many times the players have played before.

You should only change your conclusion if someone were able to show you not only that they have played cards all day every day for years, but additionally that they have played all day every day for years *and* that nothing like this has ever happened before. Then your evidence would change. Then your evidence would be that one time in very many attempts something very unlikely happened. Then this might not be surprising and could perhaps be explained by an appeal to random chance.

But that is not the position the multiverse objectors are in. Not only can scientists not tell us that there are other universes, but, even if they could, none of them are claiming to be able to tell us whether or not those universes, if they do exist, are finely tuned for life. For all we know, *if* other universes exist, maybe *many* of them are finely tuned to the otherwise vastly improbable parameters for life, and thereby further confirm the conclusion that Someone designed the system. As my colleague John Lennox once responded when asked whether he thinks there are other universes, "I've heard rumors that there is a heaven."

This universe, the one universe we have observed, is finely tuned for life. That is our actual evidence—one out of one. And that is just as unlikely to occur by chance no matter how many universes there are.

Note also the irony in this multiverse objection. In order to avoid positing God, people have posited other universes—something we can't see, can't touch, can't perform experiments on, can't prove scientifically. But it's precisely these qualities that were supposed to be points against God!

I actually think this is an unfair criticism of belief in God, because we *can* design experimental tests for God. We can wait until we die and observe the results. Or, better yet, we can pray to God sincerely to reveal Himself to us and see what happens. That experiment is a significant part of the story of how I came to faith.[29] But the multiverse response to the Fine-Tuning Argument does seem guilty of precisely what theism is often wrongly accused of. We have no way of testing, verifying, or falsifying the multiverse theory.

In response to the evidence for fine-tuning in the universe, the Stanford University physicist Andrei Linde raises the possibility of our universe being a product of design by some super-technological alien culture.[30] Likewise, astrophysicist John Gribbin says "serious consideration" should be given to the hypothesis that "our Universe is an artificial construct, manufactured deliberately by intelligent beings in another universe."[31] The fact that proposals of this sort are cropping up in the scholarly literature as strained efforts to avoid having to admit the existence of God is itself testimony to the strength of the Fine-Tuning Argument.

The facts cause even Richard Dawkins to entertain the possibility of intelligent design. He was asked in an interview, "What do you think is the possibility that intelligent design might turn out to be the answer to some issues in genetics or in evolution?" And Dawkins responded,

> Well, it could come about in the following way. It could be that at some earlier time, somewhere in the universe, a civilization evolved…to a very, very high level of technology, and designed a form of life that they seeded onto, perhaps, this planet. Now that is a possibility, and an intriguing possibility. And I suppose it's possible that you might find evidence for that if you look at the details of biochemistry and molecular biology; you might find a signature of some sort of designer.[32]

Interesting, isn't it? It reveals that Dawkins' real problem is not with intelligent design, but rather with *divine* design. I think Linde and Dawkins are grasping in the right direction. To share another of my favorite John Lennox lines, "There is indeed extraterrestrial intelligence, and His name is God."[33]

How far does the Fine-Tuning Argument get us? All the way to Christianity? No. We'll need other arguments for that. But, nonetheless, fine-tuning gets us further than you might think. What would something have to be like in order to fulfill the role of fine tuner of the universe?

The fine tuner needs to be able to determine the universe's fundamental parameters. Therefore, he needs to be very powerful and very intelligent. The fine tuner needs to be there at the beginning of the universe to set its parameters. This favors the idea of the fine tuner having always existed—his being eternal—or at any rate his being very ancient. We can also infer that the fine tuner desired to create life, and specifically intelligent sentient life that could enter into relationship, that could love, and that could display virtues. This favors the fine tuner being personal, moral, and relational.[34]

What we should conclude is that there is an eternally existent, highly intelligent, highly powerful, personal and moral designer of the universe who values relationships, love, and virtue. That sounds a lot like the God I worship.

From Science to God

It is too simple to assume that science can explain everything there is to be explained. Even that claim itself, "Truth can only be known scientifically," cannot be scientifically proven. Moreover, in stark contrast to the assumption that the advancement of science disproves God, two of the most significant scientific advances of the last century—that the universe has a beginning and that it is finely tuned for life—both point strongly to God. Further, without God, we have no reason to trust the regularity or the comprehensibility of the universe that underlies the entire scientific enterprise. Far from the advancement of science undermining God, God is the only thing that makes science possible! It is therefore not surprising to me that a recent survey found that among American evangelical Christians, scientists tend to be more active in their faith than nonscientists.[35]

God's Two Poems

We see God's signature in His design of the universe. We also see God's signature in the design running through individual lives.

Typically, people think science and miracles are at odds. That's what I once thought as I read the back cover of that book that tried to explain away all the miracles of Jesus. But in fact, it's only within the regularity of science that God can reveal Himself to us miraculously. It is science that makes miracles possible! It's only because scientifically virgins don't get pregnant that God can reveal Himself in a virgin birth. It's only because scientifically people don't rise from the dead that God can reveal Himself through a resurrection. And likewise, God can reveal Himself in each of our lives.

The more I talk with people, the more convinced I am that the experience of miracles is universal. I like asking people, even the most scientific of people, "Have you ever had an experience that made you think there might be a God?" Usually there is an awkward lull and then some nervous laughter, but, if you wait long enough, almost without fail the person will say, "Well, there was this one time when…" And then they will tell you a remarkable story that has God's signature all over it!

Most of the people I speak to have amazing stories, but they're worried that they are the only one. They're worried that others will think they're weird. They start to wonder if maybe it's all just in their heads. We need to share our stories, and we need to invite others to share their stories as well.

Here's a recent story of seeing God's finely tuned design in an individual life. A student from China showed up at a university open forum where I was speaking. One of my colleagues, Daniel, greeted her, and she said her name was "Alva." My colleague replied, "That's an interesting name; what does it mean?" Alva responded, "It means 'by grace washed white as snow.'"

Daniel's eyes went wide, and he asked Alva if she was a Christian. She said, "No, not at all." Daniel said, "Do you realize that your name is basically the heart of the Christian message?" She had no idea; she had just chosen this for her English name because she liked the sound of it.

Daniel began to explain the Christian message to her, and she was increasingly being drawn to God. Then the talk started, and halfway through the talk I quoted and put up on a PowerPoint slide, "Though your sins are like scarlet, they shall be as *white as snow*"

(Isaiah 1:18). Daniel excitedly tapped the shoulder of Alva, who looked astonished, and said, "I told you; that's your name!"

At the end of the talk, Daniel and another of our colleagues continued to explain to Alva the love that God has for her, and the sacrifice that He made for her. Alva decided she wanted to be a Christian, and my friends had the supreme privilege of praying with her to affirm that commitment.

There is one more detail to the story that fills me with awe. My talk for that night was already typed and printed before the week began, and the PowerPoint was done. But at lunchtime of that same day, my wife, Jo, and I had a distinct sense that something was missing from the talk. So we rushed home after a lunchtime event, and we added just one additional handwritten page to the talk and just one additional PowerPoint slide.

What did that slide read? Isaiah 1:18: "Though your sins are like scarlet, they shall be as white as snow." God beautifully crafted all the details of that day so He could reach out to that one young woman named Alva.

There are two things in the Bible that are spoken of as God's poem. First, Romans 1:20: "For since the creation of the world God's invisible qualities…have been clearly seen, being understood from what has been made." The Greek word for "what has been made" is *poiemasin*, from which we get the word *poem*. God's creation is His poem.

Second, there is Ephesians 2:8–10: "For it is by grace you have been saved, through faith—and this is not from yourselves, it is the gift of God—not by works, so that no one can boast. For we are God's handiwork, created in Christ Jesus to do good works, which God prepared in advance for us to do." For we are God's "handiwork." Another translation says we are His "masterpiece," and this is the same word—*poiema*.

God not only designed the universe; He designed Alva, and He named her, and He has plans for her life as carefully fine-tuned as His plan for the cosmos. And the same is true of each of us.

> The universe began.
> Its laws are stable and sustained.
> It is knowable.
> It is finely tuned for life.

May that signify to us that our lives began only because God chose us before the foundation of the world. May that signify that it is God who brings stability to our identity and sustains us through even the worst that this life has to offer. Because of God, we can know that we have a purpose. And, if we will let Him, God will fine-tune us for life—a life free of shame and guilt, a life full of love, joy, peace, patience, kindness, generosity, faithfulness, gentleness, and self-control (Galatians 5:22–23).

Just like people are supposed to be able to look at the universe and see it as a poem that must have been written by God, people are supposed to be able to look at the lives of those who follow God and say, "There is a poem that must have been written by God," and "Whoever is the author of that poem, I want Him to be the Author of my life, too."

The Bible says that our lives are "letters" lived, "known and read by everyone" (2 Corinthians 3:2). The universe points to God; I am convinced of that. But people will only be open to seeing that if they can also look at the lives of God's people and see new birth, stability of character and identity, a deep knowledge of who we are, and a confident sense that we were designed for a great, life-giving purpose.

Is your life an argument for God's existence? If we want people to see the universe for the poem that it is, we need to be the poem that we are intended to be. When people look at us, what do they see? Do they see blind chance? Do they see randomness? Or do they see the finely tuned poetry of God?

When people can look to the Christian community and see the design of a loving God, that is when people will consider joining that community in affirming, "The heavens declare the glory of God; and the firmament shows His handiwork. Day unto day utters speech, and night unto night reveals knowledge" (Psalm 19:1–2 NKJV).

CHAPTER 4

PLURALISM

❧

"All paths are equally valid."

Vince Vitale

I love sports. Always have. It is hard to find a sport I don't like. But here is a sporting experience I would never want to have.

Imagine being thrown into a game without knowing when it started, when it will finish, what the objective of the game is, or what the rules are. What would you do? You'd probably ask the other players around you to answer those four questions for you.

What if they responded with many different answers? Or what if they simply carried on playing, uninterested in your questions and looking at you oddly for asking them?

Next, you would look to a coach for help, but what if the coach was standing there, looking at the chaos, and yelling, "Great job, guys! You're all doing great! Keep going! We've got a first-place trophy waiting for all of you!"

Finally, you would turn to find the referee or umpire for definitive answers to your questions. But what if the players had gotten frustrated with the referee's calls and sent him home?

And now imagine the conversations about the game on the drive home. They would be completely meaningless. It is our knowledge of the start, the finish, the objective, and the rules of a game that provide us with the freedom to play it and to enjoy it in a meaningful way.

Sadly, this is not just a game; this is a reality for many who are struggling to live a meaningful life in a pluralistic culture. As a society, we are losing the answers to these four crucial questions:

Origin—Where did I come from?
Meaning—Why am I here?
Morality—How should I live?
Destiny—Where am I headed?

Recently I was on a university campus in Chicago and had the privilege of engaging with a variety of students about life's biggest questions. One day we set up a whiteboard on a main thoroughfare that read, "What is the meaning of life?" Columns across the top of the board offered a variety of choices—for example, personal success, to pass on one's genes, there is no meaning, to love others, etc. My lasting memory is of students walking up to the board, taking the marker in hand, staring at the different options, and then standing there, paralyzed, sometimes for minutes on end.

Many of the students whom we spoke to, when asked why they were finding it so difficult, said that it was because they didn't feel we should have to choose. "Why can't I pick more than one?" was the constant refrain. These students weren't saying there is no such thing as truth. Most of them realized that, as philosopher Roger Scruton puts it, "A writer who says that there are no truths...is asking you not to believe him. So don't."[1] It also wasn't that these students were *relativists* about truth, reducing truth to mere individual preference; rather, they were *pluralists* about truth. They believed in objective truth but wanted to say that we are all grasping at that truth in equally valid ways.

Three Bad Assumptions and Three Good Desires

Before we know how to respond to pluralism,[2] or any approach to truth, we need to ask what motivates it, and we need not to assume that, just because two people are pluralists, they are pluralists for the same underlying reason. It is the deeper motivations that we need to identify and speak to if we are to address individuals rather than a theory.

Pluralism about truth can be motivated by at least three bad assumptions and three good desires. First, the questionable assumptions.

1. Equal Claims

Some people adopt a pluralist approach to truth because they have the false assumption that all, or at least many of, the major ways of seeing the world are fundamentally in agreement. On the most important points, they are all saying basically the same thing.

I recently met a woman on the street in Chicago who told me, "I think religion is a good thing. I think all the religions are the same." Some would want to revise her comment: "I think religion is a *bad* thing. I think all religions are the same." Nonetheless, a lot of people are in agreement that the major religions, and even the major worldviews more generally, are fundamentally the same.

This is a common and also dangerous mistake. The more you study them, the clearer it becomes that while the major worldviews are sometimes superficially similar, they are fundamentally very different and often at odds.

Take Islam and Christianity. The very three things you need to believe in Christianity in order to be reconciled to God—that Jesus is God, that He died on the cross, and that He rose from the dead[3]—Islam asserts are completely wrong to believe,[4] and believing in Jesus' deity will even send a person to hell.[5]

But let's boil our assessment of worldviews down even further, to what we care about most: love and the future. One of my favorite questions to ask people is, "What causes 80% of your stress in life?" The first time I asked that question of someone, without missing a beat they responded, "People like you asking me questions like that!" I then asked what causes the other 20%, and we had a great conversation.

So often when I ask about what causes stress and anxiety, the answers boil down to one of these two concerns: Am I loved? What does the future hold? Christianity, Islam, and secular humanism, arguably the world's three most influential worldviews, have radically different things to say about what we care about most.

How Are We Loved?

First, Islam. The Qur'an has extremely little to say of God's love, and Al-Ghazali, arguably the most influential Muslim after Muhammad, pronounced that "[Allah] remains above the feeling of love."[6] In the few instances where God's love is referenced in the Qur'an, it's clear that any love Allah has for human persons is reserved only for those who have *earned* it. Allah loves those who "do good" (Sura 2:195; 3:134, 148; 5:93), the "just" (5:42; 60:8) and the "even-handed" (49:9), those who are "mindful of him" (9:4, 7), those who "turn to him" and "keep themselves clean" (2:222), and those who "never knowingly persist in doing wrong" (3:135), and Allah "truly loves those who fight in solid lines for his cause" (61:4). If those are the conditions for meriting Allah's love, the list of those loved by Allah must be a short list.

In stark contrast to its minimal references to God's love, the Qur'an emphasizes repeatedly that there are people whom Allah does not love. We are told that Allah does not love evildoers (3:57, 140), corrupters (5:64; 28:77), or transgressors (2:190; 5:87; 7:55). He does not love the arrogant, the boastful (4:36; 31:18), the conceited, the miserly (57:24), or ungrateful sinners (2:276). He "does not love anyone given to treachery or sin" (4:107), and he does not love those who ignore his commands (3:32); he is "certainly the enemy" of disbelievers (2:98).[7]

On the crucial question of love, Islam is not only different than Christianity, but in some key respects directly opposite to it. In Islam, if you love and obey Allah, he may love you back. In Christianity, Jesus explicitly objects to only loving those who love you first: "If you love those who love you, what credit is that to you? Even sinners love those who love them" (Luke 6:32). In Christianity, "God demonstrates his own love for us in this: While we were still sinners, Christ died for us" (Romans 5:8). While we were everything that is unlovable, God loved us enough to give His life for us. In Christianity, "This is love: not that we loved God, but that he loved us and sent his Son as an atoning sacrifice for our sins. Dear friends, since God so loved us, we also ought to love one another" (1 John 4:10–11). Christianity does not ask us to live good lives so that God might love us; it is because God loved us first that we are emboldened to live lives of goodness and love. On the question of love, Christianity and Islam are not just different, but the order of love is completely reversed.

One other person whom Allah does not like is the one who is "wasteful" (6:141; 7:31), sometimes translated as the one who is "prodigal." Jesus has something very different to say about the prodigal. In one of the most famous stories every told, He depicts God as a loving father longing for his prodigal son to come home (Luke 15:11–32). The prodigal son has given his father every reason not to love him: demanding his inheritance early (which in that ancient culture was basically to wish his father dead), abandoning his family, wasting on wild, meaningless living what his father had worked his whole life to provide. The prodigal was proud, ungrateful, unjust, corrupt—an evildoer.

And yet at the mere sight of the prodigal son, when he is still far off in the distance, the father hikes up his long robe, exposes his legs, and takes off running (something deeply shameful for an ancient Middle Eastern man to do). He kisses his son (the text literally says that he falls on his son's neck) and embraces him and welcomes him home with the best robe (probably the father's own), a ring on his finger (probably a signet ring denoting the authority to act on behalf of the family), and sandals for his feet (a sign of freedom). What a picture of intimacy!

I have long wondered what the prodigal son was thinking when he saw his father sprinting toward him from afar. He knew he did not deserve his father's love. He probably thought the father had been weighing his deeds and was running to give him what he deserved.

There will be a day when each of us sees God running toward us. I wonder what you picture when you picture that meeting. What emotion do you see on God's face as He sprints toward you?

How are you loved? In Christianity, you are loved with the love of a running father. Not *if* you've been keeping yourself pure and clean, not *if* you look the way you're supposed to look or get the job you're supposed to get, not even *if* you've been serving Him and spending time with Him.

God's love is *no-ifs love*. And that is why the Bible alone can claim this: "For I am convinced that neither death nor life, neither angels nor demons, neither the present nor the future, nor any powers, neither height nor depth, nor anything else in all creation, will be able to separate us from the love of God that is in Christ Jesus our Lord" (Romans 8:38–39). Nothing can separate you from God's love, and nothing can diminish God's love for you. Nothing.

We are all prodigals in our own way, and Allah has no love for prodigal children. Why? Because he's not a father. In the Qur'an,

Allah is not once called "father." In fact, the Qur'an says explicitly that "Allah does not beget" (112:3), thereby excluding fatherhood. In the New Testament alone, God is called "Father" over two hundred times.[8]

And this explains why Islam has to deny the three core beliefs of Christianity that we began with—Jesus' divinity, death, and resurrection. Only a God who is also a loving parent would come to suffer alongside His children, would be willing to die for His children, and would battle death itself if it meant seeing His children again. Islam can't understand Jesus' suffering and death because it doesn't understand God's love.

Islam only allows for the relationship of servitude toward Allah. Interestingly, being accepted as his father's "hired servant" (Luke 15:19) is the best the prodigal son thought he could hope for. But Jesus says, "I no longer call you servants...Instead, I have called you friends" (John 15:15). God is not only our father but He is our friend, our brother (Hebrews 2:11), our lover (Song of Songs 5:2), our bridegroom (Isaiah 62:5), our spouse (Isaiah 54:5). He is our mother hen who longs to gather us under protective wings (Matthew 23:37). In Islam, to claim a relationship of intimacy with Allah is blasphemous, still today punishable in extreme ways in some parts of the world. The Bible is at pains to show through every possible metaphor that what God desires most of us is intimate, loving relationship.

I find it telling that when we think of God's intellect, we quickly acknowledge that it must far surpass any human intellect. But when we think of God's love, we rarely think of His love as stronger than that of a human parent. Why is that? Is it because deep down we doubt whether we are lovable? From the perspective of Christianity, as small as our minds are compared to the totality of everything that could be known, that is how small our conception of God's love is compared to the reality of its extravagance.

How Should We Love?

How we believe ourselves to be loved is perhaps the single most important belief for any person, because how we are loved will determine how we love. Likewise, how we love will influence how those around us love, and how those around them love, meaning that the consequences of how we love will stretch far beyond our perception in both time and space. This is why it is absolutely critical whom your god says you should love.

Growing up, my friends and family came closest to playing the role of God in my life, and our attitude was, "If someone is good to you, be ten times as good to them; but if someone wrongs you, give them hell." Seek to love those who love you, but deny love to those who oppose you.

Culturally, most of us were what I have heard called "Chreasters"—we felt the need to attend church on Christmas and Easter, but our understanding of the Christian faith was very thin. Unbeknownst to us, our approach to loving others was actually much closer to Islam than it was to Christianity. The Qur'an says that until people believe in Allah alone, "enmity and hatred" is a "good example" of the stance Muslims should take toward non-Muslims (60:4).

Muslims hold to a doctrine of abrogation, which claims that Muhammad's later and most developed teachings should be weighted more heavily than his earlier teachings.[9] Sura 9, which was written just a couple of years before Muhammad's death, and hence among the Qur'an's most developed views, enjoins Muslims to attack and assault people to bring them into submission to Allah: "...wherever you encounter the idolaters, kill them, seize them, besiege them, wait for them at every lookout post" (9:5); "Fight those of the People of the Book who do not [truly] believe in God and the Last Day, who do not forbid what God and His Messenger have forbidden, who do not obey the rule of justice, until they pay the tax promptly and agree to submit" (9:29); "If you do not go out and fight, God will punish you severely and put others in your place" (9:39); "You who believe, fight the disbelievers near you and let them find you standing firm" (9:123). Muhammad modeled submission to these commands, fighting in or ordering at least twenty-five battles during the last ten years of his life.[10]

Christianity's most fully developed commands are the direct words of Jesus: "Love your enemies and pray for those who persecute you" (Matthew 5:44); "Do good to those who hate you, bless those who curse you, pray for those who mistreat you. If someone slaps you on one cheek, turn to them the other also. If someone takes your coat, do not withhold your shirt from them. Give to everyone who asks you, and if anyone takes what belongs to you, do not demand it back. Do to others as you would have them do to you" (Luke 6:27–31).

The contrast could not be starker. It was precisely the fact that Jesus spent time with and showered love upon those who were not submitted to God that infuriated the religious leaders of His day (Luke 5:30; 7:34). From Jesus' perspective, "If you love those who love you, what credit is that to you? Even sinners love those who love them. And if you do good to those who are good to you, what credit is that to you? Even sinners do that. And if you lend to those from whom you expect repayment, what credit is that to you? Even sinners lend to sinners, expecting to be repaid in full. But love your enemies, do good to them, and lend to them without expecting to get anything back. Then your reward will be great, and you will be children of the Most High, because he is kind to the ungrateful and wicked. Be merciful, just as your Father is merciful" (Luke 6:32–36). All too often in Islam it is thought that people will be rewarded for killing enemies. In Christianity, it is putting your enemy's life ahead of your own that is rewarded.

In his campaign for the Democratic nomination for president of the United States, Bernie Sanders described his views about God as such: "Everyone believes in the Golden Rule, and we call that god." This is the pluralism I have been addressing, and it is completely unfounded. The Golden Rule: "Do to others as you would have them do to you." Most people don't believe in this. The secular worldview of my cultural upbringing certainly didn't. Islam certainly doesn't. Still fewer live by it. The Golden Rule was radically distinctive when Jesus first spoke it, and it is radically distinctive today.

We all follow a god, whether supernatural or secular. How does your god feel about those who oppose him? Who does your god ask you to love? No two questions could be more critical for the human race.

Where Are We Headed?

Ultimate destiny tells us a huge amount about present reality.

You can tell a lot about someone by where they are headed. Take the trajectory of your life—the trajectory of your character, morals, choices, ideals, dreams, and relationships. Imagine extending an honest assessment of that trajectory by ten, twenty, thirty years. Where are you headed? For better or for worse, the answer to that question says a lot about who we are today.

Likewise, you can tell a lot about the essence of a worldview by what it has to say about human destiny. This is why, as Ravi puts it, "When you start a train of thought, it's important to check the ticket to see where it is going to let you off."

Among the future-oriented refrains of my youth were, "You need to put a roof over your head and food on the table," "You only live once," "The world is your oyster," "You can do whatever you put your mind to," "You make your own destiny."

Years later, I opened the Bible and was surprised at what I found: "The Son of Man has no place to lay his head" (Matthew 8:20), "Do not worry about your life, what you will eat or drink" (Matthew 6:25), "Whoever lives by believing in me will never die" (John 11:26),

"Our citizenship is in heaven" (Philippians 3:20), "Apart from me you can do nothing" (John 15:5), "Many are the plans in a person's heart, but it is the LORD's purpose that prevails" (Proverbs 19:21).

Once again, Christianity and the secular values of my youth were very different. And even once I became convinced that some sort of divine being existed, the major religions still had radically different things to say about where I was headed.

"All paths lead to God" is a tempting sentence. It has a certain positivity to it. But in actuality only Christianity even claims to lead to God.[11] The Christian destination is an intimate, flourishing, life-giving relationship with God Himself: "Now this is eternal life: that they know you, the only true God, and Jesus Christ, whom you have sent" (John 17:3); "Here I am! I stand at the door and knock. If anyone hears my voice and opens the door, I will come in and eat with that person, and they with me" (Revelation 3:20). Primarily, for a Christian, heaven is not a place but a person; it is not a reward but a relationship.

The Christianization of Western culture has sometimes resulted in us projecting the destination of intimate friendship with God onto other religious worldviews. But in fact this is distinctively Christian. In Buddhism and some traditions of Hinduism, the destination of Nirvana is the cessation of self and the elimination of desire, two essential components of personal relationship. According to tradition, it was on the very night that his son was born that Gautama Buddha left to pursue his life of detachment from anything or anyone that could cause him suffering. Contrast this with Jesus Christ, who did everything He possibly could to attach Himself to our suffering in His pursuit of relationship with us.

Likewise, the destination of Islam is not relationship with Allah. The paradise spoken of in Islam is one in which Allah is almost entirely absent.[12] Instead, paradise is depicted as a place of carnal pleasure: wine, sex, perpetual virgins, young boys who wait on men

(55:56–57, 70–78; 56:34–40). Hasn't this paradise already been tried and found wanting? How many who have reached the pinnacle of earthly pleasure have testified that it is anything but paradise, that ultimately our longing for authentic relationship cannot be satisfied by anything else?

How Do We Get There?

Christianity is distinctive in its claim to lead to God. But, actually, there's a twist. If we are being precise, even Christianity doesn't claim to lead us to find God. In fact, it claims the opposite. It claims that God came to find us: "For the Son of Man came to seek and to save the lost" (Luke 19:10).

Once more I am struck by the fact that the ideology of my cultural background was much closer to Islam than to Christianity. I accepted that "you can't rely on anyone but yourself," that "nothing is free in life," and that "you get what you deserve."

Islam affirms a similar inability to rely on anyone else for what is most important in life. If you fail to uphold the mandatory Pillars of Islam, no one can save you. In the words of the Qur'an, "We have bound each human being's destiny to his neck" (17:13), and "that man will only have what he has worked toward" (53:38–39). "No soul will bear another's burden" (17:15). In another place, "No burdened soul will bear the burden of another: even if a heavily laden soul should cry for help, none of its load would be carried, not even by a close relative" (35:18). Judgment day is "the Day when no soul will be able to do anything for another" (82:19).

Buddhism and Hinduism are in agreement in so far as it is only through the personal effort of pursuing the four noble truths or following the noble eightfold path or meriting good karma—in other words, it is only on the basis of what you *do*—that one attains the goal of enlightenment.

Here again, Jesus stands alone. He urges us, "Come to me, all you who are weary and burdened, and I will give you rest. Take my yoke upon you and learn from me, for I am gentle and humble in heart, and you will find rest for your souls. For my yoke is easy and my burden is light" (Matthew 11:28–30). Jesus explicitly offers to bear our burdens for us: "'He Himself bore our sins' in his body on the cross" (1 Peter 2:24). Salvation is therefore not something we earn but a "free gift" (Romans 6:23): "by grace you have been saved through faith. And this is not your own doing; it is the gift of God, not a result of works, so that no one may boast" (Ephesians 2:8–9 ESV). Contrary to every other major belief system, the Christian God "does not treat us as our sins deserve or repay us according to our iniquities" (Psalm 103:10). So great is His love.

Because where we are headed in Christianity is based on what God has already done and not on what we might do, we can be assured of our destiny in a way that is not possible in Islam. No one can know in Islam if he has done enough. Even if the scales tip in his favor on the last day, Allah's sovereignty is such that he is not bound by the scales. For even those who obey Allah, "the punishment of their Lord is not something to feel safe from" (70:28). The Qur'an instructs even Muhammad to say, "I do not know what will be done with me or you" (46:9).

In Christianity, there is a promise of salvation for those who trust Jesus. Explaining his motivation for writing, one of the biblical authors says, "I write these things to you who believe in the name of the Son of God so that you may *know* that you have eternal life" (1 John 5:13). Likewise, Paul says, "If you confess with your mouth that Jesus is Lord and believe in your heart that God raised him from the dead, you *will* be saved" (Romans 10:9 ESV). Many other verses could be cited in support. Jesus Christ's starting point is everyone else's finish line—the assurance of salvation!

We can have this assurance because in Christianity we are not asked to build the eternal roofs over our heads. When told by His disciples that they don't know the way to their ultimate destiny, Jesus responded, "Do not let your hearts be troubled. You believe in God; believe also in me. My Father's house has many rooms; if that were not so, would I have told you that I am going there to prepare a place for you? And if I go and prepare a place for you, I will come back and take you to be with me that you also may be where I am. You know the way to the place where I am going" (John 14:1–4). They knew the way because they knew Jesus, and He is the way.

A Muslim taxi driver once told me, "I'm terrified of judgment. Any Muslim will tell you that." After I explained that in Christianity we don't need to fear judgment because Jesus bore our judgment, he responded, with heavy emotion on his face, "It's a beautiful story. I wish it were true."

In Christianity, Jesus conceived of our eternal home, He purchased it, He is preparing it, and one day He will move us into it. He is the architect, the buyer, the decorator, and the moving company. This could not be further from having to put a roof over our own heads. This is getting so much more than we have striven for or could ever deserve.

So to return to our question, do all paths lead to God? No. None do. Some claim to lead us to some sort of reward or enlightenment. Naturalistic worldviews must admit that ultimately we are headed nowhere—for personal death and species extinction. Even Christianity claims not that we are led to God but that God's love led Him to us.

When it comes to what keeps us up at night—Am I loved? What does my future hold?—we are faced with a choice between two fundamentally very different ways of viewing the world. Must we fight to earn love or are we free to enjoy it? Must others fight to earn our love or will we share it freely? Is our future uncertain or is it secure? And will it include the relationship we long for most?

2. Equally Rational Claims

Faith Is Blind

A second reason that some are tempted by the thought that all or many worldviews are equally valid is because the various views are taken to be on equal intellectual footing.

Perhaps the most common reason for thinking this is an assumption that faith is opposed to reason, that faith is by definition blind. We can have evidence and facts about scientific and historical claims, but when it comes to big picture philosophical claims about God, meaning, morality, love, and destiny, it's all just a blind leap in the dark and therefore equally valid or invalid.

I don't have space here to share with you a lot of the evidence that was instrumental in my own journey to faith. However, I can encourage you that conceiving of faith as opposed to or in any way in tension with reason is not a Christian understanding of faith. Quite clearly, if you take the time to look, this is not how the Bible understands faith, nor is it how the earliest followers of Christianity understood faith.

As a Princeton undergraduate studying philosophy, when I first began investigating the Christian faith, evidence and reasoning were extremely important to me. I knew that if Christianity meant "pretending to know things you don't know,"[13] it was not for me. But when I finally opened the Bible, that is not at all what I found.

I found the Bible praising the people of Berea for their high intellectual standards and saying they were "of more noble character than those in Thessalonica" not due to blind faith but because they "examined the Scriptures every day to see if what Paul said was true" (Acts 17:11). I found that the one clause that Jesus added to the foremost Jewish commandment to love God with your heart, soul, and strength was to also love God "with all your *mind*" (Luke 10:27).

I learned that, according to the Bible, the transformation that occurs in a person when they trust in Christ happens not by some sort of brain-dismissing self-delusion but by "the renewing of your *mind*" (Romans 12:2).

As I continued reading, I found that the "acts" that Jesus' followers are described as performing in the biblical book *The Acts of the Apostles* include "reasoning," "arguing," "persuading," "examining," "debating," "disputing," "explaining," "defending," "refuting," "convincing," and even "proving." All those concepts are used, and that's just in that one book! On top of that, the most frequent description used in the New Testament to refer to someone's conversion to Christianity is to say they were "persuaded." If you commit to having a strong grasp of the intellectual case for Christianity, as the disciples did, I believe you will find what they found—that the case for Christianity is very strong.

Perhaps the most vital evidence for the Christian faith lies in the resurrection. The Bible says that God has given "proof" to "everyone" by "raising [Jesus] from the dead" (Acts 17:31). That is a big claim, and, what's more, it is a highly falsifiable claim. Buddha said look to the wisdom of my teaching; that is a very subjective measurement. Muhammad said look to the beauty and eloquence of the Qur'an; again, tough to prove one way or another. But Jesus provided an objective standard for His authority: "After three days I will rise again" (Matthew 27:63). That's a dangerous claim to make. If the authorities had simply produced Jesus' dead body, the claim would have been falsified. But they never did.[14]

I have vivid memories of exploring Christianity for the first time during my studies at Princeton. I was absolutely floored by the strength of the evidence for the miraculous resurrection of Jesus. I had never even considered that there could be rational arguments for such a claim. It was beyond conceivable to me that one of the most respected and influential philosophers of the last half century—Professor Richard Swinburne of Oxford University, a scholar known especially for his aptitude in evaluating evidence—could argue in a book published by Oxford University Press that, based on the available historical evidence today, it is 97% likely that Jesus miraculously rose from the dead.[15]

With my head and heart spinning from this entirely new treasure of inquiry, I arranged to meet with the two top New Testament professors at the university. They were not Christians, and I thought surely, being experts in the field, they would be able to provide me with plausible theories that could explain the relevant data without appealing to a miraculous resurrection.

One of the professors glanced toward a mass hallucination theory without conviction. This is a theory that is riddled with problems, and as a result it has earned no credibility in the scholarly literature. The other professor told me that, as a historian, he was not interested in the question. The presumption seemed to be that as soon as we start talking about the miraculous, we are no longer talking about history. I have never been able to figure out why he thought this. I began to wonder whether G. K. Chesterton was right: "The Christian ideal has not been tried and found wanting. It has been found difficult; and left untried."[16]

If you have not looked into the evidence for the resurrection of Jesus, please do. There is nothing like this early, public, multiple-attested, eyewitness-based evidence in any other religion. Having now studied the evidence at Princeton and Oxford, I am only more astounded at how remarkable it is.

Many people have heard one or two pieces of supposed evidence against God and have jumped to a conclusion without ever bothering to make a thorough investigation. Too much is at stake here to cut inquiry short. How devastating it would be to stand before God one day and have nothing to say but "I never cared enough to look into You." If God made us, He would ensure that a sincere intellectual search would point in His direction. That is exactly what I and countless others have found, and what many other sincere seekers continue to find every day.

Faith Is Arrogant

Others question the intellectual soundness of Christian faith not because they see faith as blind, but because affirming one worldview to the exclusion of others is taken to be arrogant.

A Christian should never be quick to dismiss this objection. It is an objection that should concern us deeply. When I ask my students, "Why might someone think that Christianity is arrogant?" I am hoping one of the first responses is, "They might have met some arrogant-acting Christians."

We must look first to the beam in our own behavior before looking for the speck in another's criticism. We must also be willing to ask for forgiveness, because there is no place for arrogance in Christianity. Christianity is inherently humbling. Any truth we are privileged to in Christianity is because God was gracious enough to share it. We didn't earn it; we don't deserve it. God's generosity toward us is our only gain.

Some people, however, are far too quick to label truth claims as arrogant. Simply the fact that others disagree can't be what makes a claim arrogant. If diversity in religious opinion makes Christianity arrogant, why not draw the same conclusion in philosophy, politics, or even science? No one would think a claim in one of those domains was arrogant just because others thought differently. If we thought that, we would have to label pretty much the entirety of philosophical and political discourse, as well as a great deal of scientific discourse, as arrogant. So why do we hold religious beliefs to a different standard?

Moreover, if the disagreement of others were enough to make a claim arrogant, then the claim "the disagreement of others makes a claim arrogant" would itself be arrogant, for many disagree with *that* claim! In fact, many more worldwide and throughout history disagree with that claim than accept it. The same could be said for the claims of atheism and religious pluralism as well. Even claiming the seemingly humble position of agnosticism—claiming you don't know the truth—would be arrogant, because many (in fact, most) people disagree with agnosticism.

We all make exclusive truth claims, even if our truth claim is that we shouldn't make truth claims. We can't get around saying other people are wrong. On the assumption that any exclusive truth claim is arrogant, it becomes nearly impossible to find a claim that is not arrogant.

But perhaps there is a more reasonable concern underlying the charge of arrogance. Grab a scrap of paper and draw a circle. Let that circle represent everything there is to be known—what would be known by an omniscient being. Now draw a second circle within the first circle to represent proportionally the percentage of the totality of all possible knowledge that you personally know.

Given how big the universe is and how small we are, or for that matter how small the universe is (think of nanotechnology) and how big we are, isn't it arrogant to claim that we know the truth? Even if what you know currently points toward a certain truth claim, there is so much else out there that could potentially challenge your current belief. Is it really rational to hold it with any degree of confidence?

Perhaps the reason all our truth claims are on equal intellectual footing is because they are all highly intellectually unjustified! Given the gap between our finite minds and the infinity to be known, perhaps all our worldviews are equally valid only in the sense that they are equally invalid.

I am sympathetic to this objection. Even if we cannot help making truth claims, maybe it is arrogant to be confident about our truth claims when we are so limited in our understanding. The implications of this thought are frightening. Take our ethical beliefs, for instance. If we cannot have any confidence in them, what practices that we now approve of and are complicit in will be considered horrendously evil several hundred years from now? And who will be right, us or them? That's a scary thought.

I see only one way of not getting sucked into this knowledge-sapping black hole: God entering our circle in order to reveal and verify the truth.

Every worldview that relies on us, as finite human persons, being able to reason to the truth is vulnerable to this objection. The only worldviews that can avoid it are worldviews that are revealed to humankind by Someone much more knowledgeable than we are, by Someone so knowledgeable that He determined the size and intricacy of the universe rather than being constrained by it, by Someone for whom the entire universe fits within His circle of knowledge.

The idea of divine revelation is often derided in secular culture. But criticism without alternative is empty. Biblical ethics are quickly dismissed. Dismissed in favor of what? Today's ethics? Tomorrow's ethics? The ethics of my culture? The ethics of your culture?

Only revelation can bring stability and reliability to our knowledge. Either we have knowledge by revelation, or else we are in real epistemological trouble—caught in the arrogance of claiming that somehow we, in our little corner of the universe, in our little sliver of history, have managed to discover the truth about the deepest question of life. Those are our choices: a great ignorance or a great God.

Ironically, although the charge of religious arrogance needs to be taken seriously, it turns out that faith in God is the only way to avoid the charge of arrogance. Only a God who reveals Himself can save us from arrogance about the most important questions of life.

3. Equal Impact

A third misconception that can lead to an "all paths are equally valid" view is the assumption that, at the end of the day, the practical payoff of all the major worldviews is pretty much the same.

Not long ago I had a debate with an atheist philosopher, and at one point we were asked to speak about how our differing worldviews allow us to deal practically with personal suffering. My interlocutor implied he didn't think that Christianity offered a real advantage over atheism in this regard, citing the fact that, at the end of the day, whether it is a Christian funeral or an atheist funeral, everyone is devastated.[17]

I disagreed. The last funeral I had been to happened to be a Christian funeral. It was a celebration of the life that had been and of the life that was to come, not just superficially but deeply and authentically. The brother of the deceased invited people to show their appreciation for his brother's life with a round of applause, and, before we knew what was happening, all over this posh village church, people had climbed up onto the pews and were pumping their arms and hooting and hollering louder and more joyfully than any sporting match I have ever been to. The cheering carried on, as time reached out and embraced eternity, until every face was smiling—no, beaming—through tears, and every inch of the room was filled with hope. It was one of the great privileges of my life to have witnessed and participated in this true farewell.

This was a man who died in his thirties. I wish you could have been there. I can remember thinking to myself during the funeral service, *If only that atheist philosopher could see this, he would have no choice but to retract his statement.*

A college student recently said to me on the campus of Portland State University, "I think there is a universal human longing for peace, and I think that points to the reality of something that can fulfill that longing, sort of like how hunger points to the reality of food." So far I was following. But then he concluded, "So I think it's a good idea to believe in something, whatever that is." He had this assumption that all big picture worldviews would meet this universal human need more or less equally well, that the practical payoff would be more or less the same.

But that is not true. Any old worldview will not do. Any old god will not do. The ancient Greek gods were fickle in their dealings with humankind, as likely to bring anxiety as to bring peace. Allah will not bring peace but rather a fear of judgment. The indifference of a deist god will not bring peace. Those who have most "successfully" worshipped sex and money testify that those gods will not bring peace. Many people have never said yes to God because they have never been presented with a God who can actually bring peace.

Last year a student of mine named Ariel was diagnosed with a cavernoma (cells in her brain that are prone to bleeding). She was told that they will bleed again, and that her options are either to undergo a surgery that will, at best, leave her severely disabled, or to do nothing and live with a life expectancy of less than five years. She is twenty-three years old.

The week after receiving this news, Ariel came to class to update her classmates, who had also become dear friends. She talked them through her medical condition with an incredible poise, comforting them along the way by smiling and cracking jokes.

Then she shared with us three insights that she had found comfort in as she had processed what is happening: First, she said, "God has good plans for my life, and I believe He won't take me until His purposes for my life have been fulfilled." She continued, "Jesus knew what it was to only have a few years left to make an impact on this earth, and yet He could say 'my time has not yet fully come' (John 7:8), and He could still see each day as a day to serve God and serve others." And then her final encouragement: "You know, my condition has made me more aware of the fact that my body is going to grow weaker, and that I could die at any time. But actually that doesn't make me any different from anyone else. That's true of every one of us. I may be more aware of it, but every one of us has to ask the question of how we are going to live, given that today could be our final day."

I had the privilege of interviewing Ariel about what she's been through while she was still recovering from the concussion that prompted her diagnosis. With dark glasses on to protect her eyes, which had become painfully sensitive to light, she shared with me that there was a point at which she found herself looking in the mirror, testing the limited mobility she had on her right side. And she can remember thinking to herself, *Is this the healthiest I am ever going to be? Is this the strongest I am ever going to be? Is this the prettiest I am ever going to be?*

Then she told me of the peacefulness that came over her as she remembered the answer to those questions: "No. Absolutely not."

Ariel spoke about the joy of knowing that one day her body will be able to do far more than it ever has before. I know she loves to snowboard, so I asked her if she thought there would be snowboarding in the life to come, and I wish you could have heard how unhesitatingly and how confidently she responded, "Absolutely! And soccer, too!" And I wish you could have seen the radiant smile on her face as she said it.

The atheist philosopher I debated was wrong. Christianity is not just about believing some new ideas. It is a real, personal, life-giving relationship with the "Prince of Peace" (Isaiah 9:6), and that is why it makes the most concrete and tangible difference to the strength and comfort we can have through even the worst that this life has to offer, as well as to the hope we can have that we are not headed for death but rather for greater and greater life.

Three Good Desires

Often even more important than identifying what we need to *deny* in a worldview that we disagree with is identifying what we need to *affirm*.

Every way of seeing the world seeks to explain human desires and to explore whether reality will lead to their fulfillment. Often these desires are good, at least in their uncorrupted forms. Often the problem is not with the desires but rather that we settle for a merely partial fulfillment of them. As C. S. Lewis puts it, we are "like an ignorant child who wants to go on making mud pies in a slum because he cannot imagine what is meant by the offer of a holiday at the sea."[18]

What this means is that even when an "ism" needs to be rejected, the motivation lying behind the "ism" may need to be endorsed and encouraged. As far as I can see, there are at least three good, God-given desires that find only a partial and distorted fulfillment in pluralism.

1. Equal Value

The Danger of Disagreement

First, many of us sense deep down, at least on our better days, that we must be committed to the equal value of every single person.

Shouldn't we therefore shun claims that *our* truth is the right one? Doesn't disagreeing lead to devaluing which leads to intolerance which ends in violence? This is a good worry. Indeed, this progression seems to be tested and proven nearly every day as we watch the news across the world and in our own country. And isn't religion right at the root of this problem? Religion makes you believe things fiercely and disagree with others fiercely, and the result is the devaluation of other people.

There is a popular tradition that Gandhi once tried to go to church, but was turned away at the door with a racist slur. The words of the Indian philosopher Bara Dada, sometimes attributed to Gandhi himself, would have been an understandable reaction to such an experience: "Jesus is ideal and wonderful, but you Christians—you are not like Him."[19] I have heard this story about Gandhi several times, and, whenever I do, my mind floods with all the things I have done that have probably kept people from the Christian faith, with all the times that I have failed to live up to the life of love and moral courage to which Jesus has called me. So, on the one hand, I am very sympathetic to and saddened by this objection.

Thankfully, many others I know, and myself too, have encountered Christian communities whose generous welcome and committed love have surpassed anything for which our hearts had dared to dream. These have been profoundly healing communities that you can describe as "family" and as "home" and really *mean* it.

When something, such as religion, can produce immense evil, our temptation can be to reject it straightaway. But oftentimes, that something can produce immense evil signifies that it can also produce immense good. And from this we should conclude not that the thing in question is *bad*, but rather that it is *powerful*, and that we should do everything we can to use that power for good.

For instance, a child's parent can be the most nurturing, enabling, and joy-giving force in that child's life. But precisely by virtue of the powerful connection shared between parent and child, the parent can also be a life-destroying force for darkness. We could say the same of both the depth of relational bond and the numerous forms of abuse made possible by marriage. Again, splitting the atom offered a new depth of insight into the universe and an extension of our technological power. It brought us a robust alternative fuel, but the very same technology also brought the ability to destroy huge numbers of lives. Where power excels, so does the potential to bless *or* to curse. Should we get rid not only of religion but of marriage, family, and research science, too?

Perhaps, then, the reason Christianity can seem to be at the root of *either* the depth of our self-giving service *or* our miserly hate is because there is power to be found in reaching out to the divine. And perhaps the fact that we have often used this power to bad ends tells us more about the state of our hearts than it does about the source of the power.

What, therefore, should we conclude the mixed legacy of the Christian community tells us about Christianity? Bad things have been done in the name of Christianity. They have also been done in the name of atheism. If the twentieth century taught us anything, it taught us that removing religion from society is not the answer. The twentieth century was the most murderous century of all time, and the worst of those murderers (Hitler, Stalin, Lenin, Mussolini, and Mao) turned to atheistic philosophies for their justification. Atheists would not want atheism to be judged based on the worst things done in the name of atheism any more than Christians would want Christianity to be judged based on the worst things done in its name. Just because something is done in the name of something does not mean it is a true representation of that thing.

So we have to ask, What is authentic Christianity, and what are its consequences? Violence done in God's name is expressly disobeying Jesus Christ's own teaching to love our enemies, to pray for those who persecute us, and to turn the other cheek when slapped. The one time that a sword was raised in Jesus' presence in the name of religion, He rebuked Peter with the words, "Put your sword back in its place, for all who draw the sword will die by the sword" (Matthew 26:52). It is no coincidence that the one slash of the sword that was taken, before Jesus' rebuke, cut off an ear; violence is not only inherently contradictory to the message of Christianity, but it causes it to fall on deaf ears.[20]

If anything characterized the life that Jesus lived, the life right at the center of how we are to model our lives as Christians, it is that He valued, spent time with, and cared for those who were different and those on the margins of society: foreigners, women, adulterers, tax collectors, even those who murdered Him. He looked down from the Cross at those who were killing Him—those who could not be more starkly opposed to Him—and the words that came out of His mouth were "Father, forgive them" (Luke 23:34).

Right at the crux of Christianity is the claim that even when someone is most opposed to you, the Christian response—indeed, Christ's response—is to value, to love, and to forgive. Religion has at times had violent consequences. Some religious leaders have had violent consequences. But Jesus Christ hasn't. And what I follow first and foremost, what all authentic Christians follow first and foremost, is not a religion or an institution or a set of rules, but Jesus Himself.

In the children's game "pass the parcel," you have a gift wrapped up in a box, then wrapped again with additional layers. Within each layer is a smaller token gift, usually a candy. As the box gets passed around the circle, each child hopes that when the music stops, the layer they rip off will be the last, revealing the main gift itself.

Imagine a child thinking they had reached the center gift when they really hadn't? They tear off a layer and think they have been given a useless box and a single candy—a sour one they don't even like! They might throw the box away without ever realizing that something far more precious was inside.

If we raise an objection to Christianity, we need to be careful that we aren't just targeting the outer wrapping. That stuff can be put to the side while we continue our pursuit of the central gift. We can acknowledge that some Christians, or some identifying themselves as Christians, have behaved shamefully without throwing away the whole package.

The central gift of the Christian message has never been the claim that Christians will be morally perfect. The real gift at the center is the claim that Jesus of Nazareth willingly went to His death for our sakes and victoriously rose from the dead. And neither the actions of Christians in the tenth century nor the twenty-first can cast doubt on *Christ's* actions in the first century.[21]

The Care of Authentic Christianity

You can judge a tree by its fruit (Matthew 7:17). And when you judge authentic Christianity—Christianity that follows Jesus—by its fruit, you find a very good tree.

In 2008, atheist journalist Matthew Parris, writing in *The Times*, commended the fruit of the "enormous contribution that Christian evangelism makes in Africa: sharply distinct from the work of secular NGOs, government projects, and international aid efforts.... In Africa, Christianity changes people's hearts. It brings spiritual transformation. The rebirth is real. The change is good." Parris arrived at the shocking judgment, "As an atheist, I truly believe Africa needs God."[22]

Reflecting on the last two centuries of American history, atheist Princeton philosopher Jeffrey Stout, the former president of the American Academy of Religion, reminds us that many of the greatest social victories of that time period—the abolition of slavery, women's suffrage, the civil rights victories of the 1960s—would not have been possible without the help of Christian citizens acting in ways motivated by their Christian convictions.[23] This leads Stout to argue for what he calls "The Folly of Secularism."[24] If secularists succeed in minimizing religious influence in the public sphere, they will have little chance of fulfilling many of their own goals, because history shows that most of America's greatest societal accomplishments have depended on the support of Christians motivated by their Christian beliefs.

Turning the clock of history back further, it was precisely the fruit of authentic Christianity that caused it to spread exponentially in the first place. The early Church had an enormous role in poverty relief, so enormous that the fierce persecutor of Christians, Emperor Julian the Apostate, while complaining in a letter that despite all his efforts he could not keep the Church from growing, exclaimed,

> Why then do we...not observe how godlessness has been helped on, especially by their philanthropy to strangers, by the care which they take in the burial of the dead, and by the sobriety of living which they feign?... For it is disgraceful when no Jew is a beggar and the impious Galileans support our poor in addition to their own, that ours are seen to be in want of aid from us.... Do not, therefore, let us allow others to outvie us in good deeds, while we ourselves are disgraced by sloth.[25]

Perhaps even more remarkable was the way Christians cared for the sick. Of those who survived the plagues of the first few centuries (e.g., the Antonine Plague (A.D. 165–180) and the Plague of Cyprian (250–270))—when diseased people were thrust out into the streets to die, physicians literally headed for the hills, and "No one did to another what he himself wished to experience"[26]—so many of them had a Christian to thank for it. You were statistically more likely to survive if you knew a Christian because many Christians, following Christ, were among the only people willing to remain in the cities and risk their lives in order to unite themselves with those suffering. And this despite the facts that Christians were being blamed for the Cyprian Plague and that it began as Christians were being persecuted—forced, in the Decian Persecution, to either perform a sacrifice to the Roman gods and emperor or be killed.

Bishop Dionysius, bishop of Alexander at the time, recorded that...

> Most of our brother Christians showed unbounded love and loyalty, never sparing themselves and thinking only of one another. Heedless of danger, they took charge of the sick, attending to their every need and ministering to them in Christ, and with them departed this life serenely happy; for they were infected by others with the disease, drawing on themselves the sickness of their neighbors and cheerfully accepting their pains. Many, in nursing and curing others, transferred their death to themselves and died in their stead.[27]

Fast-forward eighteen hundred years and read the accounts of medical missionaries in West Africa, and this fruit of the Christian faith remains all but identical, as evidenced recently by Ebola medical missionaries being named *Time* magazine's 2014 "Person of the Year."[28]

The Vindication of Value

Experience has taught us to fear that disagreement will lead to devaluing which will lead to intolerance which will lead to violence. We therefore worry, *Do we need to cut this off at the root?* If we adopt pluralism (no matter how incoherent), and thereby refuse to disagree, then this insidious trajectory will never get started.

But, of course, even our refusal to disagree is a disagreement with all of those who think we should not refuse to disagree. Try as we might, disagreement is not going away; it is inseparable from content-filled discussion, and therefore from free, meaningful society. The problem is not disagreement but rather that we have lost the ability to disagree well. If we are to reclaim that ability, we will need a worldview that is uncompromising in its refusal to let disagreement lead to the undervaluing of any person. (I will return to consider the countercultural nature of Christian disagreement more extensively in Chapter 8.)

Christianity is that worldview. For all people to have equal value, there has to be something about each human person that is equally true and that cannot change. What is it?

Any naturalistic answer to this question will not do, because our natural endowments are distributed along a spectrum. Some are less intelligent than others, less healthy, less useful for society, less good looking, less wealthy, less capable of passing on their genes, less moral.

Even if currently you measure up well by some of these standards, one day you won't. We will age, we will weaken, and our financial worth will fluctuate. Morally, we will lack consistency. Physically, every atom in our bodies may be different seven years from now. Who are we if every single thing about us is only temporary and changeable? By any naturalistic standard, human value is fleeting and graduated, with some coming out less valuable than others.[29]

What is it about a human person that is equally true of every other human person and can never be lost, and therefore can justify the equal value of every person and the universality and inalienability of human rights? Only the love of God. God's love is the one and only thing that is equal for every single person. God's love is the one and only thing that will never change and cannot be lost. Here we circle back to the significance of the Christian God being a father—a parent—because a good parent loves his children equally, unwaveringly, and no matter what.

You are not valuable because you can pass on genes; you are valuable because before your genes ever came together you were loved by God and chosen by Him. God does not value only those who survive as the fittest; He gave His life for the unfittest. The measure of human value is not biological, intellectual, financial, moral, or aesthetic; it is personal—measured by the value-conferring love of a personal God.

As much as we worry about the dangers of disagreement, disagreement is inevitable. It is part of living a meaningful life where people have freedom of speech. What we need is not the end to disagreement but the reality of a love big enough to inspire us to disagree without devaluing.

Here I know of only one option, the same option endorsed by atheist philosopher Jürgen Habermas:

> Universalistic egalitarianism, from which sprang the ideals of freedom and a collective life in solidarity, the autonomous conduct of life and emancipation, the individual morality of conscience, human rights and democracy, is the direct legacy of the Judaic ethic of justice and the Christian ethic of love. This legacy, substantially unchanged, has been the object of continual critical appropriation and reinterpretation. To this day, there is no alternative to it.[30]

2. Equal Opportunity

A second motivation for pluralism that is worth affirming is a desire for people to have equal access to the truth or equal opportunity to come to know the truth. At its core, this is a desire for fairness. But in a pluralistic age, with so many competing truth claims and with people exposed to such differing truth claims, it is tempting to think that the one way to be fair to everyone is to accept all views as equally valid.

This motivates a rejection of the exclusive claims of Christianity, in particular Jesus' declaration: "I am the way and the truth and the life. No one comes to the Father except through me" (John 14:6).

How can Christianity claim "There is no other name…by which we must be saved" (Acts 4:12) when so many have never even heard Jesus' name? "Surely," the objection goes, "you just believe that because of when and where you were born."

However, in one sense pluralism is actually among the most unfair of all truth claims, because so few people throughout time and across the globe have been exposed to or are even psychologically capable of believing in pluralism. To believe in pluralism, you would very likely have to have been born in a wealthy country in the last century—an extremely narrow slice of time and space.

This leads to what could be called the exclusivism or perhaps the ethnocentricity of pluralism, and for that matter of atheism and agnosticism as well. Christians are sometimes charged with exclusivism or ethnocentricity based on the fact that they are claiming to have a privileged knowledge of an objective, universal truth, while (supposedly) ignoring the fact that many people disagree with them.

But it is incredibly ironic for any atheist, agnostic, or pluralist to level this sort of objection, because they are all much worse off with respect to the very same point. Those who say "every view is valid" in an attempt to be all-inclusive are in that very sentence excluding the vast majority of the world's population who insist that many views are deeply flawed. It turns out that inclusivism is a highly exclusive claim and that Christianity is more inclusive than inclusivism. Otherwise put, so-called inclusivists exclude many more than so-called exclusivists!

Think of it this way: Imagine you were on the TV show *Who Wants to Be a Millionaire?* and you get a question you don't know how to answer. A lot of money is at stake, and you decide to "poll the audience." When you do, 98% of the audience says you should vote for answer "A." But you're feeling lucky. You choose "C."

You'd get blasted in the papers for your irrationalism! But this is precisely what someone is doing if they adopt atheism, agnosticism, or pluralism today. They are saying that a few countries in twenty-first-century Northern Europe have it right, and everyone else, not only today but throughout all history, has it wrong.

Even the slightest bit of global and historical perspective shows that calling atheism, pluralism, and even agnosticism minority positions is a radical understatement. Almost every great thinker throughout history has believed that one or more gods exist and that some views about gods are right and some views about gods are wrong. Since the time the questions could be considered, these beliefs have been nearly universal among those who have carefully considered them. A belief is not wrong just because others think differently. However, if just about everyone thinks the same, that needs to be taken seriously. Top philosopher Linda Zagzebski takes this *consensus gentium*, or "agreement of the people," to be an effective argument for theism.[31]

One might object, though, that on *Who Wants to Be a Millionaire?* we are generally only interested in polling a modern audience. With a scientific question, for instance, we would be much less interested in what people throughout all history have thought. Even so, with respect to the question of God's existence, still today there are far more theists than nontheists, and, according to many experts, including leading sociologist Peter Berger, there is no reason to think that is going to change:

> When I started out my work in sociology of religion, almost everyone in the field believed in what generally was called secularization theory, which [is] a thesis that modernity leads to decline of religion. The more modernity, the less religion.… I changed my mind not because of any religious or philosophical changes on my own, but simply because I concluded that the evidence simply did not support this thesis. And I was not the only one. Almost everyone in the field came to the

same conclusion.... Contrary to that theory...if you look at the contemporary world, to describe it as secular is impossible. The real situation is that most of the world is as religious as it ever was. You have enormous explosions of religion in the world.... In fact, you can say every major religious tradition has been going through a period of resurgence in the last thirty, forty years or so. Hinduism, Buddhism, Judaism, you name it; anything but secularization.[32]

Even polling a modern audience continues to point overwhelmingly to God. Moreover, we should only trust modern people over others if modernity has provided some sort of new evidence about God to which those who lived in early ages were not privy. What is this new evidence that is supposed to point against God? Would it be scientific evidence? I have argued against this in Chapter 3. Would it be that we are better situated due to moral progress? The moral tragedies of the twentieth century make that very doubtful.

Another objection claims that polling the audience doesn't point to God but rather to a large array of different gods reflecting all the different religions of the world. That's true, but polling the audience does show widespread agreement that something supernaturally powerful and intelligent is required to explain the universe. That, therefore, should be our starting point. If witnesses in a courtroom couldn't agree on who they saw but were all in agreement that they saw someone, you would not deny that they saw anyone because they couldn't agree on who they saw. You would accept that they saw someone and continue to seek evidence about who it was. That is just what I have been recommending.

Access to pluralism, atheism, and agnosticism may be unfairly distributed, but that doesn't yet show that access to Christianity is not also unfair. Is unfair access to the truth a warranted criticism of Christianity?

The starting point for a Christian response to this question is belief in an all-powerful, all-loving God who desires for every person to come to know and embrace the truth. The Bible is explicit about this: God "wants *all* people to be saved" (1 Timothy 2:4) and does not want "*anyone* to perish" (2 Peter 3:9). Israel was specially chosen, but the reason they were chosen was not to be favorites but to bring God's message to the rest of the world. As Abraham was told, "through your offspring *all* nations on earth will be blessed" (Genesis 22:18).

Next, we can zero in on the life of Jesus. His life begins with His identity being supernaturally revealed to magi (foreign astrologer-magicians who would have worshipped foreign gods). God took what they knew—the stars—and He took what they had—elements of magic (gold, frankincense, and myrrh)—and in His grace He used that to lead them to the truth. Then Jesus' life ends with His plea to His disciples to "go and make disciples of all nations" (Matthew 28:19). These are the bookends of Jesus' life—both an introduction and a conclusion that specify God's commitment to those outside the bounds of who would naturally hear about Him. As with any good book, the introduction and the conclusion reveal the core of everything in between—in this case, the life of Jesus, which consistently surprised both His friends and His enemies by never dismissing anyone as too foreign, stupid, disabled, or immoral to be worth God's time.

Even when I don't know exactly how God makes sure that everyone is given fair access to the truth, the bookends of Jesus' life and the story between them assure me that He is committed to reaching out to every single person.

I concede the objection that some seem to be unfairly in the dark, but God concedes it too. In fact, it is *His* objection. He has initiated a community, the Church, with the expressed goal to proclaim the good news to the ends of the earth. He explicitly says His desire is not for people to just believe based on where they are born. When we as Christians treat people with unfairness by not caring enough to share God's message with them, no one is more disappointed or objects more strongly than God Himself.

Yet, thankfully, God can make up for our lack. We are not able to go back in time to tell those who lived before Jesus, but we can be assured that God will give those who never knew of Jesus a chance to know and accept Him. We can know this because, in Hebrews 11 and elsewhere, the Bible counts a variety of people who lived before Jesus as saved. They trusted God by looking forward to His saving action in hope as we trust God by looking back on Jesus' sacrifice with gratitude.

And if God can reach those separated from Jesus by time, He can reach those separated from Him by place or culture as well. I personally have heard an astounding number of testimonies of Jesus reaching people through dreams and other miraculous ways in some of the most unreachable places in the world. Many of these miracles have happened in the lives of students, friends, and colleagues of mine whom I trust and respect deeply. God is big enough to reach everyone, and I have seen Him reveal Himself in the most extraordinary of ways in the most unlikely of circumstances.

Moreover, I know that, for several of my loved ones, they have been most aware of God, and God has reached out to them most earnestly, when it looked like their death might be near. We don't know how God is interacting with people as they approach death or even in their dying moments. Some scientists suggest that in one's final moments the brain often goes into a turbo mode that puts the world into slow motion and draws out those last moments.[33] It took only his final breath for the criminal who hung next to Jesus to be saved.

What I find perhaps the most challenging case of potential unfairness is when someone seems to have sought God and not found Him—when God seems hidden. I have wrestled through this frustration with several close friends, and I have found reflection on the nature of human relationships to be helpful. When I was nineteen, I wanted nothing more and was seeking wholeheartedly to get married. Now, looking back, I can see that my relationship with my wife is far stronger and more stable for coming later than it would have been then, even though that meant that at nineteen I didn't get what I wanted and I didn't get what I was sincerely seeking.

God's timing is sometimes different than our timing. Sure, God could miraculously make His existence obvious to all of us. But that would not get Him even one inch closer to His ultimate goal. Everyone would drop to their knees in shock. But would they be dropping to their knees in adoration or in fear? There would be no way to tell.

God's end game is not intellectual belief—"the demons believe… and shudder" (James 2:19). The word for *belief* in the Bible is perhaps best translated "trust," and trust cannot be forced; it must be developed over time. God's desire is a genuine two-sided relationship, and relationships are unique to every individual. For some, a quick courtship works; for others, it would be disastrous. Rushing into a relationship too quickly can be dangerous. Speaking personally, for all the best relationships in my life, I've had to fight for them; they didn't come ready-made, but they are all the more valuable to me because of this.

Blaise Pascal, the brilliant mathematician, physicist, inventor, and philosopher, suggested that a God who was after relationship would be "willing to appear openly to those who seek Him with all their heart, and to be hidden from those who flee from Him with all their heart." Therefore, Pascal thinks, we should not be surprised if "There is enough light for those who only desire to see, and enough obscurity for those who have a contrary disposition."[34] God would desire to reveal Himself clearly to those who desire Him, but not forcibly to those who don't. He wants us to follow Him not because He is overpowering, but because we trust Him.

To be honest, when all this is considered, I personally find it surprising that God is as obvious as He is. I have already mentioned how often, when I ask people whether they have experienced anything that made them think there might be a God, I can hardly believe the neon signposts to God that people have seen while continuing to deny Him.

Many others find themselves drawing unexpected conclusions when they finally take the time to engage in a reasoned search for God. I recently was told of a conversation in which a Christian friend of mine was explaining to another friend why God's desire for relationship means that He won't always announce Himself so miraculously that we have no choice but to believe in Him. The nonbelieving friend was following the argument, and then, before fully processing her thought, she said, "Wouldn't it be cool if God came in disguise? That way we could get to know Him but not be overwhelmed by Him?" Apparently you could see the look of shock on her face as she realized she had unintentionally made an argument for the Incarnation of Christ, the very belief that she was supposed to be objecting to!

Could it possibly be that "what may be known about God is plain to [people], because God has made it plain to them"? Do we not have access to the truth, or do we "suppress the truth" (Romans 1:18–19)?

God makes a promise: "If you look for me wholeheartedly, you *will* find me" (Jeremiah 29:13 NLT). God's timing will not always be our timing, and God's timing may not always seem fair. But fairness is only perceivable retrospectively. If all you saw was one day in the life of my family, depending on the specific day and the specific situation, you could easily conclude that my parents favored me or my brother over the other. Imagine if the only day you witnessed was my birthday. But if you have known my family for years, you could only conclude that my parents love my brother and me equally and have been fair in their treatment of us. In the same way, the Bible says that, when we look back over our entire lives from the perspective of eternity, anyone who does not accept God will be "without excuse" (Romans 1:20). We don't know everything about how God reveals Himself, but we can say this: All who want Him will find Him.

The greatest test of whether or not someone is committed to fairness is whether they make an exception for themselves. Jesus did not. He did not exempt Himself from suffering, from death, or even from the experience of feeling far from God. He chose to accept what He did not deserve so that we could trust that He came to serve. We know He will be fair to everyone because He was willing to be unfair to Himself.

Just believing something because of when and where you were born might be true of atheism; it might be truth of pluralism. But it is not true of Christianity. Jesus is a God loving enough and big enough to break in everywhere. Either we have a God who is committed to and capable of reaching people everywhere or we have a secular god that indeed people only believe in because of where they are born. Faced with that choice, my belief in God is part and parcel of my commitment to fairness for every single person.

3. Equally United

A final admirable motivation that can lead to an attraction to pluralism is a longing for unity with other people, a longing for community. That is a good longing; unity and community are indeed what we were created for. We long to see things the same way, to be in agreement, to be working with one another and not against one another. We're sick of tension and insecure about what others think of us. We long for a community full of friends who are absolutely loyal and whom you can be absolutely yourself around without judgment or controversy. However, merely avoiding disagreement and refusing to acknowledge difference, rather than working through these things, can lead only to a façade of the community we actually desire.

A commitment to worldview pluralism can be a yearning for the community we haven't yet formed. Acting as if there is a depth of relational unity, when that unity has not been hard won, is promiscuity. We want the benefit of communion without the hard work, sacrifice, and service of others that it takes to get there. But the semblance of relational unity when it does not reflect the depth of the actual relationships will bring no more satisfaction than sexual union when it does not reflect a true giving of oneself. In both cases, the façade of union can only be maintained by not sticking around long enough, whether in conversation or in each other's presence, for reality to set in.

In what might be called belief promiscuity, we jump from belief to belief depending on whom we are with. We are willing to temporarily unite ourselves with many different truth claims so long as they keep relationships easy and fun.

Though it rears its head differently in each age, this temptation is ancient. In Old Testament times, it was the temptation to worship idols—to have, rather than one God, a collection of gods that would suit each whim and need and that would give the allusion of unity with neighboring tribes. Pluralism trades physical idols for ideological ones, but at its core is very similar. It remains a promiscuous position, affirming many gods but accountable to none. It is the ideological equivalent of the person who is never ready to commit to a relationship and so keeps playing the field, picking and choosing as they like.

Perhaps sometimes it is okay to treat objects that way—it's okay for me to trade in my surfboard for a different one that I like more. But it's never okay to treat people that way. The question, therefore, is whether truth is a *person*. Christianity claims that it is; Jesus says "I am the truth" (John 14:6).

We must not endorse a promiscuous approach to relationships, no more in our approach to truth than in our approach to sex. If relating to the truth is relating to a person, then relating to the truth will require the same loyalty, commitment, and consistency necessary for any strong relationship. Then it is no wonder that the belief promiscuity underlying pluralism ultimately leaves us feeling intellectually empty.

Once again, we find that the underlying desire motivating pluralism is not too strong but too weak. We are called not to a façade of unity, but to a deep communion for all eternity. Paul says, "I urge you to live a life worthy of the calling you have received. Be completely humble and gentle; be patient, bearing with one another in love. Make every effort to keep the unity of the Spirit through the bond of peace" (Ephesians 4:1–3). True community cannot be superficial. It takes patience; it takes bearing with one another; it takes effort.

But it is so worth it. My own experience is that, at its best, God's Spirit provides a vision for and the empowering to live in an incredible richness of community. We often wish we could see a miracle. I have seen so many miracles in Christian community. I've seen people who could not sleep from anxiety sleeping long and peacefully; people who would never admit that they were wrong falling in love with asking for and receiving forgiveness; formerly selfish, unkind people in humility valuing others above themselves (Philippians 2:3); formerly angry, resentful people expressing genuine love for those who have wronged them.

Why is it that we only count physical transformations among the miraculous? If by next year I were running as fast as Usain Bolt, I would call that a flat-out miracle. But time and again in the context of Christian community, I have seen psychological and emotional transformations even more unlikely than that. When God is at the center of it, the community that is possible is miraculous and unparalleled. We *can* find the unity we long for, not by bypassing disagreement but by finding a love big enough to disagree well and by finding a truth big enough to unite us.

Conclusion

As I was finishing this chapter, I popped downstairs to throw out the recycling, and on my neighbor's recycling bin I saw a sticker that caught my eye. It had a large Christian cross in the center and these words underneath: "Surfing is my religion."

We don't want to choose! And before we know it we can't choose. Someone asks us what life is all about, and we find ourselves standing in front of a whiteboard with a marker in hand, paralyzed. If all answers are valid, then none are motivating. To leave open all theoretical possibilities is to strip away any concrete way forward. We think we are giving ourselves more options and more tolerance and more freedom, but we wind up standing in front of a whiteboard unable to move our arm. Is that freedom?

Sometimes we don't want to choose because we have misconceptions, but other times we don't want to choose for good reasons—because we are committed to universal human value and to fairness, and because we long for authentic, life-giving community. The question is, Where are these to be found? Where are we to find a love unconditional enough to ground human equality, a justice powerful enough to ensure no one is overlooked, a communion deep enough to last?

Science as a singular truth won't satisfy. Pluralism and its multiplicity of truth are under-motivated. So where do we go from here?

CHAPTER 5

HUMANISM

"We don't need God."

Ravi Zacharias

Trying to define *humanism* without running afoul of some scholar is a tough chore. In *The Humanist Tradition in the West,* Alan Bullock described humanism and humanists as "Words that no one has ever succeeded in defining to anyone else's satisfaction, protean words which mean very different things to different people and leave lexicographers and encyclopaedists with a feeling of exasperation and frustration."[1]

Nevertheless, there is no shortage of attempts to define the term. Humanism likes to see itself as "beyond agnosticism."[2] This challenge, like nailing Jell-O to the wall, is not surprising because the very philosophy is so subject to the definer. The old adage used to be, "If a Cretan tells you all Cretans are liars, can you believe him?" Now we have to ask, if a human defines what it means to be human, can you trust his definition? Is not some level of transcendence needed to be right in the definition?

An examination of several different works that focus on what is called humanism shows the broad range that it covers. For example, philosopher Norman Geisler chooses to deal with more recent struggles to define humanism from the nineteenth century, focusing on the role of Julian Huxley, who shaped so much of the modern view on it.[3] Tom Kitwood, in his book *What Is Human?* written years ago, goes back to the Renaissance, which is of course fair to the history of this tradition. His book covers humanism, existentialism, and the Christian faith. He points out, as do others, that some of the earliest humanists would have considered themselves to be committed Christians.

In 2014, the UK-based Theos think tank put out a highly informative work titled, *The Case for Christian Humanism: Why Christians Should Believe in Humanism, and the Humanists in Christianity,* by Angus Ritchie and Nick Spencer. The former Archbishop of Canterbury, Rowan Williams, lent his voice to it by writing the foreword. That alone ought to remind us of the elasticity of the term and how subjective trying to define it becomes, depending on how one defines the idea for starters, and the ramifications of the way it is believed.

In 2007, Anthony Kronman, Sterling Professor of Law at Yale, wrote a book titled, *Education's End: Why Our Colleges and Universities Have Given Up on the Meaning of Life.* A major chapter in the book is "Secular Humanism." It is fascinating to me that he assumes two realities—that the search for meaning is essential to life, and that universities should be leading the way in that search. In my travels, I have asked several students who they think should be taking the lead in the search for the meaning of life and almost never do I hear that it should be universities.

Over the entrance to Uppsala University in Sweden are the words, "To think free is great, but to think right is greater."[4] When we did a series of forums there, a survey was done among the students to find out how many of them agreed with their motto. More than half of them disagreed. So on the opening night, I asked them if they felt they were right in disagreeing with their own motto, and a chuckle went through the audience. Dare I suggest they had not even given what it said a thought? What they really wanted was just to be free. "I don't want anybody telling me how to think" is really the motto in Western education today.

Kronman calls for secular humanism to retake the high ground and believes that the university is the place for it to happen. His book is fascinating to read, both for its reach and its inability to come even close to a convincing answer. As an apologist for humanism, Kronman makes a remarkable statement about why humanism came to be and why it needs to be revived. But one wonders whether it's a battle cry or the Last Post:

> Secular humanism was born at a moment of doubt. When the pieties of the antebellum college began to lose their power and a culture of diversity and doubt took their place, the tradition of offering instruction in the meaning of life—on which American higher education had been based from the start—could survive only in an altered form. Secular humanism made this possible. It offered a way of keeping the question of life's meaning at the center of academic attention and pursuing it in a disciplined way, while recognizing the pluralistic and skeptical beliefs that had undermined the authority of the old order and the credibility of its principal premise: that there is a single right way to live in God's ordered and intelligible world.
>
> The doubts that brought this older order crashing down made it seem to some that no school could now claim authority to do what every school before had done, to instruct its students in the meaning of life. But secular humanism showed how this was still possible. It was a source of confidence in an age of doubt and for those teachers who embraced it, a new kind of faith, the only one allowed them in the disenchanted world they now inhabited.

Today we need secular humanism for the opposite reason, not as a bulwark against doubt but as a solvent of our certainties. We need it to help us challenge the pieties that condition our lives in deep and unnoticed ways. The revival of secular humanism is needed to help us to be doubtful again.[5]

In his plea to give secular humanism the magisterium in the search for meaning that science has in its materialistic terrain, Kronman starts with two premises. One, that the university, thanks to Europe, lost its way and became research institutions rather than incubators for creative and serious thought. Second, as he opines, "Deeper questions of values are left in the hands of those motivated by religious conviction—a disturbing and dangerous development."[6] Doubt about religion gave birth to humanism, so why should we relinquish the responsibility of being authoritative to religion? That, in effect, is the position.

His basic argument leads to five propositions as to why secular humanism must provide the philosophical backdrop to find meaning in life:

1. There is more than one good answer to the meaning of life.
2. The number of answers to life is limited and impossible to study in an organized way.
3. It is impossible to reconcile these answers to what bring meaning to life and thus, one has to choose among them.
4. The best way to explore these answers is by studying the great works of philosophy, literature, and art in which they are presented.
5. Any study should also include conversations or discussions between the various proponents of the various views, such as Augustine, Plato, Hobbes, Paine, Burke, Elliot, Dante, Virgil, Homer.[7]

A handful of Christian philosophers and scholars who were called to respond to Kronman did so in a symposium in September 2007 under the sponsorship of *Comment*.[8] They spared no emotion in wondering what caused such a distorted address of a theme so lofty. John Seel summed up his dismay, "Provocative but flawed," in a critique that is worth reading. Seel goes on to demonstrate that Kronman's argument is nothing more than a warmed up version of existentialism. "Moderns want meaning with autonomy. It's not possible," Seel counters.

Steven Garber, Director of the Washington Institute for Faith, reminds Kronman of Nietzsche's warning that such a pursuit was fraught with peril with the death of God, and of Vaclav Havel's reluctant reminder that, if indeed there is no God, such questions as Kronman addresses are written in the sand and blown by the wind. C. S. Lewis's *The Abolition of Man* foresaw the likes of this sentiment and talked of it as the ultimate denuding of what it meant to be human. Probably the most telling of the hollowness of Kronman's position is written by Aaron Belz, professor of English at Saint Louis University:

> However, learning to think beyond the mess of daily life by becoming fluent in Augustine, Plato, Aristotle, Tolstoy, et al, whom Anthony Kronman takes for contributors in the canon of great thought, is not enough to prevent a person from becoming the Unabomber, or even a run of the mill hustling Machiavellian capitalist.... [T]here's no salvation in familiarity with "great ideas."[9]

I might add that this theme of humanism has been long examined in the movies and been found wanting. Movies such as *The Dead Poets Society* and *Irrational Man* betray the hollow foundation of such cosmetically attired illusions and the inner decay that destroys the soul.

Fascinating thoughts here. One is tempted to digress and debate just this in passing, but I shall resist and save a critique for later. It goes to show several things by way of agreement. First and foremost, that the greatest quest in life is for meaning. When there is a decisive break from the shared meanings of the past, there is not merely a cultural revolution from the outside but a struggle within the human spirit to find coherence and values that are fulfilling within and "tolerant" on the outside. In that sense, Kronman has done everyone a favor by focusing on this important quest at which young lives are stifled and for which our educational institutions have no answers. It also underscores the value our society places on higher education.

I just wonder if his reading has been so inspiring to him personally that he had to make a case for it by saying, "Hey, come look at what I found!" It would be like finding spices and thinking you've found a recipe. He has taken musings and ideas to be the answer when those answers are either clearly in contradiction to each other or nothing more than an accompaniment for life, the main performer.

Interestingly, his book is dedicated to his mother, with the words, "When I was six and asked her, 'What's beyond the stars?' she said, 'That's a metaphysical question,' and made it clear by the tone of her voice that questions of this sort are the most important kind." I would be eager to know how high an education she had, and to ask her whether she is at peace that these most important questions on life's meaning are now answered by professors and not by parents.

I am reminded of the time I was speaking in Moscow at one of their universities and my interpreter told me of the time he was a little boy and asked his mother if Stalin would ever die. His mother replied, "What did your teacher say? Ask your teacher that question." I have absolutely no doubt that Stalin saw himself as a defender of the meaning of life. Therein is the rub, and secular humanism, being avowedly pluralistic and in effect relativistic, continues to cast doubt and breed contradictory certainties.

Seel was right that the pursuit becomes the answer, sort of like in *Fiddler on the Roof*, precariously holding on to something because there is no other way, because if you bend too far you will break. It is an ideal that has built-in tensions and has proved itself unable to deliver what it promised. The obvious was not seen by Kronman. Secularism may have been born in doubt, but maybe it has failed because the listener doubts the answers it provides. The built-in limitation of secular humanism is to stifle the absolute in favor of the quicksand of multiple choice.

The Roots of Humanism

Here I have to meaningfully, if not comprehensively, describe the term because of the very nature of the ideology as a category of thinking. The word *humanist* was first coined in the period of the Renaissance. I well remember in my lectures with Don Cupitt, the clergyman turned atheist at Cambridge University, how often he harked back to the Renaissance as the womb of modern secularism.

Ironically though, many of the Renaissance humanists were devout Christians, if not in their doctrine, then in their frame of reference. Prior to the Renaissance, most of the influential intellectuals were theologians as well, men such as Augustine, Anselm, and Aquinas. Human values were indistinguishable from Christian values and were taken as one born from the other. But the Renaissance became the womb from which a non-Christian value base emerged until it moved in more recent times to an anti-Christian position.

For starters, early humanists had no determined will to evict God, but had in mind the locus of authority from whence they got their belief. The Church power base was suspect, not the existence of God. This is key, and this authority within the Church that led to an authoritarianism of human destiny laid the groundwork for the overthrow of the Church, in secular terms by the philosophes or the thinkers, and in Christian terms by the likes of Wycliffe, Huss, Savon-arola, Luther, and Calvin that formed the bedrock of the Reformation movement. So often, secular thinkers ignore that. Luther's biggest obstacle was the Church. He was not so much against the abolition of priesthood as he was the abolition of the laity. That was precisely the secular person's trumpet sound, "private inquiry" and reasoning.

For the humanists, their revolution started with the arts, moved into the disciplines of the sciences, and finally into formal education and the expulsion of spirituality that was used by the ecclesiastical hierarchy to suppress the individual. The Church was not mistaken only in its interpretation of science; it was also mistaken in its inter-pretation of Scripture. And by the way, the Aristotelian view, sup-ported by a Ptolemaic geocentric cosmology, was then the reigning view of science.

Aristotle laid no claim to Christianity but provided a metanar-rative for cosmology. So did others at that time. Aristotle assumed intuitively that celestial motion was circular because that was the perfect motion, something that philosophically is still assumed in Eastern thought. This view was held for a thousand years until, cen-turies later, the combination of Copernicus and Kepler in the six-teenth and seventeenth centuries moved to a heliocentric cosmol-ogy and elliptical movement of the heavenly bodies that changed everything from previous speculation.

Kitwood tells the story of a priest who mentioned to his supe-rior that he had seen spots on the sun, to which he received the reply, "I have studied Aristotle and he nowhere mentions spots. Try changing your spectacles."[10] It took Galileo in the early seventeenth century, though advised by his friends not to muddy the Milky Way, to bring to the Church's attention that the earth did move, until he was silenced under the force of the Inquisition. That momentary victory of the Church resulted in the costliest loss across the centu-ries of the power of ecclesiastical authority.

With the French Revolution in the latter part of the eighteenth century, when the monarchy came to its end, a new chapter was written in blood when, according to Dickens, splendor rode hard on the bony shoulders of squalor and might crushed right until humanity, long oppressed, overthrew the regime with the monstrous contraption called the guillotine. Religious belief was essentially decapitated too, and the Church, once again siding with the power-side of the disjunction, was thrown onto the heap of corpses.

So while Da Vinci may have epitomized the birth of humanism in the Renaissance, he would never have envisioned the bloody entailments that would follow when humanity, long oppressed by power structures, overthrew those structures. France has never fully recovered from this and, to this day, the field of theology is viewed with great suspicion in their academic ranks.

The French philosopher Auguste Comte, born just after the French Revolution, postulated three stages of human development in thinking. The first is theological, the second metaphysical, and the third empirical. This last stage he called "Positivism." He actually even moved toward calling it a "new Religion of Humanity."[11] He envisioned sacraments, opening houses for the saints and rituals. Auguste Comte was sort of the papal figure of this new religion. And so it is that from Descartes to Comte to Sartre to Derrida...from rationalism to positivism to existentialism to postmodernism...just as India has produced more religions than any other country, France may get the honorary mention for producing more philosophies.

Voltaire, Robespierre, Rousseau, and Montaigne were trailblazers. Comte took up the cause and gave it scientific impetus. Combine that with the empiricists and the enlightenment philosophers and you have our modern times and postmodern worldview that would never fit the sciences but is gleefully held by the humanities. Enter the German higher critics of Scripture that also had its own Copernican revolution where an anthropometric world overturned a theocentric world, and you had not just universities but seminaries joining the march against theology and all talk of God.

Interestingly, in the early days of the collision between Christianity and the secular, when the locus of learning had switched from Athens to Alexandria, the conflict was really a philosophical battleground. That is why the early apologists were engaged either in the finer points of theology and the nature of God, or against the Greek philosophers in their search all the way into the mystery religions.

The Apostle Paul's address on Mars Hill was historic not only because of its location but because of its results. To this very day, two thousand years later, the street beside Mars Hill is called Dionysius Areopagas, named after Dionysius the Areopagite who was converted by that message. Some scholars speculate that he went on to become the first Bishop of Athens.

It was only post-Renaissance and post-Enlightenment that an underlying epistemological shift took place, and today's humanist is sometimes hard to differentiate from a hostile naturalist such as Dawkins. Strangely, very few Western philosophers deal with what was going on in the East during this time, especially in China and India. Both of these cultures have produced well-respected thinkers in ethics and religiosity. However, in the preamble to "The Humanist Manifesto" in 2000, it states this: "Humanism is an ethical, scientific, and philosophical outlook that has changed the world. Its heritage traces back to the philosophers and poets of ancient Greece and Rome, Confucian China, and the Charvaka movement in classical India."[12]

The American Humanist Association says, "Humanism is a progressive philosophy of life that, without theism and other supernatural beliefs, affirms our ability and responsibility to lead ethical lives of personal fulfillment that aspire to the greater good of humanity."[13] Let the reader take note of how so-called humanistic thinking has provided language for some political theorists and we see the word *progressive* bandied about now as a vision for the future with a political infrastructure. That such statements of optimism and "progress" could be made at the dawn of the twenty-first century following the bloodiest century in history strains credulity. So many new words are coined and become the new vocabulary that considers description as prescription and a new oughtness emerges out of the rubble of fallen foundations.

To use *humanism* as a catchall phrase applicable from East to West betrays an incredible blindness to the implications of even the few Eastern philosophies that they have named. From Sankara to Ramanuja in India, to Confucius and Lao Tzu in China, there were rich philosophies produced from these seminal thinkers, some of whom were not formally educated but brilliant in their philosophizing. Western philosophers and religious leaders were caught off guard when Vivekananda came to the West and called out Western prejudice for what it was. He had read their philosophers, quoted them, and dared to challenge their thinking by prescribing a spirituality that was man-centered and met an incredible need in the West itself among those that wished to do away with God but retain the mystical and the spiritual. In one way, he became the father of New Age spirituality.

Somewhat syncretistic but an able debater, he recognized the vacuum of spiritual fulfillment created by a robust humanism that had shed its Christian cloak and seized the moment. He delivered a spirituality that claimed to be wedded to science without divorcing the spirit. The long list of gurus who specialized in "scientifically verifiable results" hailed his courage and knowledge and entered our business arenas, fitness centers, and industries that influenced the popular culture to win converts to a transcendental spirituality that allowed a rigorous pursuit of the material. In fact, some of these gurus today spend more time in our courts settling who owns what of their spoils than they do sitting in solitude enjoying the mind without thought.

All that were needed were some doctorate level scholars such as Deepak Chopra to introduce it into the higher education ranks. Densely texturing his talks with words such as *quantum* and *consciousness*, he dispenses a robust humanism in academia cloaked in a cleverly worded spirituality. And scholars wonder where secular humanism dropped the ball? Ironically, Eastern philosophy was never formally taught as an academic discipline in the East, but rather was learned at the feet of teachers who instructed their followers on how to think on these issues.

To this day, guruism is conducted in one-on-one instruction and not as a formal course that brings degrees against one's name. To consider humanism to be beyond agnosticism and blur the distinction between an assured progressivism and a subtle gnosticism is a philosopher's dream for more categories.

But with the impact of higher education even in the East, changes are afloat until some intensely religious cultures, such as that of Islam, resist the method and message of the West and push back. Their schools are designed to look to the past, not to the future. They consider progressivism damnable and use the very scientific means applauded by the humanist as a means to take the future back to the past.

This growing conflict between East and West awaits us all in the future. Those who have forgotten the past are being blindsided once again with terminology that distorts and deceives its people, risking their offspring at the altar of political control through an ideology.

Test for Truth Fails Its Own Test

That caveat aside, once draped in its coat of many colors, humanism was on a march. On the building blocks of the Renaissance, John

Locke, David Hume, and others were able to influence seismic epistemological shifts in our thinking. Locke cast doubt on the certainty of our knowledge of the external world through our senses, insisting that, because we can only know the world through our own senses and experiences, we cannot know things as they really are. Hume took it further, even questioning causality until his test for meaningfulness in statements failed its own test. Here's what he said:

> If we take in our hand any volume; of divinity or school metaphysics, for instance; let us ask, does it contain any abstract reasoning concerning quantity or number? No. Does it contain any experimental reasoning concerning matter of fact and existence? No. Commit it then to the flames; for it can contain nothing but sophistry and illusion.[14]

This was the universal solvent for him in dealing with metaphysical notions and certainty. The scientific empirical method, breeding its philosophical single vision, was wrested to philosophy's advantage while, at the same time, a knife was put to the heart of metaphysics.

The problem was that this test evaporated by its own terms. I might add that this was the blunder Stephen Hawking made in his book *The Grand Design*. (Although, I daresay that it was made by design.) There he argues that gravity spawned the universe, so "it is not necessary to invoke God to light the blue touch paper and set the universe going."[15] Moreover, he contends that philosophy is dead because it hasn't kept step with modern science. Hawking's leap and philosophical conclusion is made thinking that humanism can build its entire foundation on an epistemology that is highly suspect as an explanation of why we are here in the first place.

But John Cornwell, Director of the Cambridge Science and Human Dimension Project at Jesus College and Chairman of the

Philosophy Department at Cambridge, took Hawking to task in his review of *The Grand Design*. As Cornwell noted (as has our own colleague Professor John Lennox),[16] no reputable theologians believe in this sort of hands-off God that Hawking rejects. Furthermore, said Cornwell, Hawking's charge that philosophy is dead is quite off base even in his own university where the department of history and philosophy of science has made significant strides to "keep abreast of theoretical physics for decades." As Cornwell concludes, perhaps it is actually Hawking "who is failing to keep up with the philosophers and the theologians, rather than the other way around?"[17]

There you have it. Starting off with the artists and moving through the centuries with the logical positivists and ultimately arriving at the same destination that made the blunders centuries ago betrays a hubris that is repeating the errors at the cost of human meaning.

That is, maybe, why Kronman needs to revisit his theory and recognize that the humanities have failed because they were doomed to do so by attempting to answer their own unanswerable questions, given their prejudices. He bemoans that science is the sole unquestioned authority. He considers churches to have somehow monopolized this question of meaning and desires that the humanities take their rightful place by not surrendering to either.

> The desire to understand is eternal, and in an age of forgetfulness, when our humanity is concealed by the powers we possess and the question of life's meaning is monopolized by the churches, to whom our colleges and universities have relinquished all authority to ask it, the revival of secular humanism offers a spiritual alternative to the fundamentalists who invite us to give ourselves up and to the science that invites us to forget who we are. With wonder and sobriety and courage to face our mortal selves: Let our colleges and universities be the spiritual leaders they once were and that

all of us, teachers, students, parents, citizens of the republic, need for them to be again.[18]

I am reminded of a friend who questioned her professor at her prestigious university as to why he so delighted in mocking Christianity. She was sent to the dean's office and told that she was being disruptive in the class. Rather surprised, she answered that it was the teacher who kept digressing from his subject and attacking Christians that she took issue with because it was the faith of her family and her own personal belief. In fact, her father was chair of one of the departments at the same university. The dean told her, "You are here now for an education. Up until this point your family has brainwashed you."

May I suggest that the dean would not have dared say that to a Muslim or a Hindu student. This intellectual cowardice that hides behind irenic statements calling for a pursuit of meaning in the university is blind to the reality that we live with a plurality of cultures and those cultures base their values on a completely different starting point to secular humanism. The intention to change their worldview is not only arrogant but flies in the face of mutual understanding. The university should be a place for healthy and civil discourse with the privilege of dissent. It is not a place to brainwash students that their religious faith is beneath the faith of a secular humanist.

It is interesting that in his book Kronman calls for universities to play a spiritual role. If indeed the university was a soul-making arena, the enforcement of one spirituality upon all the others just plainly would violate a student's constitutional right. In fact, the student I mentioned above went to court over her disciplinary action and won the case. The university can't have it both ways. It cannot be both a place of learning and a place of spiritual indoctrination that violates another student's spiritual heritage.

Forgotten in all of this is that the Renaissance that was birthed in the arts, or certainly enhanced by the arts, was ultimately propelled by the sciences to give justification to the supreme role of the scientific method. The begetting of logical positivism was its handmaiden. So to think that there is a groove that can give meaning without the foundation of naturalism is to ignore what history teaches us. In fact, the very rejection of the Christian faith promotes itself as being built on the exact sciences. So to build an edifice of meaning upon a foundation that took away the right of religion to be taught is to ask for special pleading.

This, in fact, reveals where humanism is both right and wrong. The humanist is right in trying to rescue humanity from mere matter, but runs afoul of reason by taking the bedrock of a materialistic assumption of why we are here and just exchanging it for a fanciful theory of "let's be nice to one another" because we are more than matter.

Humanism in Our Day

In our day, humanism, expanded by the "progressive lifestance" diving board, is defined thus in *The Humanist Magazine*:

> Humanism is a rational philosophy informed by science, inspired by art, and motivated by compassion. Affirming the dignity of each human being, it supports the maximization of individual liberty and opportunity consonant with social and planetary responsibility. It advocates the extension of participatory democracy and the expansion of the open society, standing for human rights and social justice. Free of supernaturalism, it recognizes human beings as a part of nature and holds that values—be they religious, ethical, social, or political—have their source in human experience and culture. Humanism thus derives its goals of life from

human need and interest rather than from theological or ideological abstractions....

Humanism is: A joyous alternative to religions that believe in a supernatural god and life in a hereafter.[19]

If I were to be contentious, I would describe it this way: Humanism is a rational philosophy (even if it is forced to support irrational behavior by removing absolutes) informed by science (as the final authority on origins), inspired by art (even if it has to justify the lewd and the profane), and motivated by compassion (but will kill the livelihood of people who don't subscribe to its presuppositions). Affirming the dignity of each human being (except in its mother's womb or by the ethically aberrant definitions of the likes of Peter Singer), it supports the maximization of individual liberty (except those of religious people who are forced to a privatized faith) and opportunity consonant with social and planetary responsibility (even as all definitions from the past are removed). It advocates the extension of participatory democracy (so it is a political theory) and the expansion of the open society, standing for human rights and social justice (without adherence to an absolute moral law, on which it is based). Free of supernaturalism, it recognizes human beings as a part of nature (no different from the animal, only with a higher ethic) and holds that values—be they religious, ethical, social, or political—have their source in human experience and culture (but cannot explain why our cultures are so self-justifyingly different).... Humanism thus derives its goals of life from human need (apart from the need of God) and interest rather than from theological or ideological abstractions (except for this ideological abstraction).... [Humanism] is a joyous alternative to religions that believe in a supernatural god and life in a hereafter (even as the best admit that we live in a society bereft of meaning, thereby doing away with the essentially sacred and the quest for justice).

The point I am making is that the constant accusations against religions that they divide, claim exclusivity, impose their ethic, stifle education, control sexuality...all these and scores of other criticisms are present here as well. And the reality is that, just like religions, humanism likes to think that it has arrived at a baseline, but here too there are deviations *ad infinitum*. Just like the fields of the sciences, the humanities, and Christianity, its followers do not always follow a single creed.

Norman Geisler, in *Is Man the Measure?*[20] gives eight different core beliefs under the rubric of humanism. They are:

Evolutionary Humanism (promoted by Julian Huxley)
Behavioral Humanism (promoted by B. F. Skinner)
Existential Humanism (promoted by Jean-Paul Sartre)
Pragmatic Humanism (promoted by John Dewey)
Marxist Humanism (promoted by Marx and Feuerbach)
Egocentric Humanism (promoted by Ayn Rand)
Cultural Humanism (promoted by Corliss Lamont)
Christian Humanism (promoted by C. S. Lewis, J.R.R. Tolkien, et al)

But let's get to some agreements among the different strands of humanism. All but the last in the list above would comfortably qualify under secular humanism, epitomized by Julian Huxley in his book *Religion Without Revelation*. In fact, he could be considered to be its mascot. His famous line was that God is beginning to resemble not a ruler but "the last fading smile of a cosmic Cheshire cat."[21] He proclaimed triumphantly the great relief this brought him and hoped that many others would follow him. Interestingly, he does also talk of the "spiritual-like" experience that made him deny the strictly materialistic humanism of a Karl Marx variety.

Two quotes sum up his view of man and the future:

> Twentieth-century man, it is clear, needs a new organ for dealing with destiny, a new system of religious beliefs and attitudes adapted to the new situation in which his societies now have to exist. The radically new feature of the present situation may perhaps be stated thus: Earlier religions and belief systems were largely adaptations to cope with man's ignorance and fears, with the result they came to concern themselves primarily with stability of attitude. But the need today is for a belief system adapted to cope with his knowledge and his creative possibilities; and this implies the capacity to meet, inspire, and guide change.[22]

So according to Huxley, the eviction of God and the destiny belief in Him brings means that humanism must find the answer to provide what the "rationality" of its beliefs denies. He hopes that out of all this, a feasible humanistic religion will evolve. Comte failed to bring it about. Huxley revived that search: "How that religion will take form—what rituals or celebrations it might practice, whether it will equip itself with any sort of professional body or priesthood, what buildings it will erect, what symbols it will adopt—that is something no one can prophesy."[23]

Fast-forward up to our day, and I am reminded of an article I read some years ago. Loyal D. Rue, a professor of religion and philosophy, argued that we must invent a "noble lie" since the Judeo-Christian worldview was no longer plausible in our scientific age. But without religious myths, he conceded that we are left with nihilism, which was also not a positive option. Hence, we need a convincing noble lie, one that tells us that our universe "is infused with value." He concedes that ultimately this is a "great fiction" because "the universe just is," but such a lie "attributes objective value to it" and "[w]ithout such lies, we cannot live."[24] He goes on to argue in his book *By the Grace of Guile: The Role of Deception in Natural History and Human Affairs* that "[i]t remains for the artists, the poets, the novelists, the musicians, the filmmakers, the tricksters, and the masters of illusion to winch us toward our salvation by seducing us into an embrace with a noble lie."[25]

There you have it. Humanism has reached its destination—a lie in order to keep us from eating one another up. Not having intrinsic worth of its own to give, it has to make it up because, otherwise, we will continue the path from whence we came and the weak will be chewed up and spat out by some strongman who cares not for values.

Revisiting Their Goals

When you read the oration at the funeral of Pericles, Kitwood points out that there were really four propositions:

1. Tolerance: Each one is sovereign over his choices, and each one ought to be free to choose that path without any outcry against that choice.
2. Wholeness or balance: A balanced life makes use of all human potentialities and pursuits.
3. Cooperation and generosity.
4. The principal and principled idea of self-reliance.[26]

At face value, there is a noble intent here. But what is subsumed under its imperatives is the fact that these qualities are intrinsically good. And how does one separate intrinsic good from pragmatic good or utilitarian good? Also, is this not a simplistic approach to life's very complex decisions? Think of what we face today with the advance of technology and the choices before us both in life and death. For these dead-ends and others, humanism itself keeps evolving, and hence the chameleon-like definitions.

The avowals and disavowals of humanism were scripted in three Humanist Manifestos in 1933, 1973, and a declaration dated 2003. Anyone can readily pull them up from various websites. Even after two world wars and the bloodiest century in history, the determination to evict the sacred is so strong that reality is ignored, though it stares them in the face. Big names and distinguished intellectuals have signed these documents.

Perhaps it is this blinded hubris that caused Paul Johnson, the historian, to write his book *Intellectuals*; the last paragraph of the book is worth the price of the book. The private lives of these intellectuals reveal the reason they are so against any moral reasoning that would make life at its core, sacred. The preamble to the British Humanist Association and the terrain reached years later tells the story:

> Humanists believe that man's conduct should be based on humanity, insight, and reason. He must face his problems with his own moral and intellectual resources, without looking for supernatural aid. Our concern is with this life, which we try to make worthwhile and sufficient in itself. We make no claims to special knowledge or final answers, since we regard the search for understanding as a continuing process.[27]

Making life worthwhile and self-reliant, rejecting any transcendent perspective, is at the core. From this simple platform, humanism evolved, reconfigured, revealed, and morphed into what it really wanted. As *The Humanist Magazine* declared bluntly some years ago, "What we should be fighting for is the total destruction of Christianity and its superstitions, impostures and swindles.... I unhesitatingly declare that freedom from religion's myth is of prime importance to humanity."[28]

One would have thought that the human experience would have brought a sober mindedness to their optimism, but it hasn't and possibly never will. The biggest challenge was to find a basis for ethics since God was no longer the source for ethics. So three different paths from evolutionary ethics were posited. The first is that of utilitarianism (Jeremy Bentham), which seeks the greatest happiness for the greatest number; the second is the ethic of mutual responsibility (H. J. Blackham is one of the names here); and third, to find a measurement for the increase in the breadth and length of life (Julian Huxley had the loudest voice here through Desmond Morris's *The Naked Ape*).

One more path may be added, and that is the valiant, albeit highly varnished, effort of Sam Harris in *The Moral Maze*, where he argues for "well-being." One marvels at the rehashed and reconfigured ideas presented in different terms. The emperor really has no clothes, but the language provides shelter from the storm of unreason. William Lane Craig among others has done a thorough job of showing the linguistic wordplay used in Sam Harris's argument as he tries to explain why we think in moral categories. I encourage readers to read his critique. It all boils down to a distortion of reality or a devaluation of humanity. If it weren't so serious, the hollowness of these efforts would be laughable.

When all the explaining has been done, humanity is left at the whim of the human doing the defining. Interestingly, I cannot have my own law of gravity, but it seems a person can have his or her own law of morality. At the end, the law of gravity will hold as we see humanity in a free fall, and the laws of morality will be proven in the process.

Before I move to a counter perspective in the Christian faith, take just one example from World War II. This was a humanitarian expression by some who felt humanity would be better because of their learning experience. *Doctors of Depravity* by English author Christopher Hudson and reviewed in *The Daily Mail* (March 2, 2007) tells this staggering story. The following quote from the Japanese doctor at the center of this inhumanity, as described by Hudson, says it all: "A doctor's God-given mission is to block and treat disease… but the work…we are now to embark is the complete opposite of those principles."[29]

Hudson details the horrors of what occurred under a secret medical experimentation unit, Unit 731, of the Imperial Japanese Army. More than sixty years later, a staff member who participated in several operations, most conducted upon prisoners of war with no anesthesia, described the experiments as "educational." Hudson writes that the officer confessed to dissecting ten prisoners, including two teenage girls: "He cut out their livers, kidneys, and wombs while they were still alive. Only when he cut open their hearts did they finally perish."[30]

The catalogue of horrors is unspeakable. Yet ironically, as Hudson notes, many from this unit advanced to important positions in society, including a doctor who became the leader of one of Japan's largest pharmaceutical company.

May I add, this is humanism's hatpin to the heart. And it is grounded in relativism about human value.

Many humanists and relativists get very angry with such illustrations. They are repelled more by those who bring this to light than by those who commit such acts. Frankly, it is not possible to read Hudson's book and not get nauseated by the details. But this is precisely what happens when those in power do things to others in the name of humanistic development. The reason such possibilities exist is because there is no overarching point of reference for good and no unified definition of what it means to be human.

In my next chapter, I will make my critique of humanism by exposing the relativism on which it and the dangers that result from it rely, and I will counter with Jesus' declaration of what it means to be human.

CHAPTER 6

RELATIVISM

~~~~

"True for you but not for me."

Ravi Zacharias

The Truthful Alternative

There is an old story about a Texas sheriff in pursuit of a bank robber who kept crossing back into Mexico after each heist. The sheriff finally tracks him down in a bar in his hometown but, because of the language barrier, he needs an interpreter who patiently translates line-by-line as each speaks to the other. Finally, the sheriff says to the robber, "Tell me where you've hidden all the money or I'll shoot!" The bandit proceeds to give the details of where, behind what house, beside which tree, how deep a hole, etc. The interpreter hesitates a moment and says, "He says…he says…go ahead and shoot!"

Self-interest and profit are powerful motivators in what we confess to. I often wonder how many academics really know that they don't have a solid foundation on which to build their worldview, but the pressure of the academy and job security forces them to refrain from admitting so and compels them to just go with the flow. As Vince noted previously, G. K. Chesterton said that the problem with the Christian faith is not that it has been tried and found wanting but that it has been found difficult and left untried.[1] There is, no doubt, truth in that statement. The cost of belief in a contrary climate is huge.

Yet when one looks at the persecuted Church, it is amazing how it has survived and often thrived. When Muslims boast about how fast Islam is growing, it is not a legitimate claim. Only if they remove compulsion from the lands where it is enforced can they then lay claim to their boast as fact. In most Islamic countries, one does not have the freedom to disbelieve. It is to the credit of the Christian faith that it has survived immense persecution and efforts to obliterate the faith completely. ISIS has tried to do this, while the rest of the world watches on, and yet followers of Jesus stand firm in their trust.

Christianity is a belief grounded in freedom. It is also, and here is where it contrasts most sharply with humanism, a belief in an absolute. This latter truth is where I wish to focus now. Humanism, secular humanism at least, is inextricably tied to the relativization of truth and of ethics. Humans are the measure of all things. Well, then, this measure is relative to which human person? Which human culture? Which human age? No answers are forthcoming. In this way, the failure of humanism and the failure of relativism are inextricably intertwined. All value is reduced to value according to the preferences and biases of this or that person, culture, or age.

I have written before on the technicalities and philosophical perplexities of relativism. Rather than rehearse that here, I wish to offer a better way by showing how both truth and ethics rely on the objective and universal framework provided by Christ. Along the way, I will also address the common pitfall in relativism in truth and relativism in ethics. Amid the confusion of the relativism mandated by secular humanism, Jesus makes an absolute claim about what it means to be human.

At the core of Jesus' teaching is the clear and definitive description of what it means to be human. That makes all the difference in holding together moral precepts and the meaning of life. I see four clear distinctives that bring the chronological and the logical together:

Creation
Incarnation
Transformation
Consummation

This sequence defines the Christian message of what being human really means. Sadly, as the ways part right from the first phase, so much misinformation and misrepresentation takes place.

Creation

Just use this word in an academic setting and you're finished. I have met instructors in universities who have told me in private settings of the academic pressure they are under if they even hint at a personal moral first cause in the agency needed to explain why we exist.

My friend and colleague John Lennox makes a profound case for the hermeneutics of the story of humanity as recorded in Genesis in his book *Seven Days That Divide the World.* The wide range of possibilities in what is being said merits serious consideration. It is fascinating that instead of focusing on the main idea, critics jump into the lesser points and try to destroy the whole narrative with minutiae.

The fact is that even scientists simply do not make a convincing case for an "earthbound" theory of origins. I do not speak of processes. I speak of the starting point. Science has to remain silent on it at this point, and that is why we see differences within the disciplines.

Here, for example, are Hoyle and Wickramasinghe as they calculated the odds that all the functional proteins necessary for life might form in one place by random events—a staggering 1 chance in 10 to the 40,000th power. They conclude, "It is an outrageously small probability that could not be faced even if the whole universe consisted of organic soup."[2]

Hoyle concludes in his book *Intelligent Universe*:

> Life could not have originated here on earth nor does it look as though biological evolution can be explained from within an earthbound theory of life. Genes from outside the earth are needed to drive the evolutionary process. This much can be consolidated by strictly scientific means, by experiment, observation, and calculation.[3]

He goes on to posit instead the possibility of a panspermia theory of origins. If science is willing to suspend judgment on ultimate origins, is it too much to ask that a Designer also be in the mix of possibilities? I recommend Lennox's book for serious-minded students to see what possibilities loom there. For my part, I wish to draw two implications for humankind from God as Creator.

The first is that human beings have intrinsic (and not merely relative) worth. This is not worth conveyed by state or politics or the United Nations. This is worth conveyed by being an entity designed for dignity and purpose. Where there is a Creator with a purpose, there is a law to govern the created entity.

Here may I also say in passing that for the hostile atheist to take apart the character of God without recognizing the covenantal relationship to which a people had agreed (along with its blessings and entailments) is tantamount to taking a sentence out of context and making it the whole story.

For example, if a child is to make deductions from its mother taking her to a doctor, horrendous false conclusions can emerge. The little one sees the big needle in the doctor's hand and screams, wondering why her mother into whose protecting arms she had submitted herself would stand by and do nothing. Further, the child may get more confused when she sees the mother actually paying the doctor for inflicting such pain. It could be years before the benefit of that painful visit might be seen.

Is it too much for us mortals to submit to the wisdom of a designing and caring Creator to show us how the painful effects of sin may bring us to the eternal perspective? Laws are inviolable without consequences. This is something so hard for us to grasp. King Solomon, who knew enough about the law though he flaunted it, said, "The path of the righteous is like the morning sun, shining ever brighter till the full light of day" (Proverbs 4:18). He went on to say that the "whole duty" of man was to "keep God's commandments" (Ecclesiastes 12:13 KJV). He spoke from the perspective of someone who struggled with a derelict lifestyle, finding out he had been "chasing after the wind" (Ecclesiastes 1:14).

The very word *law* evokes rebellion within our hearts. When you look at the Mosaic Law, there are 613 laws given in total. They were divided into the moral, ceremonial, and civic codes. As the Hebrew Scriptures unfold, you see other prophets distilling them down to their core and essence. In Psalm 15, David reduces them to eleven. Isaiah in 1:16–18 brings them down to six. Micah in 6:8 narrows them down to three: to do justice, love mercy, and walk humbly before your God. Habakkuk in 2:4 sees the law in its core relationship between man and God and states it in one law—that the "just would live by his faith" (KJV).

If you remove the third of Micah's three imperatives (to walk humbly before your God), you are left with the same terminology as humanism espouses: justice and compassion. The foundational difference between the two is the third imperative, walking humbly before God. How do we know this? When Jesus was teaching on the law, two trick questions were placed before Him. The first was whether it was right to pay taxes to Caesar. Jesus brilliantly asked the questioner for a coin. When the man produced the coin, Jesus asked him whose image he saw on the coin. The answer unhesitatingly given was that it was Caesar. Jesus promptly said, "So give back to Caesar what is Caesar's, and to God what is God's" (Matthew 22:21).

This was truly a defining moment. The taxation burden on the Jew was huge, and he resented having to pay it. But then came the silence that ought not to have been. The man should really have asked, "What belongs to God?" That question would have underscored what lies beneath all political and economic responsibility. And Jesus' answer would have been, "Whose image is on you?" That all-defining essence is at the heart of what it means to be human. We are made "imago dei." We are made in God's image.

This is even further underscored in the next trick question placed before Jesus: "Which is the greatest commandment?" (Matthew 22:36). Having failed to trip Him up on "God against Caesar," they tried "God against God." With 613 laws to choose from, Jesus was asked to choose one.

Amazingly, He didn't fall for it and put two together as inextricably bound. He said, "'Love the Lord your God with all your heart and with all your soul and with all your mind.'… The second is like it: 'Love your neighbor as yourself.'" Matthew records the ending of the conversation with Jesus' words, "All the Law and the Prophets hang on these two commandments" (Matthew 22:37–40). Mark then adds, "There is no commandment greater than these" (Mark 12:31).

In other words, loving God and the resulting love for humanity are not only inextricably bound, but apart from that all else of morality has no other ground on which to stand. This is the only noble truth. All else is an ignoble lie. There is no foundation without these and nothing greater than these. Truth-telling, sanctity of sex, sanctity of life, sanctity of ownership, etc., none is greater and none can be legitimate except based on the vertical relationship with God.

There you have what humanism simply does not have and is avowedly against. The logic of Jesus is compelling in what He has joined together. There is no absolute basis for loving your fellow human being without the first commandment. There is no way to claim to love God while being inhuman to your fellow human being. That which God has joined together, let no one put asunder.

That is why even the Ten Commandments hang on the hinge of redemption. When man is released from bondage to self, he or she sees the glory of the other person. You cannot be a genuine human without acknowledging the intrinsic worth given to every other human being.

My respect for the other person is not based on what they believe about me but what I believe about them. Money and things are economic and social quantities; a person is a spiritual entity. From this intrinsic worth we see a reflective splendor. The inherent value we have as humans gives us both general and particular worth.

I have told this elsewhere, but I know of no better way to illustrate this than an event that took place some years ago. In 2006, Taylor University in Upland, Indiana, experienced a great tragedy when several students and faculty were killed in a car accident.

One young woman survived the crash, and her family was by her bedside for days and weeks. But they soon realized that her answers weren't making sense to them. With all the allowances for head injury and trauma, etc., they knew something was awry, especially when she finally asked them why they kept calling her by the wrong name.

That triggered a series of interactions till it was realized that the young woman was not their daughter at all. There was an identity mistake. Without doing DNA tests, the coroner had given the wrong daughter to the family. A young woman who had died in the accident and been buried under another name was actually their daughter, and the daughter they were nursing back to strength was someone else's daughter.

All of a sudden one family was traumatized by finding out that their daughter, who they thought was dead, was still alive, while the family who thought their daughter had survived realized she was already buried. Trying to cope with the swing of emotions had to be a life-changing and mind rearranging shift for both families. How does one even fathom it all? One shortcut made by the practitioner and the ramifications were huge.

Let me take this further. What if the young woman realized that they assumed her to be who she was not but she actually preferred this family to her own and decided to play along and learn the part? Identity theft of material things is horrendous enough; identity theft of the essential is contemptible because everyone is robbed of the truth and a person who is dead is betrayed by a lie that steals her identity.

Think of the ramifications of misrepresenting our essential worth only to find out at life's end that we are not who the academics told us we were. The surviving young woman had a name and a value that justified her care and her liberation. She was of reflective splendor in her family but of intrinsic worth to all humanity. That is the balance only the Christian faith gives us right from the beginning of each life.

There is an interesting passage in the Bible in which Isaac's wife, Rebekah, was questioning God during her pregnancy as to what was going on inside her. God's answer to her was that two nations were in her womb and that the older would serve the younger. But here's the point. God doesn't say, "Two products of conception are in your womb," nor does He say, "Two babies are in your womb." God's statement is rather dramatic. "Two nations are in your womb" (Genesis 25:23).

This is how God reminds us of the value of a life. It is not just a single life. It is a lineage in play here, offspring who will determine the future. The Creator's design is not merely an individual thing. It is a plan and a link into the future.

Incarnation

Genesis 1:1 begins with "In the beginning God created…" Just three words in Hebrew. Those three words change every implication for who we are. But in the Gospel of John we are given more detail: "In the beginning was the Word, and the Word was with God, and the Word was God…. And the Word became flesh and dwelt among us…full of grace and truth" (John 1:1, 14 ESV).

The story of the Incarnation has informed and inspired humankind for centuries. It was not a noble lie; it was the noble truth. It was the single greatest life to change the history of the world. At His birth, shepherds who raised sheep for the slaughter at Passover came face-to-face with the perfect Lamb. Born into the household of a carpenter, the very framer of the universe entered history. Offered gifts from rulers from afar, He Himself was the greatest gift of all—the King of kings and Lord of lords. All the power of Rome tried to stop Him. He came to free the captives. He came to announce liberty to an enslaved world.

In our home we have a painting. In the foreground is a powerfully built Roman soldier with his military regalia, leaning on his spear. Below him in the proximate distance, he is observing a man leading a donkey, atop which is a woman in her delicate stage of late pregnancy. The contrast is unmistakable. The powers of this world arrayed with deluded strength, observing a simple family through whom the message of ultimate power was to come.

Here was Daniel's vision of a stone uncut by human hands that was going to shatter the kingdoms of this world (Daniel 2:34). Rome was conquered by the gospel. But even as Rome later mocked the gospel, her stones crumbled and she lives now only with memories of a glory that once was. Edward Gibbon tells of this in his multivolume book *The History of the Decline and Fall of the Roman Empire*. Her moral failures and hubris weakened her till the barbarians were able to scale her walls because, behind those walls, devastation had already taken place.

In the Incarnation, I see at least two implications: the absoluteness of the moral law and the supremacy of love. We will consider them one at a time.

No matter how loudly one screams platitudes, at its core humanism is relativistic. All values become relative to the individual's circumstances or culture. And at its core, relativism is self-defeating. To even say that all truth is relative is to engage in contradiction: That statement either includes itself or excludes itself. If it includes itself, it is claiming not to be always true. If it excludes itself, it is positing an absolute while denying that absolutes actually exist. So the only way that all truth can be relative is once again to engage in a solvent that dissolves itself.

Relativism becomes the quicksand of humanism, and meaning is also destroyed because one cannot find security based on a value-less culture, defined by a value-less individual. No one knows this better than our young. In her book *Finding God at Harvard*, Kelly Monroe Kullberg quotes a student saying, "The freedom of our day is the freedom to devote ourselves to any values we please, on the mere condition that we do not believe them to be true."[4]

In their book *Relativism*, Francis Beckwith and Greg Koukl get to the core of what moral relativism means and implies. They point out that classic moral systems have at least three characteristics. First, they serve as an authoritative guide for actions, regardless of tastes, preferences, customs, self-interest, etc. Second, there is a prescriptive code that follows from within the system and brings a sense of "oughtness" and of imperatives; it dictates how things should be. Third, morality is universal. These moral principles are not arbitrary and personal but are public, applying equally to all people in relevantly similar situations. That's what an objective moral law entails.

Even skeptics see this as necessary. Beckwith and Koukl quote philosopher David Hume, regarding a moral system:

> The notion of morals implies some sentiment common to all mankind which recommends the same object to general approbation and makes every man or most men agree in the same opinion or same discussion concerning it. It also implies some sentiments so universal and comprehensive as to extend to all mankind.[5]

Relativism, in effect, rejects such notions and takes away the universal "oughtness." It is interesting that relativists have shunned absolutes but demand compliance with relativism as an absolute. Functionally, it becomes no different to an amoral point of view or, for that matter, a person with no moral point of view. Our entire culture has fallen prey to a relativistic way of deciding which morals apply to them. Perilously, rather than make a prescription, relativism keeps shifting to the question, "Relative to what?"

How well I remember a news story in the 1990s on one of the major networks describing a survey of how Americans think of absolutes in language and morality. We live in what I call a "salvation by survey" culture. In the first question of this survey, a reporter was asking people on the street if they believed words had specific meanings or were dependent upon the user's way of using them. The question itself was prompted by President Clinton's famous phrase, "It all depends on what 'is' means."

Fascinatingly, the consensus was that word usage depended upon the user and the words themselves had no specific definitions with which to comply. It didn't occur to the surveyor or the surveyed that they were using words to settle the question.

But that aside, the next question was whether morality was absolute or depended upon the individual. The survey again yielded a dependence upon the individual rather than a moral standard independent of the individual. That again implicitly begs the question of whether one needed to be honest in their answer. Such is the self-stultification at work in our postmodern culture.

Ironically, the second item on the news that day was a warning to Saddam Hussein that if he didn't "stop playing word games, we would start bombing him." There it was in stark reality. Words and morals did have meaning by which we judged others but did not necessarily apply in the same measure to ourselves. That is the two-edged sword of relativism. It wounds the hand of the one who wields it. Words have ontic referents as do moral pronouncements, whether we admit it or not. Vince will expand on this point in his chapter on hedonism.

Going beyond the moral law, Jesus teaches the eight beatitudes where He not only reverses common assumptions, but teaches how He transcends the law (Matthew 5:1–12). The *poor in spirit* inherit His kingdom because those who see their poverty of spirit call upon the Lord to enrich them. It is not the arrogant that ultimately inherit; it is the humble.

The Sermon on the Mount lives beyond the law to an even higher calling: "You have heard that it was said…But I say unto you…" (Matthew 5:21–48 NKJV). We talk of the letter of the law and the spirit of the law. Jesus goes beyond that to make even the spirit of the law look merely as an intention. The beatitudes take us to a kingdom ethic that makes God's work in our lives the ultimate liberation.

Gautama Buddha was on to a half-truth when he said that suffering is eliminated when we cease to desire. If you don't desire anything, you never feel deprived. But instead of that, Jesus encourages us to hunger and thirst after righteousness. That is a positive desire that takes you beyond the absence of suffering to the presence of joy and His peace.

Life should not be a process of merely escaping suffering. The starting point of a created order redefines everything. That is why on Easter Sunday we see who was really alive and who was essentially dead. Or, in the case of the man who was born blind that Jesus healed, we learn that spiritual blindness is a supreme malady depriving one of what really is real.

During the Iraq war, a woman soldier lost her hand when it was blown off by an explosive device that landed near her. As she was being rushed to the hospital, she kept crying out, not for the hand she had lost but for the ring that was on that hand—her wedding ring. One of her fighting mates returned to the place, found the hand, and brought back her ring.

What an amazing transposition of values. The ring was the band that symbolized her love and union with her husband. In a dramatic realization of what really mattered, she could live without the hand but wept for the loss of the symbol of the spiritual bond of a love.

In some of life's most defining moments, we find depths of value that shallow moments never reveal. Squandering our existence in the shallow end of life, we miss all that is found in the deep end of discovery and beauty.

That leads me beyond law to the supremacy of love—love the Supreme Ethic.

Creation defines essence. Essence addresses existence. Not the other way around. If existence were to define essence, we slide down the path of a meaningless, relativistic array of choices with punctuated meanings but no ultimate meaning, and life does indeed become "a tale told by an idiot full of sound and fury, signifying nothing."[6]

There is a high priced watch that is advertised thus: "You don't really own a Patek Philippe; you just guard it for the next generation."

If existence defines essence, that's not only true of a high priced watch, it is true of anything you claim to "own." Solomon bemoaned that temporary grasp. It is only being protected for the next generation. Ironically, that selling line is for that which keeps time. All "valuable" possessions have a shelf life.

This is where the teaching of Jesus rises to a unique height. Jesus talks of the three great excellences: Faith, Hope, and Love. All three of these are postures of the mind that every human being clings to in life. Some are put aside at the end, and others meet their essence in eternity. You cannot really function without any of them, though the one that we often try to function without is the most important of them all.

Faith and hope are impossible to live without. One can attempt to live without love, but in doing so one has lived without the most glorious possession of the heart and soul. From parents to children, it is a posture of the mind that we sing about, write about, dream about, and often rob ourselves of.

I am now a grandfather and loving this stage of life. Our oldest grandson, Jude, is about five years old. It's a sentimental thing for me to watch him put his bag on his back and trot off to school, albeit at the kindergarten stage. He doesn't like to go because it's a long day for the little guy. But he loves to come home every afternoon.

When he was about three-and-a-half years old, his mother had misplaced her car keys at home and finally in frustration said, "I must be losing my mind!" At that, Jude came over toward her and said, "Mommy, whatever you do, please don't ever lose your heart, because I'm in there."

In his psalms, David says that "Out of the mouths of babes...you have ordained praise" (Psalm 8:2 NHEB). Children awaken us to the splendor of love in a way adults seldom do. Why? Because our love can be a scheming one. A child expresses it as a genuine "need" love.

C. S. Lewis would remind us that the climax of love is "appreciative love" in worship.[7]

Whether we ever graduate to appreciation love or not, we know deep within us the longing for a consummate relationship that blends the sacred and the expression in total fulfillment. That is impossible without love given and love received. How is that love possible?

In every other worldview, at best life precedes love. Only in the Christian faith does love precede life. The God of love has created us for His purpose, supremely found in loving God and our fellow human beings. Love succeeds life. It is both here and hereafter. You enjoy it, you spend it, you inherit it in still grander terms.

You don't just protect it for the next generation. Your reality is that the next generation will multiply it and ultimately enjoy it together with you in eternity. It is like a seed that is sown and the resulting fruit is tasted and enjoyed by all.

Transformation

For that kind of love, something has to die if the greater passion is to live. That is what Jesus calls the new birth, or "conversion."

As Vince has mentioned, some years ago, the prominent writer Matthew Parris wrote an incredible article in *The Times* (December 27, 2008) in which he said that the only answer for Africa was not more aid but the "evangelistic message of conversion." Anyone who knows Parris knows that his beliefs as an atheist are anything but supportive of the gospel message. Parris himself affirms this.

Yet, as he visited Malawi, where he had been raised, he saw the spiraling down of life in Africa and said it would take not more NGOs to lift Africa up but the transformed heart that the message of Jesus promises. He acknowledged that he felt torn as an atheist but was forced to admit the unique aspect of transformation that only the Christian faith promised.

Here's how he ended his article:

> Those who want Africa to walk tall amid twenty-first-century
> global competition must not kid themselves that providing
> the material means or even the know-how that accompanies
> what we call development will make the change. A whole
> belief system must first be supplanted. And I'm afraid it has
> to be supplanted by another. Removing Christian evange-
> lism from the African equation may leave the continent at
> the mercy of a malign fusion of Nike, the witch doctor, the
> mobile phone, and the machete.[8]

The truth is that this truth is not just for Africa but for all humankind. The machete is limited. The destructive power within reach of
the so-called "advanced countries" (which is a debatable term) has
cataclysmic possibilities. Our ethics may be relative, but our meth-
ods can be absolute.

Jesus called for a changed heart not only for the destructive, the
derelict, and the destitute, but also for the sophisticated, the successful, and the skilled. This heart change is the only bypass for
that which would otherwise kill. It takes a brazen self-confidence to
think we can find our own way out of this human predicament of
self and pride.

In the call for transformation, the teaching of Jesus is clear. First,
that the problem is not of the intellect but of the spirit. Walk into
a prison and see the difference between self-justification and true
remorse. I know a billionaire businessman who, about to launch a
billion dollar venture, asked me to pray for him and for the project
as he entered into it. As we walked away from the site about eleven
o'clock at night, he said, "Once upon a time I wouldn't have agreed
with your prayer when you prayed for God's will in this venture. I

would have wanted it whether God wanted it or not. Now I say with all my heart that I only want this if God wills it for me."

When the submission of the tender was approved, he called me and said, "You're the first one I am calling to tell you that my bid has been accepted." There is a world of a difference between wanting my way and wanting God's way.

In surrendering, one wins. In dying, one lives. That is what Jesus means when He asks us to deny ourselves. It is the willingness to accept God's claim upon one's life before pursuing one's own ideals. That starting point is really the beginning of victory. The funeral at which real life for each of us begins is the burying of one's own pride and self-sufficiency.

I remember as a young man, some of us teasing one of my friends who was getting married that he was losing his freedom. That banter ended when he looked at us and said, "You've got that wrong. The truth is that I am now really free…free to love…free to be committed to a meaningful relationship. You guys are still handcuffed."

Those are not just words. Properly understood, they describe what surrender and death to self bring—a life for which one was designed. Most of us try to build first and only read the directions when we run into trouble. Following the directions helps one build to specs one's own individual destiny. That is true freedom and celebration.

Consummation

Some years ago I was in Jerusalem, researching and writing my book *Light in the Shadow of Jihad*. I had a fascinating conversation with a professor of religions at the leading university there and was quite surprised by one of his comments that totally took me off guard. "You are a clever man, Mr. Zacharias, but let me tell you something you don't know."

"There's a lot I don't know, sir," I replied. "Please tell me."

"I am Jewish and you are a Christian. But we do have one thing in common. Our ultimate goal is communion with God. That is a spiritual destination. Is that right?"

"Fair enough," I said, not quite sure where he was headed, but not wanting to interrupt his passionate, intense conversation.

"Yes...yes. We have that goal in common. We wish to be in communion with our maker...our God." He continued, "Before I became a professor, I worked for the Mossad...don't cut me off now...I worked for the intelligence and protection of my country." I was taken aback by his intensity and his thoughts.

"Often I would be called to the scene of a suicide bombing to pick up the broken pieces of a blown-up body. I would be shaken to see the devastation, but here's what I noticed. The young man who had blown himself up was usually wearing a lead girdle to protect that part of his anatomy that he would need in paradise.

"Yes...that's what I would notice and would be rendered silent. He was protecting that which he would use in his afterlife. I realized then how fundamentally different my belief is to his. No, it is not just political, or land driven, or revenge, or whatever. It is an ultimate belief about who we are at the very core of our being. His faith was all metaphorically defined in material terms. My faith, though sometimes symbolized by matter, transcended matter to a spiritual communion with God. We await a day and a time when our spiritual essence will shake off all these material attachments and find our destiny in God."

I was silent and reflective. It was a starkly different conversation to the one I had had with the Grand Mufti of Jerusalem the night before. This professor was right. On one side it was all about land, power, politics, ownership, control, winning, and the destruction of any who stood in the way. This, by contrast, was a conversation that defined the journey in terms of the destination.

Søren Kierkegaard had said that he had learned to define life backward and live it forward. What is the point we are aiming to reach? What is the route God has made for us to get there? All of life is a version of wandering in the wilderness so that we may discover that we are not to live by bread alone but by every word that proceeds from the mouth of God and that, no matter the trial, He will guard and protect us with the values that are confirmed in His character.

This is why Blaise Pascal said what he did in his *Pensées*:

> It is in vain, oh men, that you seek within yourselves the cure for all your miseries. All your insight only leads you to the knowledge that it is not in yourselves that you will discover the true and the good. The philosophers promised them to you and they have not been able to keep that promise. They do not know what your true good is or what your true state is. How should they have provided you with a cure for ills which they have not even understood. Your principal maladies are pride, which cuts you off from God, and sensuality, which binds you to the earth. And they have done nothing but foster at least one of these maladies. If they have given you God for your object, it has been to pander to your pride. They have made you think you are like Him and resemble Him in your nature. And those who have grasped the vanity of such a pretension have cast you down in the other abyss by making you believe that your nature is like that of the beast of the field and have led you to seek your good in lust, which is the lot of animals.[9]

The fork in the road is obvious: Pantheism deludes you into an inflated sense of who you are, and naturalism reduces you to nothing more than a thinking machine. One is self-deifying, the other is reductionistic. Neither extreme is true or empirically justifiable.

Malcolm Muggeridge talks of a performance of the musical

Godspell at which the sometime Archbishop of Canterbury, Michael Ramsey, stood to his feet applauding and shouted, "Long live God!" Taken aback by that emotive outburst from a sedate British cleric, Muggeridge said, "It was like shouting, 'Carry on, Eternity!' or 'Keep going, Infinity!'"

He added, "The incident made a deep impression on my mind because it illustrated the basic difficulty I met with when I was editor of *Punch*: that the eminent so often say and do things which are infinitely more ridiculous than anything you can invent for them."[10] Muggeridge goes on to argue for the profound difference Jesus brought to what it means to be human. All too often what we see is a self-referencing, self-exalting, self-defining, ultimately self-denuding boast. We are left, said he, with the choice of the city of men or the city of God.

The famed E. M. Blaiklock from New Zealand said that God alone knows how to exalt you without flattering you or to humble you without humiliating you. How magnificently true that is. There's the balance we need. Hence the psalmist who thought he could outrun God or sin in the shadows wrote, "Where can I flee from your presence?" (Psalm 139:7). No matter where he tried to hide, he found that God was there. Even in hell He is known by His painfully felt absence. The same David wrote in Psalm 8:3–5, 9,

> When I consider your heavens,
>   the work of your fingers,
> the moon and the stars,
>   which you have set in place,
> what is mankind that you are mindful of them,
>   human beings that you care for them?
>
> You have made them a little lower than the angels
>   and crowned them with glory and honor…

Lord, our Lord,
    how majestic is your name in all the earth.

These are the heights to which we can aspire, or we can turn our backs upon these truths and plummet to the depths of dehumanization and the relativization that follows. That is why Blaise Pascal said in *Pensées* that we humans are "the glory and the shame of the universe." Find our purpose, and ascend to glory; thwart that purpose, and descend to shame.

His way or our way?

You make the choice.

CHAPTER 7

HEDONISM

~~~~~~~~~~~~~~~~~~~~~~~~~~~~~~~~

"Whatever makes you happy."

Vince Vitale

Suppose there was a machine (maybe before long there will be!) that would give you any experience you desired. You could choose to experience winning Olympic gold, or falling in love, or making a great scientific discovery, and then the neurons in your brain would be stimulated such that you would experience a perfect simulation of actually doing these things. In reality, you would be floating in a tank of goo with electrodes hooked up to your brain. Given the choice, should you preprogram your experiences and plug into this machine for the rest of your life?[1]

I join philosopher Robert Nozick, who first devised this thought experiment in the 1970s, in thinking that we should not plug into this "experience machine." And this suggests the falsity of hedonism, a view dating back over two millennia to the Greek philosophers Democritus and Epicurus. If all that mattered were pleasure (in other words, if hedonism were true), then we should plug into the experience machine and we should encourage everyone we know to plug in as well.

We rightly care about more than just happiness or pleasure. We want to not only feel loved; we want to actually *be* loved. We want to not only dream of accomplishing our dreams; we want to actually accomplish them. We want to not only feel inside as if we have made a difference in life; we want to actually make a difference. Hedonism is not the desire of our hearts; it is all that is left when every other "ism" has failed us.

A recent academic book suggested that, on hedonistic assumptions, because some animals can feel pleasure like human persons but cannot suffer in some of the worst ways as human persons, those animals could be understood to be more valuable than humans.[2] If the acquisition of pleasure and the avoidance of pain is the measure of all, these animals score well on pleasure with fewer deductions for the complex psychological pains such as anxiety and disappointment to which the human psyche is vulnerable. This same assumption led utilitarian Jeremy Bentham to the view that "the game of push-pin [a children's game] is of equal value with the arts and sciences of music and poetry."[3] The problem here is not with the logic leading to the conclusions but with the underlying assumption of pleasure as the sole determiner of value.

Pleasure and happiness are good things, but they are not the *only* good things. We should care not only about feeling good on the inside but also about truth and about the impact that our lives have outside of ourselves. As C. S. Lewis put it, if happiness were all he was after, a good bottle of port would do the trick.[4]

People frequently tell me that they don't need God in their life because "I'm happy as I am." That's great! I believe that happiness is a gift from the God who "fills your hearts with joy" (Acts 14:17). But Christianity offers so much more than happiness. The person in the experience machine is very happy as they are. Some animals may be very happy as they are. Should we therefore plug into the experience machine or wish we were animals? In either case, the result of hedonism is the loss of humanity.

According to Christianity, there was one person in history who could have plugged into the experience machine: Jesus. In fact, He could have done one better. He could have not created at all and just eternally enjoyed the perfect pleasure of relationship within the Trinity. Or, once He had created, He could have stayed far away from the vulnerabilities of this world. He could have lived a nonhuman existence overflowing with pleasure and devoid of all pain.

Instead, He created a world that would be broken by His creatures—a world that would grieve Him in many respects—and He chose to enter that world as a human being, with all the susceptibilities to pain and suffering that human existence guarantees. God did this knowing full well that the following prophecies, astonishingly written hundreds of years before His birth, would be true of His human life:

Isaiah 53:3–9:

He was despised and rejected by mankind,
    a man of suffering, and familiar with pain.
Like one from whom people hide their faces
    he was despised, and we held him in low esteem.

Surely he took up our pain
    and bore our suffering,
yet we considered him punished by God,
    stricken by him, and afflicted.
But he was pierced for our transgressions,
    he was crushed for our iniquities;
the punishment that brought us peace was on him,
    and by his wounds we are healed.
We all, like sheep, have gone astray,
    each of us has turned to our own way;

and the Lord has laid on him
    the iniquity of us all.

He was oppressed and afflicted,
    yet he did not open his mouth;
he was led like a lamb to the slaughter,
    and as a sheep before its shearers is silent,
    so he did not open his mouth.

By oppression and judgment he was taken away.
    Yet who of his generation protested?
For he was cut off from the land of the living;
    for the transgression of my people he was punished.
He was assigned a grave with the wicked,
    and with the rich in his death,
though he had done no violence,
    nor was any deceit in his mouth.

Psalm 22:14–18:

I am poured out like water,
    and all my bones are out of joint.
My heart has turned to wax;
    it has melted within me.
My mouth is dried up like a potsherd,
    and my tongue sticks to the roof of my mouth;
    you lay me in the dust of death.
Dogs surround me,
    a pack of villains encircles me;
    they pierce my hands and my feet.
All my bones are on display;
    people stare and gloat over me.

They divide my clothes among them
    and cast lots for my garment.

This is the life that Jesus *chose*. As He put it, "No one takes [my life] from me, but I lay it down of my own accord" (John 10:18). In choosing this life over a life of infinite, uninterrupted pleasure, and yet living the most universally lauded life of all time, Jesus' life is a powerful and sustained argument against hedonism.

Jesus in Trouble

There is a tendency to forget how troubling Jesus' life was. We tend to sanitize it, perhaps in part because that makes it easier for us to rationalize the comforts we cling to in our own lives.

Jesus is remembered as a good moral teacher, wise and respected, loved by the masses, a celebrity who enjoyed performing miracles and being praised for it. He was "Jesus Christ Superstar." And who doesn't take great pleasure in being a star? Of course, there was that unfortunate incident on a cross, but we shy away from its gruesomeness and count it an anomaly in an otherwise pleasurable life.

The reality is that the Cross was a fitting end to a consistently challenging and often uncomfortable life. Jesus knew the discomfort of having nowhere to lay His head at night (Luke 9:58). He knew what it is to be so frustrated with a dear friend that it warranted the rebuke, "Get behind me, Satan!" (Mark 8:33). He knew anger with unjust authorities who acted like "hypocrites" (Matthew 23:13), "blind fools" (Matthew 23:17), and a "brood of vipers" (Matthew 23:33). He knew the deep sadness of having what was most sacred to Him trampled on: "My house will be a house of prayer; but you have made it 'a den of robbers'" (Luke 19:46). Jesus lived with the emotions that the night before His death culminated in the words, "My soul is overwhelmed with sorrow to the point of death" (Matthew 26:38). Jesus died with the emotion of rejection: "My God, my God, why have you forsaken me?" (Mark 15:34).

The life that Jesus chose was not just one that had a troubled ending; it was one that was full of trouble from start to finish. He was born with a king seeking to kill Him and He died at the hands of those seeking to kill a King.

Jesus lived a troubling life, but more than that He actively went looking for trouble. There was one day when a large crowd had lined up on the shore of the Sea of Galilee to hear Jesus speak. The crowd was so large and so eager that Jesus got into a boat and taught them from just offshore. When evening came, Jesus decided to leave the crowd behind and said to His disciples, "Let us go over to the other side" (Mark 4:35). So they set off and traveled through a furious storm that almost sunk the boat.

When they arrived on the other side, Jesus engaged a man who is described as having an evil spirit: "This man lived in the tombs, and no one could bind him anymore, not even with a chain. For he had often been chained hand and foot, but he tore the chains apart and broke the irons on his feet. No one was strong enough to subdue him. Night and day among the tombs and in the hills he would cry out and cut himself with stones" (Mark 5:3–5). This man, who "had not worn clothes" for a long time (Luke 8:27), fell on his knees in front of Jesus, and Jesus said to him, "Come out of the man, you evil spirit!" (Mark 5:8 NLT).

When the people who lived nearby came to see what was happening, "they saw the man who had been possessed by the legion of demons, sitting there, dressed and in his right mind" (Mark 5:15). Then Jesus got back in His boat and crossed over to the other side of the Sea of Galilee, and again a large crowd gathered around him.

This is the life that Jesus lived. He is seemingly in the middle of an ideal teaching opportunity on the scenic banks of the Sea of Galilee. He has a massive audience that has come to hear Him speak, and they are eager to hear more. He can continue awing the crowd with His wisdom and enjoying the accolades of adoring fans.

But Jesus has a better idea: "Let's go over to the other side." Let's cross the Sea of Galilee, at night—the eight-mile-wide Sea of Galilee surrounded by high mountains and known for sudden, violent storms. "Why can't this trip wait until morning, Jesus?" "Well, there's an incredibly violent and incredibly strong demon-possessed man on the other side, and I'd like to go talk with him and see if I can help him."

That man is the kind of guy who if you see him on the street, you cross over to the other side. Not Jesus. Jesus crossed over to this man's side. Jesus went looking for trouble, not because it was easier or more pleasurable, but because it was most loving. And once Jesus had gotten into the trouble He was looking for, it appears in Mark 5:21, as well as in Luke 8:37 and Matthew 9:1, that Jesus promptly crossed back over to the initial side of the sea. It seems that Jesus made this ridiculous trip just to heal this one troubled man.

I imagine there were a lot of days like this for those who hung out with Jesus—days when Jesus didn't go looking for His own pleasure but went looking for other people's hurt. He went looking for trouble because it was in the place of trouble that God had work to do; it was in the place of trouble that healing needed to take place.

Here is how Jesus understood His life purpose: "The Spirit of the Lord is on me because he has anointed me to preach good news to the poor. He has sent me to proclaim freedom for the prisoners and recovery of sight for the blind, to set the oppressed free, to proclaim the year of the Lord's favor" (Luke 4:18–19). The poor, prisoners, the blind, the oppressed, the one in seven children who will run away from home before the age of eighteen, the eight hundred and forty children who will die from hunger or easily treatable diseases by the time you are done reading this chapter—not those who could promise Him pleasure but those who needed His help. Jesus went looking for trouble, not for trouble's sake but because there are a lot of people in trouble. He went looking for trouble because that's what it took to save us.

Jesus the Troublemaker

Jesus was also a troublemaker. He made trouble in the lives of His followers because following Him meant following Him into trouble.

Christians often speak about how Jesus died so that we would not have to. That is absolutely true; in His extravagant and unthinkable love, God accepted our sin and shame and suffering on Himself so that we could be free of it. But just as true is that Jesus died so that we *would* die. Jesus died so that we might find in Him the courage to lay down our lives for others the way He has laid down His life for us.

Jesus said it this way: "My command is this: Love each other as I have loved you. Greater love has no one than this: to lay down one's life for one's friends" (John 15:12–13). And John and Jesus' other disciples embraced this high calling: "This is how we know what love is: Jesus Christ laid down his life for us. And we ought to lay down our lives for our brothers and sisters" (1 John 3:16).

Jeremy Bentham believed that "nature has placed mankind under the governance of two sovereign masters, pain and pleasure."[5] But for Jesus and those who follow Him, these counterfeit gods are neither sovereign nor masters. Jesus calls His followers not to the endless, exhausting pursuit of pleasure, nor to the futile evasion of pain, but to to sacrificial love. I have heard the contrast expressed simply and sharply: In a culture that says be yourself, look after yourself, express yourself, trust yourself, and treat yourself, Jesus said "deny [yourself] and take up [your] cross daily and follow me" (Luke 9:23), knowing that "if they persecuted me, they will persecute you also" (John 15:20).

I remember meeting with an Oxford University student over

several weeks to discuss his questions about God and Christianity. When it seemed as though things were making sense to him and that he was persuaded by the intellectual case, I asked him what was holding him back from making the decision to be a Christian. He responded, "I guess I'm just weighing up what's in it for me." My heart sank. He had missed it. He had missed that what Jesus calls us to is so much greater than that—a life lived not just for oneself but for others and for truth and for beauty and for goodness.

I am so thankful that Jesus' response to me was not to "weigh up what was in it for Him." His response was precisely the opposite: He "did not come to be served, but to serve, and to give his life as a ransom for many" (Mark 10:45). The only scale Jesus cared about was the one that weighed up what was in it for us.

My coauthor and friend Ravi Zacharias was recently asked in an interview, "Do you enjoy your ministry?" There was an extended pause. Ravi needed a moment because he simply hadn't considered the question, and that is one of the things I admire most about Ravi. He never asked, "Will this bring me the most happiness and pleasure?" He asked whether this was what he was called to and whether this was a way that he could serve others well. After thinking about it, Ravi responded, "There are many moments that I enjoy deeply."

Are there many moments of pleasure in the Christian life? Absolutely. And even better than that there is a deep and steadfast joy that comes from knowing you have a purpose and from always being able to rest in the presence of the One who loves you most. But pleasure and joy are only gifts we can receive with integrity when they are the result not of plugging into the experience machine but of living with the love of Christ in our real and troubled world.

God is a troublemaker. He goes looking for trouble and He asks His followers to go looking for trouble with Him. So what trouble is He calling you into, in order for you to be His agent of healing? Every follower of Christ must be able to answer that question.

Getting into Trouble with Money

Sadly, often we are too distracted by "What's in it for us?" to ask what trouble God is calling us into, and there are no two greater distractions than money and sex. When it comes to money, do we plug into the experience machine? The atheist philosopher Peter Singer, who on many points I could not disagree with more adamantly, makes a chilling and challenging argument that we do plug into the experience machine. It goes something like this:

> There's a guy walking along train tracks and he realizes he's dropped his iPhone a few steps back. He looks forward and sees that a train is coming, and at the same time he also sees a young child tied to the tracks, screaming for help. He can easily untie the child in time, but he realizes he only has time either to untie the child or to go back and pick up his iPhone. He also hears noise to his right, so he looks, and he sees that the child's family is trying to get to him, but they are stuck behind a barbed wire fence, helpless to rescue him. The family sees the man and screams desperately to him to save their child. The man looks at the child, looks at the family, and then casually walks back and picks up his iPhone. The child and his family weep and wail until the train runs him over, dismembering him and scattering his body parts.

When later interviewed about the situation, the man said,

> "I know I could have easily saved that child, but I really like my iPhone, and if I had let the train crush it, I'd have had to buy another one, and that would mean I wouldn't have had that extra cash to buy the new TV that I really want. It just wasn't worth saving the child. It's not my problem."[6]

If we were watching the news and saw this interview, we would respond with outrage! We would think the man was an absolute monster. But are we any different?

In many places in our world, about two hundred dollars can turn a sickly, dying two-year-old into a healthy six-year-old. What many of us spend on personal luxury and personal pleasure is far more than enough to get a dying child through the most vulnerable period; it's enough to save his life.

Are there any differences between us and the monster walking along the train tracks? Yes, there are a couple. We are farther away from the people we could save, whereas he was close enough to hear the screams of the tied-up child. Another difference is that many others besides us could help save people in life-threatening situations around the world, whereas in Singer's example only the one man was in position to save the child.

But it takes only a second's reflection to see that these differences do not make the slightest moral difference. All they do is make it easier for us to turn a blind eye. All they do is make it easier for us to plug into the experience machine, shutting out the outside world so that we can be untroubled by our purchases of internal pleasure.

Jesus challenges us—He pleads with us—not to plug in, and His plea has integrity because He followed it first: "For you know the grace of our Lord Jesus Christ, that though he was rich, yet for your sake he became poor, so that you through his poverty might become rich" (2 Corinthians 8:9). Jesus became poor that we might become rich. Literally. He literally gave up heavenly comfort and luxury to come live in human poverty because that's what it took to meet us in our trouble and pull us out of it.

If you looked at the last page of my bank statement, what would you conclude? I just pulled it up online: iTunes, Netflix, MLB.com. None of these things are bad things, but "where your treasure is, there your heart will be also" (Matthew 6:21). Is my heart breaking at the trouble of the real world or is it delighting in the deception of my personalized experience machine?

Now, I am very aware that there are a lot of complicated questions to ask when it comes to using money well. When and where do we give, when and where do we save, when and where do we invest in the economy? All tough questions and ones I am wrestling with. But what I do know is that my heart has to be aligned with the message of Jesus. And that message, plain and simple, is that people are worth dying for. His death was the price to give us life. So are we dying to pay for others' lives? Or are others dying to pay for our pleasure machines?

Getting into Trouble with Sex

One of the very first things that stuck out to me about Christianity was its countercultural approach to sex. "No sex before marriage! You're kidding me, right?" To me, this seemed downright weird; it was evidence of how outdated Christianity was. It reminded me of the old laws you can find in many states that, while technically still on the books, were obviously made for a different era and are no longer relevant.

For example, I have heard that, in Baltimore, there is technically a law stating that it is illegal to take a lion to the movies. (It's pretty disturbing to think that at some point it was necessary to make that law.) Or, supposedly, in Oklahoma—this is my favorite—it's illegal to have a sleeping donkey in your bathtub after seven o'clock in the evening! (What would make you think that it's appropriate to have a sleeping donkey in your bathtub before seven o'clock?)

That is how I used to see the Christian practice of not having sex before marriage—a weird, outdated, sexually repressive, impossible-to-follow rule. A rule meant to spoil my fun and restrict my pleasure. In college, one guy was trying to explain his Christian faith, and he said, "I used to drink, I used to party, I used to have sex. But now I'm a Christian and I don't do these things anymore." And I thought, with full sarcasm, *Yeah, sounds great. Where can I sign up?* This is how I used to perceive Christianity—ridiculous rules that would be more fun to break than to follow.

I certainly was not alone in thinking that Christianity seemed downright weird when it came to sex. I can distinctly remember telling my two best friends, after I had become a Christian, that I had made the decision not to have sex again until marriage. They looked at me as though I had three heads.

Then, when Jo and I were about to get married, one of our friends came to give us a wedding card a few days early, because she wasn't going to be able to make it to the wedding. We opened the card in front of her and read it, and when we started laughing hysterically, she looked at us with an expression that said, "Why are you laughing at my lovely card?"

We turned the card around and showed her that, when she was signing off, she meant to write, "Wishing you all the *best*," but she must have been thinking about how weird it was that Jo and I hadn't had sex together yet, and without knowing it she had signed off, "Wishing you all the *sex*." Definitely our favorite wedding card!

So not having sex before marriage can seem pretty odd and outdated, but my thinking about this has changed radically. Let me try to explain why. The way we use words is important. Even slight errors with our words can have significant consequences. Early on in our dating relationship, Jo had bought a bicycle to get around town, but she bought a really heavy bike, and every time she would go to ride it she would start off wobbling down the street before it finally straightened out. She asked me, "Why do I wobble on this bike?" And I said, "Oh, that's because you have such a heavy frame." After a long silence, I saw the look of death (*my* death!) on Jo's face, and I exclaimed, "THE BIKE! The BIKE has a heavy frame!"

Minor error in words; major difference. Words are powerful. When I look back on the worst moments in my life, they are not fist fights; they are not the times I've been physically injured; they are not even times I've failed miserably. They are words. They are the times I was lied to, or the times when people said one thing to my face and something very different behind my back. They are the times when the words that were spoken *did not reflect what someone actually meant.*

Why do Christians make a big deal about sex? It's not just because of some arbitrary, outdated rule. It's because *sex* is a type of word—a symbolic word, a physical word. Sexual "intercourse" is a very appropriate name, because sex *says* something. Causing another to be fulfilled sexually is the strongest word in our physical language. It's the word that says "all of me for all of you, always."

Words have meanings that are formed and stabilized over hundreds and thousands of years, and we inherit these meanings whether we like it or not. You can't just snap your fingers and decide to change the meaning of a word. I can try to use the word *cheeseburger* to mean "hot dog," but I'm still going to wind up with a cheeseburger on my plate. Likewise, I can decide to use the word *ugly* to mean "pretty," but I'm not going to make any friends in the process. And even if for some unimaginable reason my wife agreed for us to use the word *ugly* to mean "pretty," I guarantee that if I called her ugly, it would not feel good, because you can't just up and change the long established meaning of a word. The etymological roots and the psychological roots that intertwine with them run deep, and severing a fully grown tree from its roots can only lead to decay.[7]

The same is true with the physical word of *sex*. We cannot just decide for it to mean less than what it actually means. Sex has an objective meaning regardless of whether we "meant it that way." That's why when we push sexual interaction beyond where a relationship actually is, we say something we don't mean. We lie. And that's why when relationships that have been sexual don't work out, there is such a deep sense of having been lied to, betrayed, violated; it feels like a broken promise, because it is.

I think God wanted Jo and me to wait to have sex with each other because, when we did use that word, He wanted us to know that it really meant what it felt like it meant—"all of me for all of you, always." God wanted Jo and me to be able to trust that when we said something to each other, whether verbally or physically, it was the truth. And God wanted Jo to know that as much as I would have enjoyed having sex with her before we were married, she is worth waiting for. Being careful with her heart is more important than rushing to fulfill my own desires.

Now, I know there's a lot more to say on this topic, but this is just one of many examples in my life where I have come to find that God's rules are not outdated. They're not an attempt to spoil our fun, they're not going to make us boring, and they're not some arbitrary test to get Him to love us. They are a gift because He already loves us, and He wants the best for us. In fact, I can say without any hesitation or doubt that following Jesus has led to the most honest and life-giving relationships I have ever known.

C. S. Lewis warned of *verbicide*[8]—a fatal separation of words and meaning; literally, "the murdering of words." In essence, he was warning against the experience machine, against plugging into the experience of the pleasurable but deceptive words of a false reality. We are now living through what Lewis foresaw.

Today, the Christian vision for sex and marriage is radically countercultural. However, might recent history suggest that the idea of a more clearly delineated vision for sex is not such a crazy idea? When I look at the last fifty-plus years in the West, one of the conclusions that I come to is that when we experimented as a society with a sexual revolution that severed sex from any proper meaning and purpose and context, the results were largely and gravely antithetical to human flourishing. The results have included drastic rises in divorce, addiction to pornography, marital unfaithfulness, abortion, and sex trafficking, to name just a few. My colleague Michael Ramsden puts it poignantly: "Whenever you try to break God's law, you wind up proving God's law while breaking yourself in the process." This summarizes the history of sexual ethics in the last half-century. Ironically, it is the hedonistic view of sex—anyone, anytime—that is outdated. We tried that. It didn't work.

It didn't work at a societal level, and I can attest that it doesn't work at a personal level either. In my old life, when I tried to use sex without any established meaning or parameters, it got me into serious trouble. I really hurt people, even the people who meant the most to me, and I nearly lost my most cherished friendships in the process. When I sat down and reflected on the recent history of the West and on my own life, it made me take a second look at Christian ethics. I realized that it's not at all crazy to think that a God who cares about human flourishing would give us clear guidelines about what the powerful word *sex* means and how it can be most lovingly spoken.

Authentic Christianity is marked by saying there is a better way than hedonism, especially when it comes to money and sex. A second-century defense of Christianity, attempting to explain the Christian faith to a culture that found it foreign, reads thus: "[Christians] have a common table but not a common bed."[9] Nearly two thousand years later, we are invited into that same noble calling, to respond to others' hurt with our resources and to tell the truth with our bodies.

When Trouble Comes Looking

Hedonism fails. Sexual fulfillment has never fulfilled anyone. Financial security has never made anyone secure in their identity. Those who have made the most money and had the most sex attest time and time again that hedonism leaves one empty. So many who gave their lives to hedonism wound up in the company of Oscar Wilde:

> The gods had given me almost everything. But I let myself be lured into long spells of senseless and sensual ease.... Tired of being on the heights, I deliberately went to the depths in search for new sensation. What the paradox was to me in the sphere of thought, perversity became to me in the sphere of passion. I grew careless of the lives of others. I took pleasure where it pleased me, and passed on. I forgot that every little action of the common day makes or unmakes character, and that therefore what one has done in the secret chamber, one has some day to cry aloud from the housetop. I ceased to be lord over myself. I was no longer the captain of my soul, and did not know it. I allowed pleasure to dominate me. I ended in horrible disgrace. There is only one thing for me now, absolute humility.[10]

To the contrary, I have never met someone who wishes they had been less generous with their money. I have never met someone who regrets reserving sex for their spouse. We know hedonism doesn't work. We know that the one thing that is most certain not to lead to pleasure is the pursuit of pleasure.

Hedonism fails for those who pursue pleasure as their god. But let us not forget that the pursuit of pleasure is a luxury that many millions of people cannot afford. For so many in our world, hedonism is not even a live option; life is too broken and full of suffering to even attempt the luxury of hedonism.

During the time that I have been writing this chapter, this exclusivism of hedonism could not have been clearer or more pronounced. There have been terrorist bombings in Brussels that have killed thirty-two people and a savage attack in an Orlando nightclub that took the lives of forty-nine. A man drove a truck through a crowded street in Nice, murdering eighty-four men, women, and children. A good friend in his thirties has been diagnosed with stage IV cancer. I received the following message from another dear friend: "This very hour is the six-year anniversary of my suicide attempt. I feel vulnerable, alone and forsaken. Please could you pray for me?"

When we unplug from the experience machine, the reality that we wake up to is that not everyone is given the opportunity to be happy. Many have that opportunity brutally stripped away from them. In a broken world, hedonism is not a worldview that will work for the majority.[11]

Hedonism fails whether we pursue pleasure or whether we are denied the pursuit of pleasure. The most important questions, therefore, are, How must we respond to hedonism's failure? And how can we stand with those who have suffered the brunt of that failure?

First, with tears. When Jesus arrived at His friend Lazarus' tomb, He wept. The language used implies that He wept bitterly. Jesus urges us not to allow dry eyes to disqualify our support of those who have suffered. No one plugged into the experience machine of indifference will be of any help to those who are hurting. Only once we have cried with those suffering and with their loved ones will we be qualified to offer a meaningful response.

Second, we need to call the brokenness of this world absolutely, unqualifiedly, incontrovertibly evil. Too often I have heard it blithely debated in philosophical armchairs whether there is any such thing as real, objective good and evil. Increasingly, I now hear this from students on college campuses: "Good and evil are nothing more than subjective evolutionary byproducts. Haven't you read Richard Dawkins?" "There is, at bottom, no design, no purpose, no evil and no good, nothing but blind, pitiless indifference."[12]

This is not good enough! It is not good enough for those who are suffering the horrors of this world. It is not good enough for the families of those who are suffering. Let us respond to the brokenness of our world by repenting of any time that we have let philosophers or popularizers of philosophy convince us that the denial of good and evil is an adequate position. Let us repent of the fact that we have allowed today's youth to regard this as an adequate position. And let us have the courage to ask who could possibly be in position to provide an objective morality that transcends the fickleness of human opinion and the fluidity of human culture, and that therefore allows us to call good "good" and to call evil "evil."

A third response that the failure of hedonism demands of us: We must believe that every single human life is sacred and valuable and worth protecting, and that must manifest itself in a love for others that is unconditional—a love that precedes any and all questions; a love that is not dependent on "Do you look like me?" or "Do you act like me?" or "Do you agree with me?" or "Do you benefit me?" or "Do you add to my happiness?" That is the only love that qualifies as Christian love.

"While we were still sinners, Christ died for us" (Romans 5:8). What this means is that, even when the answer to every one of these questions was a clear no, Jesus loved us with such aversion to conditions, with such an aversion to prioritizing His own comfort or pleasure, that He gave His life for us. Without asking any of these questions, He preferred to die than to watch us die.

Let us repent of when in our hedonistic fixation we have asked questions before opening our hearts to love. May we be adamant that it is never okay to treat people as anything other than sacred and absolutely worthy of dignity and respect.

Fourth, when faced with unspeakable evil, we need justice. We need to know that repulsive hate and its consequences will not be overlooked. We need to know horrendous evils are not just going to fade into the rapidly deteriorating memory of history.

Yale theologian Miroslav Volf says he only came to understand

God's commitment to justice after his homeland (the former Yugoslavia) was ravaged by war. Two hundred thousand killed and three million displaced demanded this response from Volf:

> Though I used to complain about the indecency of the idea of God's wrath, I came to think that I would have to rebel against a God who *wasn't* wrathful at the sight of the world's evil. God isn't wrathful in spite of being love. God is wrathful *because* God is love.[13]

In view of the incessant evil and suffering of our broken world, we need a god who is fully and equally committed to both love and justice. The Christian God is the only god who meets this condition. It is precisely because of how much God loves every single person who was run over in Nice that He is so committed to justice.

Fifth, those who suffer cannot be left to suffer alone. As we struggle to even imagine what so many of those suffering around the world are going through, let us trust that God will be with them.

I do not believe those who recently have been killed in America, Belgium, France, and so many other places were alone when they died. Not one of them was alone. I believe the God who loves them was with them and was reaching out to them even in those final moments. And I believe the reason His presence with them at that time could have been a source of comfort and strength is because He knows firsthand what it is to have a child brutally murdered, and He knows what it is to be hated, captured, tortured, and murdered. He chose to go through it Himself so that He could be meaningfully present in those last moments to those who face unspeakable evil today.

This is a God worth following. But following Him means making serious sacrifices in order to be meaningfully present to those who are suffering. Are we?

Finally, we need hope. We need hope that evil will not have the last word in our world. A few years ago I saw a commercial that depicted a baby being born, and then in thirty seconds it fast-forwarded through the child's entire life until before you knew it he was old and gray and hunched over, and finally he fell down and crashed into a grave.

Then words flashed across the screen: "Life is short. Play more Xbox." Really? Is that the best we've got? Life is short, and it's fragile. Is the answer really just to play more Xbox—to distract yourself and try not to think about it, to plug into an Xbox experience machine because there's nothing you can do about it anyway?

The future that the Bible offers is so very different:

> God's dwelling place is now among the people, and he will dwell with them. They will be his people, and God himself will be with them and be their God. "He will wipe every tear from their eyes. There will be no more death" or mourning or crying or pain, for the old order of things has passed away (Revelation 21:3–4).

Let us hope with those for whom hedonism is not an option. Let us hope with them that death need not be our end. Let us hope that God is with each one, until the very end, offering this hope.

Hedonism fails, and we know it fails. It fails regardless of whether you pursue pleasure or you are denied the pursuit of pleasure. And yet, if we are brave enough to consider the questions and answer them honestly, how much of our lives are lived worshiping at the altar of pleasure? What percentage of our lives are spent plugged into an experience machine? Who is getting hurt in the process? And what opportunities for honest relationship are passing us by?

Jesus does want us to be happy—absolutely. And He promises that we can live in happiness for all eternity. But Jesus doesn't *just* want us to be happy. His call on our lives is much grander and nobler than that. As He modeled, He wants us to respond with integrity to the failure of hedonism. He wants us to have tears for others. He wants those tears to unite us with a God who shed tears—a God of love and of justice. He wants following that God to lead us to the sacrificial love and service of others that alone brings not only pleasure but forgiveness, peace, purpose, and hope—the very fullness of life (John 10:10).

William Butler Yeats once said, "Too long a sacrifice can make a stone of the heart."[14] Perhaps, especially when that sacrifice lacks purpose. But even more true is, "Too *little* sacrifice can make a stone of the heart." We know we are called to a life greater than what hedonism offers; we know we are called to more than plugging into an experience machine. What we don't know is whether we have the strength to say no to our selfishness and yes to sacrificial love.

What that suggests is that our problem with hedonism is not an intellectual problem but a heart problem. No "ism" offers a change of heart, and that is why every "ism"—no matter how ideologically captivating—so frequently succumbs to hedonism in practice.

There is only one who offers a change of heart: the God of Christianity. He promises, "I will give you a new heart and put a new spirit within you; and I will remove from you your heart of stone and give you a heart of flesh" (Ezekiel 36:26).

He calls us to more than hedonism; He calls us to the challenging but supremely meaningful life that I think we know deep down we were made for. He calls us to a life that one day, not far off, we can look back on with gratitude. And if we will just ask Him, He will give us the heart, the spirit, and the strength needed to live that life.

Chapter 8

Love the Truth

Vince Vitale

Playing with the Truth

The first sentence in this chapter is false. Is it? Think about it.

This is the feeling we often have about the truth. Whatever we say about it, we're told we've got it wrong:

"There is no truth." Is that true?

"There is absolute truth." You are a narrow-minded extremist!

You're either stupid or you're dangerous. Not great options. With the truth, it seems as though we can't win.

So what do we do? We keep our mouths shut. It's no wonder that discussion of truth has all but disappeared from modern Western discourse. And when it is discussed, the discussion is very confused. The line between truth and falsity is growing ever blurrier. There's the truth, and then there's the _naked_ truth. There's the honest truth, and then there's the _God's_ honest truth. Lies are okay as long as they are white. Truth is buried because it hurts.

We affirm the gospel truth while taking it to be obvious that the gospel is false. We swear to the God who told us not to swear (Matthew 5:34) and in whom we don't believe.

We've become skilled at manipulating the truth. We *stretch* the truth and *bend* the truth and *twist* the truth. When we want something to be false, we knock on wood. When we want something to be true, we cross our fingers. Which wooden cross are we trusting in?

We make truth claims "literal" when they are metaphorical: "I am literally dying for a coffee." If we want someone to have confidence that we are actually telling the truth, we need to add a qualifier: "in truth" or "truth be told" or "to tell you the truth." Even then confidence will be low because truth is not our default setting but merely a special occurrence: the "*moment* of truth."

We hate that people won't accept us for who we truly are, but we spend most of our time on social media trying to convince people we are someone we are not. We hate that we don't trust our leaders, but we no longer expect the truth from them. As I write this, having 11% of America believe that you are "honest and trustworthy" is good enough to have a 9% lead in the race to be the next president of the United States.

Partial Truths

In which battle did Napoleon die? His last one. Where was the Declaration of Independence signed? At the bottom. What do you have if you have three oranges in one hand, and five in the other? Big hands.[1]

Partial truths can be as uninformative and misleading as lies, and because we like thinking we are in the know and we hate feeling ignorant, presenting partial truths as the whole truth is very much in our human nature.

The history of science is one of the great affirmers of this. Lord Kelvin, the great nineteenth-century physicist, thought that the output of radiant energy from the sun must be due to the one mechanism he could identify as a possible source of such energy—gravitational compression. In one sense this is true; gravitational compression does account for heat from the sun. However, solar heat has more to do with nuclear fusion. We now know that most of the energy that is converted into sunshine comes not from gravitational compression but from the release of nuclear binding energy when atomic nuclei in the sun's core bump into one another and fuse. Kelvin didn't know, indeed he couldn't have known, about this additional mechanism because it relied on fundamental discoveries in physics that had not yet taken place.[2]

Countless similar examples could be cited. The moral of the story is, don't assume that in discovering a partial truth you have discovered the whole truth. Our tendency is to assume that what we know is all there is to know. Ravi and I have argued that this is the same tendency at work in the secular "isms" considered in this book. Each takes a partial explanation and claims for it explanatory omnipotence.

> Scientism: The partial truth is that science explains a lot. But we forget that it cannot explain itself, and it cannot explain many of the most important things in life.

> Relativism: The partial truth is that refusing to see things from another's perspective is dangerous and lacks love. But we forget that this relies on there being an objective perspective according to which those different from us are valuable and worthy of respect.

> Pantheism: The partial truth is that the divine is everywhere and that union with the divine is our destiny. But that union is not the union of sameness but the union of relationship.

Pluralism: The partial truth is that no worldview has a monopoly on truth. But we mistake this for all worldviews being equally true.

Humanism: Human persons were indeed made for greatness. But greatness results from divine grace and strength, not human self-reliance.

Hedonism: Pleasure is good. But it is not *all* that is good.

Every "ism" considered is an example of elevating a partial explanation of truth to the divine status of explaining all truth.

Partial truths can be funny. They can also be very dangerous, because, as with Kelvin's investigation of sunshine, they can act to cut off inquiry before important questions have been fully illuminated. As the poet Alfred Tennyson put it, "A lie which is half a truth is ever the blackest of lies."[3]

Truth as Power Play

Sadly, our mistreatment of truth goes even deeper than our tendency to exaggerate partial truths.

If tomorrow you woke up with the superpower of knowing the future, what would you do? For many of us, I bet it wouldn't be long until we placed some bets—until we found a way to use that knowledge to take other people's money. Or imagine that tomorrow you were told the exact location of an invaluable treasure in another part of the world. What would you do? We would immediately start thinking about how we can get to that treasure before anyone else learns of it.

Truth is power. Many of us can remember a time as a child when we caught a sibling doing something they were not supposed to be doing. And what did we do? We held that truth over our sibling's head like a guillotine: "I'm telling Dad unless you do whatever I want." Even at a young age, we understood that truth is power. And we understood, instinctually, how to wield that truth into not having to do the dishes for the rest of the week.[4] Even though we didn't yet know the word, we were blackmailing—using privileged knowledge to get someone to do something that benefits us. We were making a power play.

The problem is that we never grew up. Name-calling turned to gossip; tattling turned to calculated breaches of confidentiality. But we still see truth as something to be used to our advantage and to others' disadvantage.

I remember watching a Yankees game a few years ago. It was a critical moment in the game, and who else stepped up to bat but Derek Jeter—baseball's ambassador of integrity for an entire generation. An inside fastball was thrown and Jeter winced in pain, clenching his teeth and shaking off his hand as a "hit by pitch" was called and he took first base. Then the replay gave us all a surprise. The ball never hit Jeter. It had passed right by. But only Jeter knew that. He had taken privileged knowledge and used it to his advantage, and to the disadvantage of the Tampa Bay Rays.

And here's the real shocker: Jeter was lauded on both sides for his lie, by both players and coaches. One of the other team's coaches said he wished his players had more of that sort of "gamesmanship," that win-at-all-costs attitude and resourcefulness.

We live in a culture where almost every moment we are caught in a power play with the truth. We are forced to vote for candidates who seemingly have no limit to the extent that they will twist the truth for their advantage. We are forced to buy products and policies from companies that bury the truth in the fine print. Each day we see three thousand advertisements, each one capitalizing on privileged knowledge about what we like, what we will respond to, what will play to our subconscious fears and desires. Each one capitalizes on the fact that we won't register that the models on the billboards have not only been airbrushed and colored, but their very dimensions have been distorted. The advertisements are literally not true (I literally mean "literally"), but only the advertiser knows that truth.[5]

Why is truth distorted in this way? To sell more products so that you can chase an image that it is not biologically possible to achieve. In this consumeristic crossfire, self-image and self-worth are left fractured and insecure. The National Center for Health Statistics reported in April 2016 that suicide rose 24% in America between 1999 and 2014. It is at a thirty-year high, and it has tripled among ten- to fourteen-year-old girls. Truth is not a game.

Truth is power, and we are power hungry; our appetite has increased as we have grown. The problem is, the more powerful something is the more tempting it is to use and the harder it is to control; there's a reason people covet sports cars and also a reason they are much more expensive to insure. And we are living in an ever increasingly powerful world where the internet and social media in particular allow us to share, withhold, and distort the truth with greater and greater frequency and with greater and greater influence.

Agreeing to Disagree

Exaggeration and power play are not intrinsic to truth. The problem is not with the truth but with our relationship to the truth.

I remember the first time I commented on a paper that my wife had written. She was a graduate student at the time, and I had worked hard to give her the most extensive and helpful comments that I could. I remember, as we sat down to go over it together, feeling really good about the fact that I had invested time and effort to help her.

I began by telling Jo what a great job she had done, and then we worked through my comments, suggestions, and corrections. When we were finished, I concluded, "Great job, honey!" And Jo promptly burst into tears!

Now, granted, maybe I shouldn't have used a red pen, and maybe I should have edited my comments down to less than an hour and a half. That being so, I think there was something deeper going on as well, and something generally reflective of our contemporary culture. Jo assumed my *disagreement* with her was a *devaluing* of her.

I realized in that moment that my experience of disagreement as a professional philosopher is culturally very atypical. Academic philosophy has its vices, but, at its best, one of its virtues is that it places a very high value on truth. And one result of this is that disagreeing with someone about their core beliefs is seen as a compliment and an act of service. It's a way of saying that the other person's ideas are promising enough to take seriously, so much so that you are willing to invest time and effort into them yourself. (As an aside, this is why some atheists contradict themselves when they claim that Christianity is a mental illness and then proceed to argue against it. If Christians are really mentally ill, arguing and debating rather than counseling is a very odd approach.)

If a scholar takes the time to critique my research in print, that is a great gift. And the more extensively she critiques my work, the greater the gift. Something similar is true in sports. Extensive critique by a good coach means that the coach sees potential in you, and therefore believes that putting extra time into you is a good investment. If he didn't think you could add value to the team, he wouldn't bother. In professional philosophy and in high level sports, not only is disagreement not a sign of devaluing but it is the exact opposite of devaluing.

Sadly, because truth so often has been abused as power play, experience has taught us that disagreement goes hand in hand with devaluing. We have learned that the trajectory of disagreement is from disagreement to devaluing to intolerance to violence. In fact, the opposite should be true. Disagreeing with someone who is being completely irrational is futile. Our bothering to take the time to disagree with someone should be a sign that we think we can learn from them, that there is enough truth in what they are saying that, with revisions, we believe their ideas could make a positive impact. My disagreement with you should be itself an act of valuing you.[6]

Because truth has so often been used as a weapon to manipulate, abuse, and control, many have stopped valuing truth altogether. We have lost the ability to disagree in love. Even more, we have lost the ability for disagreement to be itself an act of love. Our experience of human nature has taught us that disagreement leads to devaluing which leads to intolerance which leads to violence. Therefore, disagreement becomes an act of hate and of war.

An act of war leaves you with only two options: fight or flee. Either we wage war or we avoid it at all costs.

If we choose to wage war, we must demonize our opponents to justify our violence. Truth is our weapon as we dig up every piece of partially true dirt that we can find and exaggerate it until it has stained our enemies' reputations for good (or at least for our advantage). Here it is very difficult not to think of what the American political scene has become.

But this type of behavior is much closer to home as well. While writing this chapter, I took a break to grab a sandwich, and I ate it while walking around Oxford University. At one point during my walk, two guys just ahead of me were having a spirited conversation about a current ethical, political issue. One of them was expressing how he just couldn't understand how anyone could take the position contrary to his own. He couldn't imagine them having reasons for their view, and so he wondered out loud whether the only solution would be to shame them out of their position. His friend quickly chimed in, "Yeah, that's what we should do. We should ridicule them mercilessly in the most insensitive ways we can think of."

Then they both made a right turn and swiped their faculty cards to enter the University of Oxford Theoretical Physics building. These were probably scholars at Oxford, a place that prides itself on academic freedom and the exchange of ideas, and "merciless, insensitive ridicule" was the best they could come up with for resolving disagreement. I found myself wondering how many beliefs they hold in theoretical physics that were once or one day will be considered ridiculous.

The alternative to fighting is fleeing—completely avoiding disagreements about the truth. We spend most of our time on Facebook and Twitter where we can "like" and "retweet," but there is no option to "dislike." Because disagreement is unsafe, "safe spaces" are defined as those where disagreement is disallowed. In the rare instance when we do take issue with something, we disagree about it online so that we don't need to look the person in the eyes. Even among friends, we disagree online and then get together for dinner and act as though the disagreement never happened.

When it comes to dating, we use online sites that either imply we don't want anything serious or "match" us with someone so similar in beliefs, background, and personality that as much disagreement as possible is avoided. We no longer meet people on the street or on the bus because our earphones are in and our heads are bowed over Facebook, Twitter, Tinder, Instagram, or Snapchat. We no longer meet people at restaurants or grocery stores because everything we need or want has been designed to come to us. Culturally, we are set up to avoid disagreement. Opposites are no longer given the chance to attract.

I recently saw a video of interviews being conducted on the campus of the University of Washington.[7] Students culturally conditioned into the assumption that disagreement will lead to offense were willing to avoid disagreement at almost any cost. At one point, the interviewer, a 5'9" white man, asked a student if he would disagree if he claimed to be a 6'5" Chinese woman. The claim was obviously false, and a tape measure could have easily proven that it was false. But the college student refused to disagree. Affirming what has been called "the tyranny of political correctness," he responded, "I feel like I would be very open to saying that you are 6'5", or Chinese, or a woman." Another student was asked if she would affirm that the fully grown, adult interviewer was seven years old. She responded, "If you feel seven at heart, then so be it; yeah, good for you." Ironically, to be politically correct we must deny that anything is objectively correct.

A colleague of mine, Abdu Murray, recently encountered this same immovable aversion to disagreement on another American university campus. Here is a portion of the conversation he had:

> Student: "I don't prefer Nazism's version of the truth, but I can't say that they are wrong. My worldview requires that I don't disrespect anyone by saying that they are wrong."
> Abdu: "Wait a minute; are you telling me that you can't disagree with anyone?"
> Student: "Yes, that's right."
> Abdu: "Sure you can."
> Student: "No, I can't."
> Abdu: "You just did."

Avoiding disagreement is not possible, and trying to do so lands you in incoherence; you forfeit your ability to have intelligent conversations.

Nonetheless, I have sympathy for these students because if disagreement starts us on a course that leads to intolerance, extremism, violence, and terrorism, then irrationality may seem like a price worth paying in order to avoid disagreement. Moreover, these students are simply following what many schools and universities are teaching them. Justified by the need to create "safe spaces," speakers are increasingly no-platformed from universities for holding views that might upset those who hear them.

Campaigning against Sharia Law and for all residents of the United Kingdom to be subject to the same law resulted in Maryam Namazie being blocked from speaking at Warwick University, despite having been invited by the Warwick Atheists, Secularists, and Humanists Society. Many other recent examples could be cited. At stake here is nothing less than democracy itself—a willingness to listen to those you disagree with and to take part in the back-and-forth of reason-giving and persuasion. If we lose this in the universities, where will it survive?[8]

A positive feedback has emerged: The more disagreement is labeled as offensive, the more our children need helicopter parenting to shelter them from the offense, and the more our children are sheltered, the more offensive they find disagreement. And so on and so on until even the smallest expression of difference or disagreement is labeled a "microaggression" (the websites of several reputable American universities have recently listed "Where are you from?" as an example of a microaggression, and in 2014 the operators of "Tiger Microaggressions," a service for Princeton University students that reports the use of microaggressions, said that anything can count as a microaggression because "there are no objective definitions to words and phrases"[9]) and the only options we are left with are aggression or silence—fight or flee.[10]

It is sad that religious discourse has been no exception to this cultural ultimatum. Fight or flee: increasingly we encounter either a pluralism that refuses to disagree with anyone's beliefs about God, or a militant atheism that grasps for any partial truth to use as a weapon against God and His followers. The give-and-take of carefully listening to and thinking through opposing positions is very hard to come by. We would rather just take.

More sadly, this secular approach to truth has even seeped into the Church. We fear doubt because doubt means that disagreement is near, and disagreement is dangerous and therefore must be suppressed before it can do any damage. Hence, at the first sign of doubt, we fight or we flee.

Instead of being "merciful to those who doubt" (Jude 22), we have labeled them as dangerous and have either dismissed them by not creating a space for them to ask their questions or demonized them by treating doubt as a moral failure. These are the consistent frustrations that I hear recounted by countless students who will wait in line for hours after a university event in the hope that someone might be able and willing to answer their questions about God. They either tell me that there is nowhere that they can ask these questions or that they have been led to believe that something is wrong with them for having such questions.

We have made an enemy of doubt. The real damage, however, has come not from doubt or disagreement but because so many of our young have lost their faith when their questions were not taken seriously. So many of our young are sent off to college completely unprepared for the challenges to faith that they will face. Rather than seeing disagreement as a compliment—a sign of investment in a faith they think is worth questioning and considering—and responding in kind, we have fled from our children's questions and in turn they have fled from the Church.

Why does the Bible encourage us to be merciful to doubters? Because, as twelfth-century theologian Peter Abelard put it, "By doubting we are led to question, by questioning we arrive at the truth."[11] To this I would add only that it is not by mere questioning that we arrive at the truth, but rather by questioning that is taken seriously in the context of community and responded to with gentleness and respect.

Jo and I recently had dinner with a friend of ours who wanted to talk with us about faith. She shared with us that as a young child she asked her churchgoing mother, "Did Jesus really rise from the dead?" Her mom responded, "Nicole, don't be difficult!" That may have been the last real question that Nicole ever asked about God, and today Nicole is one of the most intellectually accomplished atheists we know.

Ignored questions lead to disbelief. Dismissed questions lead to disbelief. I will never forget the words of a student who said this shortly before making a commitment to Christ: "You actually took my questions seriously, and I was surprised to find that there were decent answers."

America as a country was established on a commitment to defend our right to disagree with one another. This is the cornerstone of democracy, and it is crumbling. It is crumbling in political discourse, public policy, the God debate, and even in the Church. Now, in many contexts what is affirmed is the right not to be disagreed with (not a freedom *of* speech but a freedom *from* speech),[12] a right wholly antithetical to democratic values. At a time when the Middle East is looking to the West to learn how to disagree, Michael Ramsden laments that increasingly the West has no wisdom to share.

We need to redeem disagreement not as an act of devaluing but as a gift. We need to redeem truth not as power play but as an opportunity to love others sacrificially.

One of mine and Jo's best memories is from a time when she confessed to me something she had done wrong. Jo started crying as she told me. When she finished telling me, I told her I forgave her and that I would be back in a moment. I ran downstairs to the shop that sells flowers below our apartment, and I bought every yellow tulip (Jo's favorite flower) that they had. I returned with two armfuls of flowers and told Jo how much I love her.

If marking Jo's essay was one of my lowest moments as a

husband, this was one of my brightest ones. I took the truth of what Jo had done wrong and turned it into an opportunity to bless her rather than an opportunity to wield power over her. In this instance, by God's grace and certainly not by my own strength, I chose not to consistently remind her of what she had done every time I needed her to look the other way or every time I wanted to guilt her into doing something for me.

I think the reason this is such a powerful and healing memory for me and Jo is not just because I used the truth as an opportunity to care for Jo but because my act of care for her was my actual disagreement with her. You see, when Jo made this confession to me, she thought her actions made her unlovable. My response was not only a statement about my commitment to use truth not to harm her but to bless her, but it was also my very disagreement with her on this crucial point. By my action I communicated that she *was* loveable and that nothing she could do could ever change that—the very opposite of what she had thought.

One of my students this past year, an Anglican minister from Northern Nigeria, was asked by a fellow student on the first day of classes, "How do you approach mission in a context in which you are viewed as the enemy?" We knew that Hassan ministered in a region terrorized by Boko Haram; we found out only later that he had been shot at twice and has a bounty on his head.

Hassan went on to explain, in a focused but matter-of-fact way that spoke to the reality of his experience, that there came a point when he had seen so many of his Christian brothers and sisters murdered for their faith that he began a conversation with a known gun dealer in order to acquire an AK-47. He had seen too much, and violence seemed to be the only answer.[13]

While he was trying to figure out where to get the money to buy the gun, he saw a young girl run by his house hawking groundnuts during school hours. He stopped her and asked why she wasn't in school, and she replied that her parents didn't have the money to send her. Hassan thought to himself, *That's not right*, and decided he and his church would pay for her schooling. He asked the girl to take him to her parents.

His stomach knotted up as she walked him across the clear dividing line between the Christian and Muslim sections of the town. He had assumed this little girl came from a Christian family; she was in fact from a Muslim family.

But Hassan had already committed to her that he would pay for her education. It took several trips to convince her parents, through the Imams and the Muslim Community Ward Head, but eventually they agreed, and Hassan and his church began paying her school fees. Soon Hassan discovered her brothers were also not in school. Then he identified another Muslim child who could not afford education, and another, and another. Hassan and his diocese are now providing education for about two hundred Muslim children in Christian schools.

Then Hassan thought, *Why are we only helping the children?* He realized that the Christian women in his region had a skill for making clothes that the Muslim women didn't have, and also that the Muslim women knew a particular style of cooking that the Christian women didn't know. One hundred and sixty Christian and Muslim women are now meeting, enjoying one another's company and conversation, and blessing one another by sharing their expertise.

Shortly before Hassan came to Oxford, some militant Muslim youths showed up at his door. He was afraid. He thought his life was in danger. He worried that they had come to collect the bounty on his head or, still worse, to hurt his family. The youths looked at him sternly and said, "Why don't you help us? You help the children; you help the women. Why don't you do anything for us?" Militant Muslim youths are asking an Anglican priest to incorporate them into his mission strategy!

Why did these young men respond so positively? After all, Hassan was disagreeing with them in a big way. He was symbolically saying we should love our enemies and pray for those who persecute us, something untrue in Islam. He also was saying that Christ should be at the center of their education. But he used truth to care for and serve them rather than as power over them. He didn't disagree with them first and then care for them second. His loving sacrifice for them was the very content of his disagreement with them. And he asked for nothing in return. That is how they knew that, despite his disagreement, he could be trusted. This is how they knew that he was someone with whom they could agree to disagree.

Note that this is vastly different from the secular virtue of "tolerance." In fact, this was *intolerance*—intolerance of that girl not having the money for school, intolerance of the Islamic beliefs that would preclude Hassan from loving and serving her, intolerance of the thought that he and his community had nothing to learn from their Islamic neighbors. Tolerance is not a Christian virtue. I hope *tolerant* is not a word that applies to me and my community. I'm not called to tolerate anyone; I'm not called to see anyone as tolerable. I'm called to love others sacrificially and to give my life for those I disagree with. Am I?

Counterculturally, it was precisely Hassan's exclusive truth claims that included his Muslim neighbors. His commitment to Christian truths excluded their beliefs, but it included them. So often when someone is told that a disagreement is with their belief and not with them as a person, the distinction is dismissed as a ruse. But in Hassan's case, it was not dismissed because the very content of Hassan's disagreement was communicated in an act that was ideologically exclusive but personally inclusive. That is a properly inclusive truth and a fitting representation of a gospel that is meant for everyone.

Hassan's actions challenge us not to "tolerance" but to "truth *in* love" (Ephesians 4:15)—not truth spoken *because* I love you, but truth spoken *in* an act of love. What would it look like for us to love those we disagree with in our very acts of disagreement? What would it look like for us to disagree with such love and personal sacrifice that people would show up on our doorstep asking for us to act on our disagreement with them?

Hassan headed back to Nigeria last week. He has been appointed the pastor of a church that borders on a Muslim portion of town. He received word several weeks ago that the church that he was being sent to pastor, which had already been burnt to the ground once, was destroyed a second time by Muslim youths when there was an attempt to rebuild it. The Muslim youths, he was informed, have said they will make sure no church will be built there again. Our team is helping to send Hassan back with a large fireproof tent for him to hold services in. If the tent is destroyed, we will send another. You should see the smile on his face when he talks about his new post. Please pray for Hassan and his family. I know he would be extremely grateful, and I know God will use your prayers powerfully.

On his last Sunday with us in Oxford, our pastor interviewed Hassan during the service. He asked Hassan, "Is it worth it?" Hassan had a quizzical look, because the answer was so obvious to him: "Of course." Then, lastly, Hassan was asked whether he had any parting words for us as a church. He said, "I beg you; do not compromise here in the West on the faith that we in Africa are dying for."

The Gospel Truth

That is one of two interviews with Hassan that I will never forget. The other came six months ago when my wife, Jo, interviewed Hassan about his story at a secular university. Most of those in attendance were not Christians, and they included politics professors, students from the politics and international relations departments, and students in the Officers' Training Corps.

221

The interview lasted for about an hour. When Hassan had finished speaking, the applause went on endlessly. It was one of the most powerful moments I have ever experienced. I have never seen anything like it. Hassan had spoken about his experiences from his Christian perspective. He had not shied away from any of his theological commitments. He had spoken completely openly about the uniqueness of Christianity, the reality of sin, and our need for a Savior. And yet the room was overflowing with appreciation and affirmation.

Immediately I thought to myself, *They don't realize it, but they are applauding the truth of the gospel!* Hassan had shared, with evident humility, about how he is risking his life for those who are against him. And that is the gospel: "While we were still sinners, Christ died for us" (Romans 5:8). Jesus knows the truth about us. He knows every time we have done something we shouldn't have. He knows every way in which we are against Him. And yet He does not hold it over our heads. He allowed it to be held over His head. He didn't make a play for power, but He set aside His power in order to love and to serve.

Jesus disagreed with us. His very coming was an act of disagreement with us—a statement that we required saving because our lives have disagreed so badly with what He intended for them. In the life that He lived, the things that He taught, and the way that He laid down his life, Jesus is the greatest expression of God's disagreement with us; and yet, simultaneously, Jesus is the greatest expression of God's love for us. Like Hassan, Jesus did not disagree with us first and then later serve us as a sort of consolation for the offense He had caused. No. Jesus' sacrifice for us was the very content of His disagreement; it was His very statement that we are sinners in need of a Savior.

Our culture sees the truth as something to be used for personal gain. Jesus "did not come to be served, but to serve" (Mark 10:45). As Christians, we talk often about Jesus being "full of grace and truth"

(John 1:14). What does that look like concretely? How do we take truth seriously without getting arrogant? How do we hold fast to an exclusive truth while being inclusive of others? We must practice gospel truth. Gospel truth is not "tolerance." Our being tolerable to God never would have motivated the sacrifice that He made. Gospel truth is sacrificial disagreement; it is disagreement defined by the generosity of an unmerited gift and the love of a personal sacrifice.

That is a far tougher form of disagreement than fighting or fleeing, but we have a high calling. The early Church's loudest disagreements were in the forms of buying back slaves into freedom, providing for the poor, and risking their lives to care for those with contagious, fatal diseases. What content were they communicating in those acts of sacrificial love? What cultural assumptions were they overtly disagreeing with? If we are prayerful enough, thoughtful enough, united enough, creative enough, disagreement can be redeemed.

We live in a society that increasingly does not value truth on the biggest questions of life. Why? Because we are afraid of truth. Because our most consistent experience of truth is the abuse of truth. The Church needs to recapture a communication of truth that is simultaneously an expression of sacrificial love. That is the model of Jesus.

Do we handle truth as Christ did? Do we disagree sacrificially? What would that look like for the different individuals and communities we disagree with? We are called to share the gospel truth, and gospel truth is by very nature sacrificial truth. How often is our disagreement with others a sacrifice for them? These are the questions that will determine the Church's impact in the critical days ahead.

Do We Fear the Truth?

Gospel truth is a truth we can trust; it is truth that elicits applause from sincere hearts even when they disagree. So why do we so often refuse to accept it?

In a word: *fear*. Some of us have probably had the experience of coming close to going on a roller coaster or close to jumping off a high diving board, and then, at the last second, thinking better of it. Why didn't I get on that roller coaster? Is it that I actually thought it wouldn't hold me and I would get hurt? No. If you had told me a million dollars were at stake and asked me to guess the correct answer to the nearest percentage point of how likely it was for me to get injured on the roller coaster, I quickly would have answered 0%.

It wasn't truth that kept me from that adventure. It was fear. Fear disempowers truth. If we're honest, very often, even when we know the truth, we let fears get in the way of accepting it. Not accepting the truth often has more to do with our emotions than with our reasoning.

Previously I mentioned the biblical claim in Romans 1 that somewhere deep down we do know the truth about God, because God has revealed it, but we "suppress" it. We know the truth, but we're afraid to accept it. This is true of our beliefs generally. Might it be true of our beliefs about God as well? Is it facts or fears that keep us from God?

When I was a graduate student at Oxford, I lived with four other graduate students, and one evening we wound up in a wide-ranging God, the universe, and the meaning of life conversation that culminated in a discussion of ghosts. Slowly, it emerged that three out of the four of them were absolutely convinced of the existence of ghosts, to the point of being adamant that they personally had either seen or interacted with ghosts in the past. These were Oxford University graduate students (some are scientists), who were more or less indifferent about God's existence, claiming near certitude about the existence of ghosts.

That conversation made me rethink my entire understanding of why these friends of mine were dismissive of God. I had assumed it was that the supernatural just seemed too unlikely. Meanwhile, they were absolutely convinced of the supernatural! Was it truth that kept them from taking God more seriously, or was it fear of some sort? Was it that they couldn't imagine Him being true, or that they didn't like the idea of Him being true?

That raises another question: What would make God scarier than ghosts?

The late Christopher Hitchens thought that Christianity, and religion in general, is so bad that it poisons everything it touches. He found the Christian description of reality abhorrent, nightmarish even. He said that, if it were true, it would be like a "celestial North Korea" where you are under constant surveillance. God would be a tyrannical authority ever watching you and ever subjecting you to His rules.

Should we agree? There are some situations in which we willingly loosen the boundaries of our autonomy and allow others into our "private" world. My wife, Jo, has a very high degree of, in a sense, "surveillance" over me. Not only is she around me during most of my waking and sleeping hours, but when she observes me, she can see me like no one else can. The subtle tones in my comments, the feelings I try to conceal—none of this is hidden to Jo. And in relationship with her, I have also subjected myself to rules—rules not to be unfaithful to her and not to quit when things get hard.

Despite her knowledge of me and the "constraints" I am under, my relationship with Jo is incredibly life-giving, not something I'm toiling under. The rules of marriage free us from worry and fill us with confidence that our relationship will be lasting. And when I consider the extent to which Jo knows me, and how exposed my true self is before her, I don't long to regain my "privacy." Quite the opposite. Knowing that I am loved by someone who knows so much about what I'm *really* like frees me to stop competing to be loved and just enjoy it.

Interestingly, our fear of others knowing the truth about us is an implicit admission that the truth about us is not always pretty. I have been told that someone once wrote anonymously to twelve highly powerful people, saying "All is discovered. Flee at once." All twelve of them left town.[14]

In 2008, the British Humanist Association, with backing from Richard Dawkins, suggested the opposite—that nothing is discovered. In what was termed "The Bus Campaign," the sides of London buses proclaimed the following message in large colorful lettering: "There's probably no God. Now stop worrying and enjoy your life." It's an amazing advert! For starters, the use of the word *probably* doesn't exactly fill you with confidence. It's a bit like saying, "That berry is probably not poisonous, so stop worrying and go ahead and enjoy it!" or "Our parachutes usually open, so go ahead and enjoy your jump!"

But note what else is implied by this advertisement. It doesn't say, "Stop worrying because whether or not there is a God, He'll be happy with the way you are living." It says, "Stop worrying because there's probably *not* a God," implying that if there *were* a God (if all *were* discovered), we might be in trouble. It might as well have read, "Stop worrying because you'll probably never get caught!"

We hide the truth because we know that some of the truth about us is not pretty, and the thought of there being someone to answer to for the darkest stuff in our lives is a scary thought. We also hide the truth because experience has taught us that we can't trust others with the truth. We don't want people to know our grades, our salaries, that we are seeing a counselor, or how messy we keep the house, because we don't trust what people will think and say behind our backs. There is good reason to be afraid of others knowing the truth about us, both because there is shameful truth to be known and because the truth has been used against us.

The reason we don't want God watching us is because we project our distrust of one another onto Him. Instead of trusting God with the truth about us, we create gods that cannot see us and cannot know us. We create gods that we can control: scientism (our technology), relativism (our perspective), humanism (our ability), pantheism (our divinity), hedonism (our pleasure). Secular gods all locate truth either in ourselves or in something impersonal. We don't want truth to be found in anyone else, because we are not convinced that we can trust anyone else with the truth.

However, we were not always so untrusting. Every time my two-year-old goddaughter, Carys, walks into a room—no matter what she is doing—she raises her hands and joyfully exclaims, "I'm here!" I love this. There is something so pure and right about it. Carys wants people to see her. She wants to be known. We don't want people to know the truth about us, because we believe they will use it as a weapon against us. Carys doesn't want anyone to miss anything that she does, because she knows she is loved.

Our struggle is we can't imagine that someone could know us fully and love us fully. Love and truth become an either/or, and hence we look to bury the truth that we might find love. But Jesus doesn't ask us to choose. His love for us is the unconditional love of a perfect parent, and He pleads with us to come to Him as children—hands raised, "I'm here!"

If God knows me *perfectly* and yet loves me *perfectly*, I haven't found a tyrant; I have found what my heart cries out for—someone whose love isn't drawn to me because of the outer performance I put on, nor driven from me because of the inner mess I hide away. Someone whose love for me is unconditional. If anything would help atheists such as Hitchens and Dawkins not to fear God and to appraise the merit of Christian evidences with more openness, it would surely be an experience of love like *this*.

Do You Love the Truth?

Fear disempowers truth; there is a difference between knowing the roller coaster will hold you and actually taking it for a ride. Therefore, if we want to live by (rather than just believe) the truth, the truth will need to be something that overcomes our fears.

Theoretical truth will not overcome fear. We know theoretically that the roller coaster will hold us, and yet we still fear. Likewise, theories will not overcome our greatest fears: the fear of not being loved, the fear of death, the fear of meaninglessness. Scientism led to the most fearful century in all human history. Relativism can't even identify our fears. Hedonism merely distracts us from our fears without addressing them. An "ism" will not get us on the roller coaster we were made to enjoy.

What will overcome our fears and provide us with the courage to face them? The hand of a loved one—the hand of someone who has committed to stay by your side and to take the ride with you. Only "love drives out fear" (1 John 4:18). And, therefore, if we want to live in the truth, love and truth will need to coincide.

This is something most of us can agree about. To be called a lover of truth is one of the highest compliments one can receive. That loving the truth is central to living a worthwhile life has been recognized across time and beliefs. Prudentius claimed in the fourth century that "Nought can be higher than the love of truth and right,"[15] and the Bible warns that people perish because they "refused to love the truth" (2 Thessalonians 2:10). But many contemporary atheists are in passionate agreement. Stephen Fry, for one, takes pride in the claim, "I am a lover of truth..."[16]

We all grasp intuitively that there is something authentic and good about being lovers of the truth. Love of truth is not a superficial love. It is not love like love of a favorite color or a favorite food.

Love of truth is supposed to be among the deepest of loves, a love deep enough to direct your life and to submit your life to.

The question is then raised, What is this thing we are supposed to love—truth? What are the things that are true? As philosophers would put it, what are the bearers of truth?

Here are the answers most commonly given to that question in philosophical scholarship today: propositions, sentences, beliefs, or facts. And here's the problem: When is the last time you loved one of those? Maybe there is a sense in which you could love a really beautifully composed sentence, but that's not the sort of love that is substantial enough to direct your entire life, and love of truth is supposed to be this deepest and highest form of love.

Into this challenge Jesus speaks astonishing words: "I am the truth" (John 14:6). It is one of the most remarkable things about Jesus' life. He does not say like the Buddha to look to the propositions and beliefs of His teaching. He does not say like Muhammad to look to the eloquence of the Qur'an's sentences. Jesus says, look to Me. He says, "You study the Scriptures diligently because you think that in them you have eternal life. These are the very Scriptures that testify about me, yet you refuse to come to me to have life" (John 5:39–40).

Jesus makes truth personal, and therefore loveable in the very deepest sense. In Christianity alone, truth is a person who is inviting every other person into a love relationship. In this way, perhaps more than any other, Jesus outshines secular gods. No ideology, idea, or "ism" ever asked, "Do you love me?" Jesus asks it repeatedly: "Do you love me? Do you love me? Do you love me?" (John 21:15–17). Jesus says you can trust the truth because truth itself will be the one to take your hand, and stay by your side, and ride with you.

If the truth is a person, the search for the truth becomes filled with the meaningfulness of pursing relationship. If all truth is ultimately grounded in the person of God, then every question asked is a question asked about a person, and every answer given is an answer received from a person. Every question about science is a question about how and why God has made and sustained the universe as He has. Every question about morality is a question about the character of God. Every question about politics and economics is a question about what it means to be made in the image of God and granted dominion over the earth. Every truth, no matter the discipline, says something about who God is and what He has done. Now you can love the truth, because every truth—being personal—is a fitting object of love.

The problem is not with truth but with what we take to be the truth bearers. If they are impersonal, they cannot be loved in the deepest sense. If they cannot be loved in the deepest sense, they cannot overcome fear. If they cannot overcome fear, we cannot live in the truth.

Christianity offers Jesus as an alternative, countercultural truth bearer. On the Cross, He literally bore the truth. He bore the truth about us—even the shameful truth. We can therefore love the truth because the bearer of truth was willing to bear the truth about us. Only a Christian can be a lover of truth, in the deepest sense of love, because only Christianity is an invitation to a personal loving relationship with the truth.

Does the Truth Love You?

Not just any truth will do. Only loving the truth will cast out fear. Only loving the truth will stop our abuse of the truth.

There is nothing worse than unreturned love. But, for many, that has been their experience of truth because, if truth is not personal, there is nothing there to love you back. For someone who loves the truth, seeking the truth in anything other than a person is inevitably a failed relationship.

However, even seeking the truth in a person will not suffice unless you know that person can be trusted, unless you know that person loves you. When asked, "Does God love you?" a university student in Chicago quickly responded no. I asked him why he thought that. He said, "I'm a bad person. I do bad things. I think bad things. I have a bad personality."

I asked him whether, years from now, he would stop loving his child if that child began to think and do bad things. "No, I would continue to love him," he responded. I then made the simple connection: "If God is a father and you are His child, wouldn't He continue to love you through both the good and the bad?" He paused, his eyes filled with tears, and he responded, "I guess that makes sense." So many people have a grave misconception about God's love. They believe His love to be less than that of a human parent rather than that of a perfect parent.

The countercultural nature of God's love is that it cannot be earned and it cannot be lost. God's love is not a response to our love but a love we are asked to respond to: "This is love: not that we loved God, but that he loved us" (1 John 4:10); "we love because he first loved us" (1 John 4:19). We struggle to love the truth because we don't believe that the truth loves us. But not only does the truth love us, He loved us first.

God loved us first because love is what He is: "God is love" (1 John 4:16). In Christianity, love is not something God might happen to do or feel; it is His very nature.

Here's what follows from all this: If God is truth *and* God is love, then truth is love, and we don't need to choose between truth and love. They are one and the same. Truth that is not loving is not truth. Love that is not committed to truth is not love.

If the truth is love itself and loves us, then we have every reason to respond by loving the truth. And if we love the truth, then we will stop fearing it, stop abusing it, and stop abusing others with it. So much is at stake when we consider the love of God. How can we be assured of it?

The more someone is willing to give up for you, the more sure you can be of their love. The more valuable something is to someone, the more they are willing to pay for it. How much was God willing to pay for you?

The following is a transcript from a video that I came across on Mother's Day. The video is of two daughters who alternate holding up index cards in order to tell the story of their mother's love:

I'm Chloe,
And I'm Annie.
We want to tell you a story about our mom.
Our mom and dad got married in 1991.
In 1992, I was born (Chloe).
A few years later, in 1994, I was born (Annie).
And finally, in 1996, our little brother was born.
We lived in a happy home with lots of love and laughter,
And a mom who loved us more than the world.
But there was an accident in 1999 that changed everything.
We were on vacation with my grandparents,
And we were going to rent a log cabin.
It was beautiful and overlooked a huge cliff.
We were so excited!
At the time, I was seven.
I was five,
And our brother was three.
When we pulled into the driveway of the house,
My parents and grandparents got out of the car to sign paperwork in the doorway.
My sister, brother, and I stayed in the car and watched from the window.

Even though my mom had her keys with her, the car some-how knocked out of gear,
And started rolling...
Toward the cliff.
As soon as my mom saw what was happening,
She did the unthinkable.
She ran in front of the SUV, determined to stop it.
We remember the look on her face right before she went under,
And we remember feeling the bump as we ran over her body.
That bump saved our lives.
It slowed the car down just enough for my grandpa to run up beside it
And pull the emergency break
Right before we went over the cliff.
The weight of the SUV on my mother's body should have killed her,
But by some miracle of miracles,
It didn't.
But it did break her back.
She is paralyzed from the waist down,
And she will never walk again.
But she says she wouldn't change it for the world because her three kids are alive and with her.
She hasn't let her wheelchair stop her from anything.
She has been at every piano recital,
Every tennis tournament,
And is the voice at the end of the phone when I'm away at college.
She is our rock
And our best friend.
She is the most amazing mother in the world.

She taught us from a young age that when people stare at us because of her wheelchair,
We should hold our head up high
And just stare back.
That is what she has done with life.
Life gave her a tough hand of cards,
But she arranged them into something beautiful.
Yes, she saved our lives in the accident in 1999,
But she saves them over and over again, each and every day.
Happy Mother's Day, Mom.
We love you more than words.[17]

Watching this video convicted me of how often we forget the rawness, and with it the love, of the Cross. Madonna made the Cross a fashion accessory. We wear crosses if they look pretty; we casually knock on wood; we jokingly cross our fingers and hope to die. Chloe and Annie "remember the look on [their mother's] face right before she went under." They "remember feeling the bump as [they] ran over her body." Do we remember the look on Jesus' face when He dropped down and gave His life for us? Do we remember the thump as the nails were pounded into His flesh?

The four-year-old son of dear friends recently asked his mom, "How did Jesus die?" "He died on a cross," my friend responded. "But *how* did he die," her son pressed again. Eventually, appreciating his question, my friend talked her son through the details of how Jesus died. She touched her son's hands and then his feet as she explained where Jesus was pierced and how He was forced to hang against that wooden cross.

Now her son looked as if he understood. He said, "I didn't know that, Mom. I knew Jesus died. I knew He came back to life. But I didn't know about the Cross."

Many of us know Jesus died. Many of us know that He came back to life. Do we know about the Cross? Do we remember when the Truth was stretched, when the Truth was twisted and bent, when the Truth was naked? Do we remember when the Truth hurt, and when the Truth was buried? Do we remember how much God gave for us, how much He paid for us, how much He loves us? And when people stare at us because we worship a crucified God, will we hold our heads up high?

In a secular age where God is increasingly deemed irrelevant to truth, we fear the truth and we abuse the truth because truth and love are disconnected. Truth has become something it was never meant to be—impersonal, offensive, a burden. But because of Jesus, we never need to doubt whether truth is on our side; we never need to doubt whether the truth loves us. Let us be lovers of the Truth, because the Truth loves us.

I was recently present when a man understood for the first time the depth of Jesus' love for him and decided he wanted to love Jesus back. This man prayed a simple but sincere affirmation of and commitment to this newfound love. And when he had finished praying, these were the very first words out of his mouth: "I have always felt alone and always had to 'wear a mask,' but now this is the first time in my life that I can take off that mask and be fully myself and fully alive!"

For the first time in his life this man could live in the truth, because for the first time in his life he trusted the truth. Now he knew that into his fear had stepped truth itself, and that truth is personal, and that Person promises—to every one of us—that, if you follow Him, "you will know the truth, and the truth will set you free" (John 8:32).

ACKNOWLEDGMENTS

Ravi Zacharias

EACH TIME I try to pen my indebtedness to someone for the completion of a work, the list always starts with the same people. My wife, Margie, who is my chief editor. Navigating that is a gift of grace for us. I smile as I say that. The truth is she spends hours on the chapters to make sure my voice is heard but that the correctness in saying it is retained. My final editor for sources and such is Danielle DuRant. She has been my research assistant for over twenty years. She knows my material well. Joey Paul, my dear friend and guide in writing, has had a profound impact on my life and writing. Thank you, Joey.

Thanks also to Lance Wubbels. Brilliant final editor to make it the way it is meant to be.

Finally, as always, my family. My three beautiful children, their spouses, and their children give me the privilege of this ministry with long hours of absence from them. One of the great privileges of eternity will be their constant presence. Because of their sacrifice, others will be in our Lord's presence as well.

Vince Vitale

WORDS COULD not exhaust the depth of my gratitude to my wife, Jo. I trust her more than anyone. Her wisdom and godly affections influence every page that I write, and her patience and steadfast support allow me to write them. To be shown such grace and trust by Ravi and Margie, for whom I have such immense admiration, is an incredible and undeserved gift for which I continually thank God.

Acknowledgments

This book would not exist without Joey Paul's outstanding vision and leadership, but I am even more thankful for his belief in me and for his friendship. My agent, Andrew Wolgemuth, was an ever superb companion through this process. His instincts and assessment were incisive at every turn, and I look forward with excitement to working with him on future projects.

Catherine Tomkins displayed characteristic excellence in her research and in the gracious disposition with which she conducted it. Martin Smith went above and beyond in the precision of his analysis and his extraordinary attention to detail. Danielle DuRant generously lent her topflight expertise in both the research and editing phases. She was as always a joy to work with. Keith Small displayed his distinguishing integration of scholarship and charitableness when advising me on several passages. Ed Clark's mathematical expertise was a great gift when consulting on a number of key points. Lance Wubbels demonstrated impressive thoroughness and thoughtfulness in his copyediting, and the manuscript benefited greatly from his efforts and care.

To no one am I more thankful than to Carla and Vince Sr., Mom and Dad, who had the love and loyalty to join me on this great adventure in search of Truth.

NOTES

CHAPTER 1

1 Maya Oppenheim, "Richard Dawkins: Atheist academic calls for religion 'to be offended at every opportunity,'" *The Independent* (23 May 2016), http://www.independent.co.uk/news/people/richard-dawkins-atheist-academic-calls-for-religion-to-be-offended-at-every-opportunity-a7043226.html. Accessed 10 Sept. 2016.

2 Ibid.

3 Robert A. Morey, *The New Atheism and the Erosion of Freedom* (Minneapolis: Bethany House Publishers, 1986), 98.

4 G. K. Chesterton observes, "It is said that Paganism is a religion of joy and Christianity of sorrow; it would be just as easy to prove that Paganism is pure sorrow and Christianity pure joy.... Man is more himself, man is more manlike, when joy is the fundamental thing in him, and grief the superficial. Melancholy should be an innocent interlude, a tender and fugitive frame of mind; praise should be the permanent pulsation of the soul. Pessimism is at best an emotional half-holiday; joy is the uproarious labor by which all things live. Yet, according to the apparent estate of man as seen by the pagan or the agnostic, this primary need of human nature can never be fulfilled. Joy ought to be expansive; but for the agnostic it must be contracted, it must cling to one corner of the world. Grief ought to be a concentration; but for the agnostic its desolation is spread through an unthinkable eternity." G. K. Chesterton, *Orthodoxy* (Chicago: Moody Publishers, 2009), 236–237, 105. Also available online at http://www.gutenberg.org/files/16769/16769-h/16769-h.htm. Accessed 10 Sept. 2016.

5 William Blake, "Mock on, mock on, Voltaire, Rousseau" in *The Norton Anthology of English Literature,* Third Edition, general editor M. H. Abrams (New York: W.W. Norton & Company, 1975), 1338.

6 Mortimer Adler, *The Synopticon: An Index to the Great Ideas, Vol. 1* (Chicago: Britannica, 1952), 543.

7 Winston Churchill, "The Munich Agreement," http://www.winstonchurchill.org/resources/speeches/1930-1938-the-wilderness/101-the-munich-agreement. Accessed 10 Sept. 2016.

8 Charles Kaiser, *The Cost of Courage* (New York: Other Press, 2015), 51.

9 "Letter to the Officers of the First Brigade of the Third Division of the Militia of Massachusetts, 11 October 1798," in *Revolutionary Services and Civil Life of General William Hull* (New York: D. Appleton & Co., 1848), 266.

10 Thomas Paine, *The Theological Works of Thomas Paine* (London: R. Carlile, 1824), 317.

11 Paul Edwards, ed., *Encyclopedia of Philosophy, Vol. 1* (New York: Macmillan, 1967), 175.

12 Étienne Borne, *Atheism* (New York: Hawthorn Books, 1961), 61.

[13] Thucydides, "The Funeral Oration of Pericles," *History of the Peloponnesian War,* M. I. Finley, editor, translated by Rex Warner (New York: Penguin Classics, 1972), excerpt online at http://teacher.sduhsd.net/tpsocialsciences/world_history/dem_ideals/pericles.htm. Accessed 10 Sept. 2016.

[14] Stephen Jay Gould, quoted by David Friend and the editors of *Life* magazine, *The Meaning of Life* (Boston: Little, Brown and Company, 1991), 33.

[15] Citation from book jacket, http://www.davidberlinski.org/devils-delusion/about.php. Accessed 10 Sept. 2016.

[16] John Barrow quoted in Julia Vitullo-Martin's "A Scientist's Scientist," http://www.uncommondescent.com/intelligent-design/barrow-to-dawkins-youre-not-really-a-scientist/. Accessed 10 Sept. 2016.

[17] G. K. Chesterton, *As I Was Saying,* ed. Robert Knille (Grand Rapids, MI: Wm. B. Eerdmans, 1984), 267.

[18] G. K. Chesterton, "A Defence of Nonsense" in *A Defence of Nonsense and Other Essays* (New York: Dodd, Mead & Company, 1911), 8.

CHAPTER 2

[1] Richard Dawkins, *The God Delusion,* reprint edition (Mariner Books: New York, 2008), 51.

[2] Malcolm Muggeridge, *A Third Testament* (New York: Ballantine Books, 1983), xix.

[3] See Richard Dawkins, *Out of Eden* (New York: Basic Books, 1992), 133: "The universe we observe has precisely the properties we should expect if there is, at the bottom, no design, no purpose, no evil and no other good. Nothing but blind, pitiless indifference. DNA neither knows nor cares. DNA just is. And we dance to its music."

[4] Edwin Hubbell Chapin, *Living Words* (Boston: N.E. Universalist Publishing House [sic.], 1866), 121.

[5] Nicholas Wolterstorff, *Lament for a Son* (Grand Rapids, MI: William B. Eerdmans, 1987), 72–73.

[6] See "Megyn Kelly to OJ's Former Lawyer: Was the 'Not Guilty' Verdict Fair?" (13 May 2016), online video interview at http://insider.foxnews.com/2016/05/13/robert-shapiro-reflects-oj-simpson-verdict-megyn-kelly-presents. Accessed 10 Sept. 2016.

CHAPTER 3

[1] Richard Dawkins, "A Challenge to Atheists," *Free Enquiry* (Vol. 22, No. 3, 2002).

[2] Alvin Plantinga, interview by Gary Gutting, "Is Atheism Irrational?" *The New York Times Opinionator,* 9 Feb. 2014, http://opinionator.blogs.nytimes.com/2014/02/09/is-atheism-irrational/?_r=0. Accessed 10 Sept. 2016.

[3] Peter van Inwagen, "Weak Darwinism," *Darwin and Catholicism: The Past and Present Dynamics of a Cultural Encounter,* edited by Louis Caruana (Edinburgh: T & T Clark, 2009), 119.

[4] Stephen Hawking, "The Beginning of the Universe," *Primordial Nucleosynthesis and Evolution of Early Universe,* edited by K. Sato and J. Audouze (Dordrecht, Netherlands: Kluwer Academic Publishers, 1990), 129, 137. Although Hawking appears to stand by this statement of his (it is included in a featured lecture on his website), his more recent work has speculated about nontheistic, scientific explanations of the beginning of the universe. My subsequent philosophical discussion of the nature of infinity is a challenge to any theory that attempts to posit an endless series of nontheistic, scientific explanations culminating in the origin of our universe.

[5] William Lane Craig and James D. Sinclair, "The *Kalām* cosmological argument," *The Blackwell Companion to Natural Theology,* edited by William Lane Craig and J. P. Moreland (West Sussex, UK: Wiley-Blackwell, 2012), 182.

[6] David Hume, *The Letters of David Hume, Volume I 1727–1765*, edited by J.Y.T. Greig (New York: Oxford University Press, 1932, Letter 91), 187.

[7] For an accessible introduction to this argument see: William Lane Craig, *On Guard* (Colorado Springs: David C. Cook, 2010).

[8] Richard Dawkins, *The God Delusion,* 10th anniversary edition (London: Transworld, 2016), 171.

[9] Albert Einstein, *Ideas and Opinions* (New York: Crown Trade Paperbacks, 1995), 292.

[10] "With me, the horrid doubt always arises whether the convictions of man's mind, which has been developed from the mind of the lower animals, are of any value or at all trustworthy. Would any one trust in the convictions of a monkey's mind, if there are any convictions in such a mind?" (Charles Darwin, "C. D. to W. Graham, July 3d, 1881," *Selected Letters on Evolution and Origin of Species,* edited by Francis Darwin (New York: Dover, 1958), 68.

[11] See C. S. Lewis, "The Cardinal Difficulty of Naturalism," *Miracles* (London: Geoffrey Bles, 1947).

[12] This argument originally appeared in the last chapter of: Alvin Plantinga, *Warrant and Proper Function* (New York: Oxford University Press, 1993). The argument was then expanded in the unpublished paper: Alvin Plantinga, "Naturalism Defeated," *Calvin.edu,* 1994, calvin.edu/academic/philosophy/virtual_library/articles/plantinga_alvin/naturalism_defeated.pdf. Accessed 10 Sept. 2016.

[13] "'Miracle Child' is Survivor," *The New York Times,* 25 Sept. 1993, nytimes.com/1993/09/25/us/miracle-child-is-survivor.html. Accessed 12 Sept. 2016.

[14] Alvin Plantinga, "Introduction," *Naturalism Defeated? Essays on Plantinga's Evolutionary Argument Against Naturalism,* edited by James Beilby (Ithaca, NY: Cornell University Press, 2002), 4.

[15] Michael Ruse, "Evolutionary Theory and Christian Ethics," *Zygon,* Vol. 21, No. 1 (1994), 20–21.

[16] A transcript of this portion of the interview can be found at: Richard Dawkins, interview by Justin Brierley, "The John Lennox—Richard Dawkins Debate," *bethinking.org,* 2008, bethinking.org/atheism/the-john-lennox-richard-dawkins-debate. Accessed 11 Sept. 2016.

[17] Charles Darwin, *The Descent of Man* (New York: D. Appleton and Company, 1871), 70.

[18] You might ask, at this point, why the natural processes of our universe result not only in great orderliness and meaning but also in great suffering. Ravi and I speak to this important question in *Why Suffering? Finding Meaning and Comfort When Life Doesn't Make Sense* (New York: FaithWords, 2014).

[19] Importantly, when we talk about finely tuned features of the universe, we're not talking about gaps in the system (and hence this is not a "God of the gaps" argument), but rather the system that was designed in the first place.

[20] With respect to this estimation, Penrose says, "I just want to give you some feeling for how special the initial state of the universe was. And for some reason, people, you know, they try to say you don't want such and such a theory or so and so a theory because that requires fine-tuning or something like that. Well, there's got to be fine-tuning. This is fine-tuning. This is incredible precision in the organization of the initial universe" (MrEpistemologist1, "The Big Bang's low entropy condition," *Youtube*, 1 Nov. 2012, https://www.youtube.com/watch?v=GvV2Xzh11r8. Accessed on 11 Sept. 2016).

[21] Fred Hoyle, *The Intelligent Universe* (London: Michael Joseph, 1981), 18–19.

[22] William Lane Craig, "Five Reasons God Exists," *God? A Debate between a Christian and an Atheist,* edited by James P. Sterba (New York: Oxford University Press, 2004), 10.

[23] Del Ratzsch, "Teleological Arguments for God's Existence," *The Stanford Encyclopedia of Philosophy*, edited by Edward N. Zalta, Winter 2009 Edition, plato.stanford.edu/archives/win2009/entries/teleological-arguments/. Accessed 11 Sept. 2016.

[24] *Collision: Christopher Hitchens vs Douglas Wilson.* Directed by Darren Doane, 2009.

[25] Fred Hoyle, "The Universe: Past and Present Reflections," *Engineering and Science,* November 1981, 12.

[26] It is interesting to note, however, that in string theory the most commonly cited number of possible universes is 10^{500}; if Penrose is anywhere near accurate in his calculation of how finely tuned the universe is (to 1 part in $10^{10^{123}}$), then 10^{500} universes still would be far too few universes to make the existence of a life-friendly universe in any way probable. In fact, the probability would remain so small that, for all practical purposes, it would amount to zero.

[27] Richard Swinburne, *The Existence of God,* Second Edition (New York: Oxford University Press, 2004), 185.

[28] John Polkinghorne and Nicholas Beale, *Questions of Truth: Fifty-one Responses to Questions about God, Science, and Belief* (Louisville, KY: Westminster John Knox Press, 2009), 13.

[29] In Chapter 4, I discuss why this experiment is sometimes thought to have failed for some people who have sought God.

[30] Linde says, "To send a long message, you must make a weird universe with complicated laws of physics. It is the only way to send information. The only people who can read this message are physicists. Since we see around us a rather weird universe, does it imply that our universe was created not by God, but a physicist hacker?" (Adrei Linde,

interviewed by Rudy Rucker, "Goodbye Big Bang," *Seek! Selected Non-Fiction* (New York: Four Walls Eight Windows, 1999).

[31] John Gribbin, *In Search of the Multiverse* (New York: Penguin Books, 2010), 173.

[32] *Expelled: No Intelligence Allowed.* Directed by Nathan Frankowski, Premise Media Corporation & Rampant Films, 2008.

[33] "Are We Alone in the Universe? John Lennox and Paul Davies." *Unbelievable?*, premierchristianradio.com/Shows/Saturday/Unbelievable/Episodes/Unbelievable-17-Apr-2010-Are-we-alone-in-the-universe-Paul-Davies-John-Lennox. Accessed 11 Sept. 2016.

[34] One might object that the evil and suffering of our world favors the idea of the fine tuner being morally flawed. See *Why Suffering? Finding Meaning and Comfort When Life Doesn't Make Sense* (New York: FaithWords, 2014) for a book-length presentation of Ravi's and my response to this challenge.

[35] "Misconceptions of science and religion found in new survey," *Rice University News & Media*, 16 Feb. 2014, news.rice.edu/2014/02/16/misconceptions-of-science-and-religion-found-in-new-study/. Accessed 11 Sept. 2016.

CHAPTER 4

[1] Roger Scruton, *Modern Philosophy: An Introduction and Survey* (London: Mandarin, 1996), 6.

[2] The ideology of *pluralism* about truth, or being a *pluralist* about truth, is not to be confused with the reality of a *pluralistic* society (that is, a society that includes people of diverse beliefs).

[3] Compare Romans 10:9: "If you confess with your mouth that Jesus is Lord and believe in your heart that God raised him from the dead, you will be saved."

[4] Sura 4:157 denies that Jesus was crucified or killed; Sura 3:59, 4:171, 43:59, and 9:30 deny the divinity of Jesus. Sura 9:30 adds, "May God thwart them! How far astray they have been led!"

[5] This is because believing that Jesus is God violates the Islamic concept of the unity of God, resulting in *shirk*, Islam's unforgiveable sin. See Sura 5:72.

[6] Al-Ghazali, *The 99 Beautiful Names of God.*

[7] Allah also does not like "those who do wrong" (Sura 42:40) or "those who reject the truth" (Sura 30:45).

[8] See Robert H. Stein, "Fatherhood of God," *Biblestudytools.com*, http://www.bible-studytools.com/dictionaries/bakers-evangelical-dictionary/fatherhood-of-god.html. Accessed 12 Sept. 2016.

[9] Sura 2:106 is the foundational text for this doctrine.

[10] See Ibn Ishaq, *The Life of Muhammad*, translated by A. Guillaume (New York: Oxford University Press, 2002). This is the earliest available biography of Muhammad and documents his conquests.

[11] I am indebted to my colleagues Andy Bannister and Tanya Walker, whom I first

heard make this point. For Tanya's discussion of it, see her chapter "But…What About Other Religions?" in *A New Kind of Apologist*, edited by Sean McDowell (Eugene, OR: Harvest House Publishers, 2016). For Andy's discussion, see Chapter 3 of his *The Atheist Who Didn't Exist* (Oxford: Monarch Books, 2015).

[12] In Islam, the most one can hope for in paradise is to look at Allah (Sura 75:22–23), but even this falls far short of a relationship. Indeed, wouldn't it leave a person longing for relationship?

[13] Peter Boghossian, *A Manual for Creating Atheists* (Durham, NC: Pitchstone Publishing, 2013), 10.

[14] For an excellent discussion of this point, see Abdu Murray, "The Substance of Hope," https://www.intouch.org/read/magazine/features/the-substance-of-hope. Accessed 17 Sept. 2016.

[15] See Richard Swinburne, *The Resurrection of God Incarnate* (New York: Oxford University Press, 2003).

[16] G. K. Chesterton, "What's Wrong with the World," *The Collected Works of G. K. Chesterton IV* (San Francisco: Ignatius Press, 1987), 62.

[17] "Why Does God Allow Suffering? Vince Vitale and Julian Baggini," *Premier Christian Radio,* 7 February 2015, premierchristianradio.com/Shows/Saturday/Unbelievable/Episodes/Unbelievable-Why-does-God-allow-suffering-Vince-Vitale-Julian-Baggini. Accessed 11 Sept. 2016.

[18] C. S. Lewis, *The Weight of Glory* (New York: Macmillan, 1949), 26.

[19] E. Stanley Jones recorded Bara Dada saying this in his book, *The Christ of the Indian Road* (New York: Abingdon Press, 1925), 114.

[20] Here I am indebted to Professor John Lennox, who makes this point with respect to using force in order to defend Jesus or His message.

[21] I am thankful to Martin Smith for identifying this analogy with "pass the parcel" and for his insightful collaboration on the point that it draws out.

[22] Matthew Parris, "As an atheist, I truly believe Africa needs God," *The Times,* 27 Dec. 2008, thetimes.co.uk/tto/opinion/columnists/matthewparris/article2044345.ece. Accessed 12 Sept. 2016.

[23] See Jeffrey Stout, *Democracy and Tradition* (Princeton: Princeton University Press, 2009), 69–70, 84–85, 91.

[24] Jeffrey Stout, "2007 Presidential Address: The Folly of Secularism," *Journal of the American Academy of Religion*, Sept. 2008. Vol. 76, No. 3 (2008), 533–544.

[25] Flavius Claudius Julianus, "To Arsacius, High Priest of Galatia," *A Few Notes on Julian and a Translation of His Public Letters,* translated by Edward James Chinnock (London: Ballantyne Press, 1901, Epistle 49), 75–77.

[26] Pontius of Carthage, "The Life and Passion of Cyprian," *The Ante-Nicene Fathers, Volume V,* edited by Rev. Alexander Roberts and James Donaldson (Edinburgh: T & T Clark), 270.

[27] "Festival Letters," quoted by Eusebius, *Ecclesiastical History* 7.22, translated by G. A. Williamson (New York: Penguin, 1965).

[28] See *Time*, "Person of the Year," 10 Dec. 2014, time.com/time-person-of-the-year-ebola-doctors/. Accessed 26 Sept. 2016.

[29] I am grateful to Joshua Fountain and Michael Lloyd for insightful discussion on this point.

[30] Jürgen Habermas, *Time of Transitions* (Cambridge: Polity Press, 2006), 150–151.

[31] Linda Zagzebski, *Epistemic Authority: A Theory of Trust, Authority, and Autonomy in Belief* (New York: Oxford University Press, 2012), 18–188.

[32] Peter Berger, "Dr. Peter Berger at the November 2011 Faith Angle Forum," *Ethics and Public Policy Centre*, eppc.org/publications/berger/. Accessed 12 Sept. 2016.

[33] V. Arstila, "Time Slows Down During Accidents," *Frontiers in Psychology*, 27 Jun. 2012, Vol. 3, No. 196 (2012), http://doi.org/10.3389/fpsyg.2012.00196. Accessed 25 Sept. 2016.

[34] Blaise Pascal, *Pensées* (New York: E. P. Dutton & Co, 1958), 430.

CHAPTER 5

[1] Alan Bullock, *The Humanist Tradition in the West* (New York; London: Norton, 1985), 8.

[2] Slogan for the Council for Secularism, https://www.secularhumanism.org/index.php. Accessed 10 Sept. 2016.

[3] See Norman Geisler, *Is Man the Measure?* (Grand Rapids, MI: Baker Book House, 1983).

[4] See http://www.uu.se/en/about-uu/traditions/thomas-torild/. Accessed 10 Sept. 2016.

[5] Anthony Kronman, *Education's End: Why Our Colleges and Universities Have Given Up on the Meaning of Life* (New Haven, CT: Yale University Press, 2007), 255.

[6] Anthony Kronman, "Why are we here? Colleges ignore life's biggest questions, and we all pay the price," *The Boston Globe* (16 Sept. 2007), http://archive.boston.com/news/globe/ideas/articles/2007/09/16/why_are_we_here/. Accessed 10 Sept. 2016.

[7] Ibid.

[8] See Symposium "A Dangerous and Disturbing Development" (21 Sept. 2007), https://www.cardus.ca/comment/article/928/a-dangerous-and-disturbing-development/. Accessed 10 Sept. 2016.

[9] Ibid.

[10] A.E.E. McKenzie, *The Major Achievements of Science* (Cambridge University Press) cited in T. M. Kitwood, *What Is Human?* (London: InterVarsity Press, 1970), 17.

[11] "The next year, Comte chose the evolution of Humanity as the new topic for his public course; this was an occasion to lay down the premises of what would become

the new Religion of Humanity." As quoted in "Auguste Comte," *Stanford Encyclopedia of Philosophy,* http://plato.stanford.edu/entries/comte/. Accessed 10 Sept. 2016.

12 See Paul Kurtz, "A Call for a New Planetary Humanism" (Humanist Manifesto 2000), https://www.secularhumanism.org/index.php/1169. Accessed 10 Sept. 2016.

13 See "What Is Humanism?" http://americanhumanist.org/Humanism. Accessed 10 Sept. 2016.

14 David Hume, *An Enquiry Concerning Human Understanding* (London: A. Millar, 1777), 166.

15 Stephen Hawking and Leonard Mlodinow, *The Grand Design,* reprint edition (New York: Bantam, 2012), 180.

16 See, e.g., John Lennox, "As a scientist I'm certain Stephen Hawking is wrong. You can't explain the universe without God," *The Daily Mail* (3 September 2010), http://www.dailymail.co.uk/debate/article-1308599/Stephen-Hawking-wrong-You-explain-universe-God.html#ixzz0yabn9HCT. Accessed 10 Sept. 2016.

17 John Cornwell, "*The Grand Design: New Answers to the Ultimate Questions of Life* by Stephen Hawking: review" in *The Telegraph* (20 Sept. 2010), online at http://www.telegraph.co.uk/culture/books/bookreviews/8006738/The-Grand-Design-New-Answers-to-the-Ultimate-Questions-of-Life-by-Stephen-Hawking-review.html. Accessed 10 Sept. 2016.

18 Kronman, *Education's End*, 259.

19 See "Definitions of Humanism," http://americanhumanist.org/humanism/definitions_of_humanism. Accessed 10 Sept. 2016.

20 Geisler, *Is Man the Measure?* (Grand Rapids, MI: Baker Book House, 1983).

21 Julian Huxley, *Religion Without Revelation* (New York: Harper, 1957), 58.

22 Ibid., 188.

23 Ibid., 205.

24 George W. Cornell, "In Light of Science Let's Begin with a Noble Lie," *Deseret News,* 20 July 1991, http://www.deseretnews.com/article/173507/IN-LIGHT-OF-SCIENCE-LETS-BEGIN-ANEW-WITH-A-NOBLE-LIE--PHILOSOPHER-SAYS.html?pg=all. Accessed 10 Sept. 2016.

25 Loyal Rue, *By the Grace of Guile: The Role of Deception in Natural History and Human Affairs* (New York: Oxford University Press, 1994), 279.

26 Kitwood, *What Is Human?*, 13.

27 Ibid., 30.

28 As quoted in Kitwood, 36.

29 Christopher Hudson, "Doctors of Depravity" (2 Mar. 2007), *The Daily Mail,* http://www.dailymail.co.uk/news/article-439776/Doctors-Depravity.html. Accessed 10 Sept. 2016.

30 Ibid.

CHAPTER 6

[1] "The Christian ideal has not been tried and found wanting. It has been found difficult; and left untried." G. K. Chesterton, "The Unfinished Temple" in *What's Wrong with the World Nonsense and Other Essays* (San Francisco: Ignatius Press, 1994), 37.

[2] Fred Hoyle and N. Chandra Wickramasinghe, *Evolution from Space* (London: J. M. Dent & Sons, 1981), 24.

[3] Fred Hoyle, *Intelligent Universe* (New York: Holt, Rinehart, and Winston, 1983), 242.

[4] Rebecca Baer Porteous quoted in Kelly Monroe Kullberg, ed., *Finding God at Harvard* (Grand Rapids, MI: Zondervan, 1996), 17.

[5] David Hume, "Universal Principle of the Closed Frame," *The Enquiry Concerning Morals*, quoted in Francis Beckwith and Greg Koukl, *Relativism: Feet Firmly Planted in Mid-Air* (Grand Rapids, MI: Baker Book House, 1998), 29.

[6] William Shakespeare, *Macbeth*, Act 5, Scene 5.

[7] See C. S. Lewis, *The Four Loves* (New York: Harcourt Brace & Company, 1988), 17.

[8] Matthew Parris, "As an Atheist, I Truly Believe Africa Needs God," *Times*, 27 Dec. 2008, http://www.timesonline.co.uk/tol/comment/columnists/matthew_parris/article5400568.ece. Accessed 10 Sept. 2016.

[9] Blaise Pascal, *Pensées*, Section VII: Morality and Doctrine, 430, http://www.bartleby.com/48/1/7.html. Accessed 10 Sept. 2016.

[10] Malcolm Muggeridge, *The End of Christendom* (Grand Rapids, MI: William B. Eerdmans, 1980), 13.

CHAPTER 7

[1] Robert Nozick, *Anarchy, State, and Utopia* (New York: Basic Books, 1974), 42–45.

[2] See Mark H. Bernstein, *The Moral Equality of Humans and Animals* (Hampshire, UK: Palgrave Macmillan, 2015).

[3] Jeremy Bentham, *The Rationale of Reward* (London: J. and H. L. Hunt, 1825), 206.

[4] C. S. Lewis, *God in the Dock: Essays on Theology and Ethics* (Grand Rapids, MI: Wm. B. Eerdmans, 2014), 48. The exact quotation from Lewis is, "I didn't go to religion to make me happy. I always knew a bottle of Port would do that. If you want a religion to make you feel really comfortable, I certainly don't recommend Christianity."

[5] Jeremy Bentham, *An Introduction to the Principles of Morals and Legislation* (Oxford: Clarendon Press, 1879), 1.

[6] This is my example, but it was inspired by reflection on Peter Unger's book *Living High and Letting Die* (OUP, 1996) and Peter Singer's article "The Singer Solution to World Poverty" (*The New York Times*, 1999).

[7] While it is true that youth especially sometimes adopt the practice of referring to one another in derogatory terms as a sign of friendship, it is telling that generally people

grow out of this practice. In other words, practices that sever etymological roots in this way are difficult to sustain. Reflection also suggests that there are some words that even adolescents are able to identify as having meanings too strong and established to be easily overridden. This is all the more the case with the word of *sex* due to the divine origin of its meaning.

[8] C. S. Lewis, *Studies in Words*, Second Edition (Cambridge, UK: Cambridge University Press, 1960), 7.

[9] "Epistle of Mathetes to Diognetus," *New Advent*, http://www.newadvent.org/fathers/0101.htm. Accessed 11 Sept. 2016.

[10] Oscar Wilde, "De Profundis," *The Collected Works of Oscar Wilde* (Hertfordshire, UK: Wordsworth Editions, 2007), 1071.

[11] Ravi and I discuss the philosophical and personal challenges of living in a broken world in our book *Why Suffering? Finding Meaning and Comfort When Life Doesn't Make Sense* (New York: FaithWords, 2014).

[12] Richard Dawkins, *River Out of Eden: A Darwinian View of Life* (New York: Basic Books, 1995), 133.

[13] Miroslav Volf, *Free of Charge: Giving and Forgiving in a Culture Stripped of Grace* (Grand Rapids, MI: Zondervan, 2005), 139.

[14] William Butler Yeats, "Easter 1916," *A Terrible Beauty Is Born* (New York: Penguin Classics, 2016).

CHAPTER 8

[1] Thank you to Nelly Wambui for making me laugh with these jokes and for her wise reflections on the relationship between truth and fact.

[2] This example is taken from Peter van Inwagen, "A Kind of Darwinism," *Science and Religion in Dialogue, Volume Two*, edited by Melville Y. Stewart (West Sussex, UK: Blackwell, 2010), 820.

[3] Alfred Tennyson, "The Grandmother," *The Works of Alfred Lord Tennyson* (Hertfordshire, UK: Wordsworth, 1994), 542–546.

[4] I am indebted to Abasiano Udofa for identifying a similar example and for his very insightful reflections on what examples of this sort say about our relationship with the truth.

[5] See Tim Piper, "dove evolution," *Youtube*, 6 Oct. 2006, 11 Sept. 2016, youtube.com/watch?v=iYhCn0jf46U. Accessed on 11 Sept. 2016.

[6] Of course, sometimes it is important to oppose an idea even when we judge it to be completely irrational. This can be the case when an idea, though irrational, threatens to have grave consequences. However, I would term this opposition rather than disagreement. Disagreement welcomes response and, in doing so, values the other. Mere opposition looks to undermine without inviting response. Unfortunately, our current political culture seems to be producing much more opposition than disagreement.

[7] Family Policy Institute of Washington, "College Kids Say the Darndest Things: On Identity," *Youtube*, 13 April 2016, youtube.com/watch?v=xfO1veFs6Ho. Accessed on 11 Sept. 2016.

[8] See Roger Scruton, "Universities' war against truth," *Spectator Life*, http://life.spectator.co.uk/2016/06/universities-war-against-truth. Accessed 2 Oct. 2016. Also see Andrew Anthony, "Is free speech in British universities under threat?" *The Observer*, https://www.theguardian.com/world/2016/jan/24/safe-spaces-universities-no-platform-free-speech-rhodes. Accessed 2 Oct. 2016.

[9] Katherine Timpf, "Princeton Students Set Up Microaggression-Reporting Service," *National Review*, 11 Dec. 2014, http://www.nationalreview.com/article/394461/princeton-students-set-microaggression-reporting-service-katherine-timpf. Accessed on 11 Sept. 2016.

[10] I am indebted to Michael Ramsden for his insightful thoughts on the relevance of helicopter parenting and microaggressions to this discussion. Michael has a unique and penetrating perspective on the wider narrative and implications of this topic, and I believe his continued work in this area will be highly significant.

[11] Peter Abelard, *Yes and No: The Complete English Translation of Peter Abelard's Sic Et Non*, translated by Priscilla Throop (Charlotte, VT: MedievalMS, 2007).

[12] See, for example, Greg Lukianoff, *Freedom from Speech* (New York: Encounter Books, 2014) and Joanna Williams, *Academic Freedom in an Age of Conformity* (New York: Palgrave Macmillan, 2016).

[13] See also Ruth Gledhill, "Meet the Christian Pastor with a £500 Bounty on His Head," *Christian Today*, 3 Dec. 2015, http://christiantoday.com/article/meet.the.christian.pastor.with.a.500.bounty.on.his.head/72441.htm. Accessed 11 Sept. 2016.

[14] This tale is most often attributed to a practical joke performed by Arthur Conan Doyle, author of the Sherlock detective fiction stories.

[15] Prudentius, "Discourse of the Martyr St. Romanus Against the Pagans," *The Poems of Prudentius*, translated by Sister M. Clement Eagan CCVI (Washington, D.C.: Catholic University of America Press, 1962), 207.

[16] Stephen Fry, *Paperweight* (London: Arrow Books, 2004), 59.

[17] Chloe Veron, "Mother's Day," *Youtube*, 12 May 2012, youtube.com/watch?v=-KA-8pL64W1I. Accessed on 11 Sept. 2016.